The Essentials of Contract Negotiation

Stefanie Jung • Peter Krebs

The Essentials of Contract Negotiation

Springer

Stefanie Jung
Faculty III
University of Siegen
Siegen, Germany

Peter Krebs
Faculty III
University of Siegen
Siegen, Germany

Translated by Melissa Dowse (University of Siegen)
Corrected by Rachel Schneider (University of Siegen)

ISBN 978-3-030-12865-4 ISBN 978-3-030-12866-1 (eBook)
https://doi.org/10.1007/978-3-030-12866-1

This Springer imprint is published by the registered company Springer Nature Switzerland AG.
The registered company address is: Gewerbestrasse 11, 6330 Cham, Switzerland

Preface

B2B negotiations are of great practical relevance. Mastering the art of negotiation can be decisive with regard to whether a contract is concluded or not. In case the parties agree on a contract, not merely the (rational) negotiation power but likewise the individual negotiation skills are a key factor to the eventual shape of the contract. Hence, employing well-trained negotiators is essential to all kinds of businesses. Acquiring negotiation skills requires much practical experience and also a certain talent. Besides, particularly dealing systematically with the topic of negotiations, learning basic skills in the field of negotiations, avoiding mistakes and the continuous aim of improving these skills is helpful. In the same way as amateur footballers in the lowest league up to the champions league all have a trainer who gives instructions, a systematic instruction to the field of negotiations is helpful for amateur negotiators as well as professional negotiators. With this work the authors want to spark the general interest for the topic of contract negotiations, help beginners and advanced negotiators to improve the quality of their negotiations and motivate researchers to deal with this exciting matter in more depth. It is worth it!

This book does not require any prior knowledge, yet it does, in parts, consciously concentrate on matters in-depth and in this context also includes references to further literature. Therefore, this reading is suitable for both beginners and advanced negotiators. On the one hand, the aim is to gather the current scientific status of the negotiation science, which is majorly influenced by the research conducted in the USA. On the other hand, the focus is on further developing or rather critically questioning present findings. Thus, it is attempted to critically analyse the different suggestions for negotiation tactics and—where possible—to make proposals for countermeasures.

This book was developed based on the German edition *Die Vertragsverhandlung – taktische, strategische und rechtliche Elemente* (2016). The underlying idea of this project was to offer an abbreviated version of the original book (which is nearly 500 pages long) that stresses the most important aspects for international negotiations. According to this idea, the title *Essentials of Contract Negotiation* was developed. Consequently, this book paves the way for a quick familiarisation with contract negotiations for practitioners and students. Therefore, the majority of the book is a (revised) translation of the original template. The revised parts include the introduction into the subject of negotiations in order to provide a quicker understanding of the subsequent text. Above that, this book also comprises a new chapter on cultural differences in negotiations. In an exemplary manner, this chapter will illustrate selected US-American, German, and Chinese peculiarities in negotiations.

At this point, we would like to take the opportunity to thank all the people involved who have helped to realise this project. First and foremost, we thank Melissa Dowse, LL.B., and Rachel Schneider (both from University of Siegen), who were responsible for the translation and linguistic revision of the texts. Without their help the project would not have been realised. On this note, many thanks go to Melissa Dowse, LL.B., for her extensive assistance on this book. Further, we thank Michael Matejek (LL.M., University of Siegen) for developing the graphics. Lastly, we would like to thank the faculty III of the University of Siegen for its financial support, which has made the publication of this book possible in the first place.

We, the authors, find great joy in dealing with the matter of contract negotiations. That is why we would be delighted if the readers of this book could find a similar fascination for the topic. Feedback, further information, suggestions and critical comments are very welcome. Conversely, we are also happy to provide advice for others.

Siegen, Germany
March 2019

Peter Krebs
Stefanie Jung

Contents

Abbreviations

5 Ps	Prior preparation prevents poor performance
ACBD	Always consult before deciding
AcP	Archiv für die civilistische Praxis (German legal journal)
Art.	Article
B2B	Business to business
B2C	Business to consumer
BAFO	Best and final offer
BATNA	Best alternative to a negotiated agreement
CBCA	Criteria-based content analysis
CIETAC	China International Economic and Trade Arbitration Commission
CMS	Compliance management systems
cf.	Confer
Chap.	Chapter
DAD approach	Decide, announce, defend approach
DDD approach	Dialogue, decide, deliver approach
DITF	Door-in-the-face
DoD	Detection of deception
EANT	Ethically ambiguous negotiation tactics
Ed.	Edition/editor
Eds.	Editors
e.g.	Exempli gratia
EI	Emotional intelligence
esp.	Especially
et seq.	Et sequentes
EU	European Union
FC approach	Full consensus approach
Fig.	Figure
FITD	Foot-in-the-door-technique
FOA	Final offer arbitration
FOG	Facts, opinions, guesses
FTF	Face-to-face

GTFT	Generous tit for tat
IACM	International Association for Conflict Management
i.e.	Id est
IO	Interpersonal orientation
LOI	Letter of intent
M&A	Mergers and acquisitions
MBTI	Myers-Briggs-type indicator
MESO	Multiple equivalent simultaneous offers
MGA	Mutual gains approach
MoU	Memorandum of understanding
NDA	Non-disclosure agreement
NOPA	No possible agreement
No.	Number
p.	Page
PON	Program on Negotiation
pp.	Pages
PRC	People's Republic of China
RFP	Request for proposal
Sect.	Section
SMART	Specific, measurable, assignable, realistic, time-related
SMARTER	Specific, measurable, assignable, realistic, time-related, evaluated, reviewed
SME	Small and medium enterprises
SOPHOP	Soft on people, hard on points
SVA	Statement validity assessment
SWOT	Strength, weakness, opportunities and threats
TFEU	Treaty on the functioning of the European Union
TFT	Tit for tat
TINA	There is no alternative
TV	Television
UCC	Uniform Commercial Code
UCLA	University of California, Los Angeles
UK	United Kingdom
U.S.	United States
USA	United States of America
Vol.	Volume
WATNA	Worst alternative to a negotiated agreement
WWW	What worked well
WWYDD	What would you do differently
ZOPA	Zone of possible agreement

List of Figures

Chapter 1
Introduction and Instructions for Use

1.1 Introductory Remarks

Contract negotiations are of great practical importance. Findings on the functioning of contract negotiations and their implementation by way of tactics and strategies can help to reach an agreement, achieve better negotiation results or make a well-informed decision against an agreement.

This work is dedicated to business contract negotiations, i.e. B2B (business to business) negotiations. Hence, the below explained findings, tactics, strategies, overall concepts as well as framework conditions can apply to negotiations between companies as well to negotiations held within the company. This does however not preclude that the same or at least similar tactics and strategies are used in the context of family negotiations, diplomatic negotiations or in negotiations between businesses and consumers (B2C) or employees. Yet, in this work these tactics and strategies are only examined from the view of business negotiations.

This composition mainly focuses on the illustration of negotiation tactics and strategies. Here, tactics refer to the specific individual steps in the course of negotiations, whereas a strategy is continuously followed throughout the entire negotiation process. Overall negotiation concepts are developed so comprehensively that they claim validity for all existing types of negotiations. The only comprehensive negotiation concept currently in existence is the Harvard negotiation approach which will also be discussed intensively throughout this work. In order to provide a better common understanding, the following sections also illustrate basic terms used in negotiations as well as tactics and techniques which are fundamental to fully grasp the basic idea of negotiations. Further, the sections will also deal with the underlying effects and the mechanisms upon which these tactics are essentially based. Moreover, this composition includes the description of technical devices which are applied during negotiations.

S. Jung, P. Krebs, *The Essentials of Contract Negotiation*,
https://doi.org/10.1007/978-3-030-12866-1_1

In summary, this book distinguishes the following basic categories:

- basic terms
- mechanisms/effects
- tactical means
- techniques
- strategies
- overall negotiation concepts
- fundamental problems within negotiations

The explanations provided refer to these basic categories. The terms discussed in the course of this book are arranged in an alphabetical order. Since the authors consider an alphabetical listing of explanations to be much more comprehensive, they deliberately decided against presenting them in a continuous text. At the same time, an alphabetical listing also offers the opportunity to link the described terms by way of a system of references (see details below under Sect. 1.2). Furthermore, the index enables the reader to select specific aspects. In this context, also the topic lists in the appendix allow the reader to deal with specific questions (instructions are described further on).

Negotiation research links several science fields, most importantly the one's dealing with psychological, legal as well as economic aspects. The same applies to findings from the field of communications science. The objective of this work is to afford a general insight into the current status of the science dealing with negotiations. Thus, this book primarily gathers the most important findings from various disciplines. Beyond that, this work also claims to make these findings more practicable, overall enabling the reader to transform these findings into the actual negotiation process or helping the reader to successfully cope with certain tactics employed by their negotiating partners. The authors of this book attempt to critically examine the illustrated tactics and techniques and also evaluate their practical applicability within company-related negotiations. On occasion, the authors also introduce entirely new suggestions (e.g. the legitimacy limits of fraudulent behaviour).

Reading this book does not require any prior knowledge—but only an actual interest in the discussed matter, which is why it can act as a general introduction into the field of contract negotiations. It can, however, be of equal interest to experienced negotiators, due to the fact that it helps explaining the underlying mechanisms of action. Based on these findings, negotiators can improve their own tactics and strategies. In this context, the given literature references allow interested readers to commence further research on individual aspects. A number of references can already be found in the descriptions within the alphabetical overview of key terms. In addition, a detailed list of the literature used can be found in the list of references which is provided for in the appendix.

Most aspects of negotiations cannot be acquired by bare reading, but rather require practice and, to a certain degree, also negotiation talent. However, it is essential to understand how both—yourself and others—negotiate, what strategies, tactics and techniques can be applied, to what extent and why they seem to be functioning, and which specific factors influence the eventual success of a tactic.

Nonetheless, dealing with this book cannot, and also should not replace actual practice of negotiations. Rather, this work aims at preparing the reader for practice, intending to support the efficient management of negotiations, and encourage negotiators to reflect their commonly used own behaviour.

Even so, the featured negotiation tactics and strategies should not be regarded as general recommendations, as some elements of the individual tactics and strategies do not comply with the commonly aspired ethical standards or are, in fact, illegal. The authors generally outline their concerns about the risks associated with certain tactics. However, since there is an omnipresent risk that the negotiating partner will make use of unethical tactics, it is vital for negotiators to be able to identify them and have knowledge on how to react appropriately.

1.2 Instructions for the Use and Structure of the Book

1.2.1 Structure of the Book

This book is divided into different chapters. To begin with, the authors give a short explanatory introduction to the issue (Sect. 1.1). In the following section (Sect. 1.2), we provide a short introduction into the proper handling of this book in order to facilitate a better approach and improve the reader's accessibility of the discussed matters. Chapter 2 then outlines the planning process and the procedure of business negotiations. In this context, the six phases of negotiations are distinguished and described:

- Preparation of negotiations (Sect. 2.1);
- start of negotiations (Sect. 2.2);
- the core phase of negotiations (Sect. 2.3);
- the agreement (Sect. 2.4);
- Implementation of the agreement (Sect. 2.5) and
- the ex-post-phase (Sect. 2.6).

Even though in-depth reading of these introductory remarks is not required in order to understand the subsequently provided explanations for negotiations, they are the key prerequisite to the proper application of the knowledge presented. An efficient realisation of the illustrated techniques and strategies is only possible based on a fundamental understanding for the structure of negotiations between companies.

Chapter 3, the main part of this book, gathers findings, tactics and strategies, complemented by additional explanations of the basic terms in alphabetical order. Chapter 4 deals with cultural differences regarding negotiations. In this context, the chapter (comparatively) focuses on the negotiation practice in the US, Germany and China. The appendix of this work includes topic lists (see further below), a comprehensive list of the literature used and a glossary of keywords.

1.2.2 Possible Ways to Approach This Book

With particular regard to the composed tactics and strategies, readers can employ various methods to approaching this book. The keywords are in alphabetical order, hence there is no specific thematical order given. Readers who know exactly what they are looking for, can easily jump from one key word to another and may therefore use this book as a mere work of reference. The lexicon-like structure is particularly suitable to look something up quickly. Readers with a particular interest in specific aspects however, can also use the index as a means of orientation. The glossary contains all the keywords which are printed in bold letters throughout the texts. All general terms (at the beginning of the definition for the key terms), as well as all synonyms and terms with a similar meaning, are printed in bold. Likewise, phrases which are thematically closely connected to the general term are also highlighted.

Example
Terms printed boldly in the description of the Harvard negotiation concept:

Harvard negotiation concept	This is the general term and can be found under the letter H.
Getting to Yes	This is a synonymous term, which is also highlighted using bold letters in the text.
Principled negotiations **Negotiations of merits** **Third way**	These are synonyms in a broader sense (bold).
SOPHOP	This is a term which is closely linked to the Harvard negotiation concept and is thus also explained in that context.
Neutral evaluation criteria:	This term is also closely linked to the Harvard negotiation concept, and is therefore also explained.

Note: Although more terms are closely linked to the Harvard negotiation concept, not all of them have been added to the exemplary list above.

Since one keyword can include a number of connected terms printed in bold, the glossary references the general term (marked with "see below").

Examples
Third way *see under* Harvard negotiation concept
Neutral evaluation criteria *see under* Harvard negotiation concept

Readers who wish to focus on specific topics can use the thematic lists (topic lists) provided in the appendix. These lists include all general terms linked to a certain subject (e.g. negotiation strategies). In order to keep these lists concise, no additional key words in bold (such as synonyms etc.) are included. Since the topic lists can be linked to one another, some lists are summarised under one general term. For instance, there is the superordinate term of "communication techniques", under which inter alia topic lists for "answering techniques" and "questioning techniques" can be found.

Readers can, of course, also read the book right from the beginning or look up certain keywords here and there. In this context, the reference technique we use serves to provide the reader with suggestions for further terms, which might also be of interest.

As already mentioned, this book does not require any specific background knowledge. Yet, not all illustrated terms are equally important for negotiators. This work rather combines the main basis of negotiations, complemented with useful additional terms. To gain a general overview of the topic, it is recommended to first of all read the following section on the general "Preparation and Negotiation Process" (Chap. 2), with the connected key words and subsequently focus on more specific aspects.

The terms are each discussed individually (in alphabetical order) but are not to be viewed isolated from one another. In fact, the illustrated techniques, tactics, and strategies are rather interlinked. To provide good linkage between the individual terms (despite the alphabetical order), the individual terms include references (marked with an arrow "→" and written in italics). Terms marked by these arrows are independent general terms that are explained (and are listed in alphabetical order). If a term is only presented in italics, it is a keyword which can be found under a different general term. In this case, the relevant general term is presented in front of an arrow, often in brackets.

Example
→ *Anchoring* – in this way, a reference to the general term of anchoring (under anchoring) is made
Anchor discreditation (→ *anchoring*) – this reference shows that the term "anchor discreditation" is further explained under the key term of "anchoring". In the index, you will find the entry: Anchor discreditation *see under* anchoring.

This reference technique allows the reader to look up certain aspects and focus on further and thematically linked terms. To provide the greatest possible comprehensibility of the presented knowledge, it is accepted that in some cases redundancies may occur.

Since the various basic categories are simply too diverse, the individual terms do not have any specific structure. However, there are several elements that are mentioned regularly. In the first place, possible synonyms for a certain term are stated. Any sources or persons particularly influencing the term will be mentioned at the beginning of the definition. To provide interested readers with further information, these references regularly include the relevant literature (in the corresponding footnote). In order to clarify for the reader, which specific key term is being explained, the term is assigned to one of the basic categories (such as tactics, techniques, strategies, framework). This is followed by the explanation of the term and possibly the illustration of the specific circumstances, general conditions, etc. For illustration purposes, examples, graphics or explanations of scientific studies are included at the end. Since certain terms may be very similar, they are differentiated from other, possibly connected, key words at the beginning or the end of the explanation.

The German version of this book uses the so-called "generic masculine" which generally also includes females even if the word is per se used in its masculine form (example: "The negotiator (…) he (…) himself"). However, during workshops and seminars the authors came to realise that women tend to take on the role of men in negotiation simulations whenever the given instruction for the negotiation simulation is written in the generic masculine form. Also in the course of discussions it is evident that most people generally imagine a male negotiator. Thus, in order to avoid potential biases—where necessary—this book uses both forms (example: "The negotiator (…) s/he (…) himself/herself").

Once again, it should be noted that not all the presented actions are advisable from a legal or even ethical point of view. The authors clearly state possible ethical concerns. Legal aspects are not included in this work as national legal orders generally differ from one another.[1] Nonetheless, it is important to be aware of (legally and) ethically questionable tactics and strategies, as there is a perpetual risk of the negotiating partner making use of these very actions. In these cases, it is crucial to firstly identify these tactics and then have corresponding reaction possibilities at hand. The choice of tactics used within negotiations depends inter alia upon the prioritisation of negotiation objectives, bargaining power, the tactic applied by the negotiating partner and the individuals' personal attitude towards negotiations. It is also influenced by many other circumstances pertaining to each individual case, which is why from the outset it is prohibited to elaborate general recommendations for negotiations.

[1] In the German (extensive) version of this book "Die Vertragsvergsverhandlung – taktische, strategische und rechtliche Elemente" (2016, 525 pages) legal aspects are included. In that work reference is usually made to German law.

Chapter 2
Preparation and Negotiation Process

Negotiations can be divided into different negotiation phases (→ *negotiation phases*). In literature, the specific number of phases differs. Be that as it may, the most important steps are

- the preparation of negotiations,
- the start of negotiations,
- the core phase of negotiations,
- the agreement,
- the implementation of the agreement and
- the ex-post-phase.

The following sections outline the most important aspects of each individual negotiation phase.

2.1 Preparation of Negotiations

Preparing the negotiations (see topic list for the specific key terms) is essential for the final success of negotiations. The → *80-20-rule* was therefore established by *Leigh L. Thompson*.[1] According to this rule, preparing negotiations is four times as important as the negotiation itself. Clearly, the significance of the preparation process cannot be generally quantified (as preparation can take up more or less time according to individual circumstances). Even so, the rule serves to highlight the importance of this phase. As *James A. Baker* once said: "*Prior preparation prevents poor performance*"[2] (*5 Ps* → *80-20-rule*).

---

[1] Thompson (2014), p. 34.

[2] Baker (2006), p. 5.

S. Jung, P. Krebs, *The Essentials of Contract Negotiation*,
https://doi.org/10.1007/978-3-030-12866-1_2

Like any other negotiation phase, the specific structuring of the preparation depends on the individual circumstances and concrete framework of the negotiations. Important factors which determine the preparation of the negotiation are:

- The negotiation object;
- the negotiating partner or the partners (→ *two negotiators*, negotiation team, for the possible actors in negotiations, see thematic list, concerning gender aspects → *gender*);
- the roles of the negotiation partners (seller, buyer etc.);
- the negotiation objective(s) (e.g. short- or long-term optimisation of company interests, improving or preventing a deterioration of the relationship to the negotiating partner, gaining attention and reputation, gaining negotiation experience, preventing certain actions/activities of the negotiating partner or third parties);
- the nature of the relationship towards the negotiating partner (e.g. one-time deal, → *permanent business relationship*);
- the personal relationship (trusting or strained relationship);
- one's own → *negotiation power* and in this respect especially one's own → *BATNA*;
- the negotiation power of the opposing party (especially the negotiating partner's BATNA) and
- the negotiation type (e.g. → *face-to-face*, → *e-mail*, → *auction*, → *renegotiations* etc. see topic list.)

To structure and professionalise the negotiations, developing a → *prenegotiation plan* which includes checklists may prove useful. The prenegotiation plan inter alia includes guidelines for the preparation of negotiations. These should be based on the negotiators' experience and the informative findings of negotiation research. The prenegotiation plan serves to remind the negotiator of any necessary preparations for negotiations. The checklists contained in the prenegotiation plan are usually used for preparatory work with the draft contract. Prenegotiation plans can be used especially for routine negotiations. In negotiations which deviate from the routine, checklists may be helpful but are perhaps incomplete. In companies, measures promoting digitalisation can contribute to make the preparation process more efficient. For instance, the use of internal systems and databases serves to support the prenegotiation plan and the experience gained in the course of previous negotiations should be utilised to further develop the preparation process (see also Sect. 2.6 concerning the ex-post-phase). In this sense, negotiations can be regarded as an iterative process.

In the first place, negotiators should determine the negotiation subject. In this regard, a buyer has to analyse his/her needs, while a seller has to develop marketable products or services to sell. Buyers search the market for potential vendors while sellers try to get in contact with potential buyers. In this context, another essential task is identifying potential negotiating partners as well as other relevant stakeholders that might influence the overall negotiation process (→ *think beyond the table*). In case of many influential stakeholders it can be helpful to draw a so-called *all-party map* (→ *think beyond the table*), i.e. a sketch that lists all relevant stakeholders and their respective interests as well as the relevant relations and potential influence. Once the parties decide to negotiate, organisational questions such as the negotiation venue (including booking the rooms etc.), the number of people attending the negotiation (→ *two negotiators*), the → *agenda*, possible → *deadlines*, the negotiation type (→ *face-to-face*, via → *e-mail*, via telephone etc. must be clarified. With the exception of very large and very small negotiations, appointing a two-person negotiation team is a sound recommendation (→ *two negotiators*) for face-to-face and even in phone negotiations. In this regard, a two-people negotiation team offers the advantage that the one who is currently not negotiating can always take on the role of the observing → *analyst*. In general, it is useful to pair up negotiators with different content specialisations e.g. a technical and an economical-juridical expert.

Moreover, the parties should priorly agree on whether negotiations will be made in the course of a → *single text negotiation*, i.e. conducting a negotiation on the basis of a single text, usually a contract draft. In this instance, also questions such as which party is in charge of providing the draft, or whether the parties will resort to using drafts provided by a third party have to be answered. It would also be possible for parties to work with → *boilerplates*, i.e. specific standard clauses or text blocks, instead of using a complete contract template. In addition, the contract can be drawn up jointly by both parties without a draft or might also be a joint proposal derived from two suggestions. In any case, the legal preparation is an essential step in the phase leading to the negotiation.

Furthermore, information is the key to the proper preparation of negotiations. In this respect, it can make sense to firstly conduct an → *information demand analysis* in order to evaluate which information is needed. The second step is then to gather this information. In this context, it should be noted that not all relevant information is available prior to the negotiation. Gathering the relevant information (see e.g. topic list "questioning techniques") is rather an ongoing task throughout all negotiation phases. Typical sources for obtaining information are the negotiation partner himself/herself as well as his/her competitors or business partners; intracompany information systems and publicly available sources (e.g. the internet, registries, relevant journals). The reliability of the information should be checked regularly (→ *detection of deception*). In this regard, it is oftentimes useful to try to obtain the information from another, independent source. However, it is not only important to conduct an → *information demand analysis*, gather the information, and consequently analyse the data, but also to reflect which information is available for the other side, which information about the own side should be disclosed in the negotiation process, and which information is confidential (→ *information control*).

With the help of the information gained, it is then necessary to determine both, one's own interests and those of the negotiating partner (if possible). Many negotiators focus merely on their own position instead of analysing underlying interests. The → *Harvard negotiation concept,* however, firmly suggests focusing on interests, because this offers the chance to find *common interests* with the negotiation partner as well as merely *diverging but not conflicting interests* (→ *Harvard negotiation concept*). An interest-based approach thereby offers the possibility to increase the mutual gains (→ *win-win strategy*) for the parties (*expanding the pie* (→ *negotiation pie*)). This can lead to a bigger → *negotiation pie*. The term negotiation pie refers to the total value of the negotiations. If the overall net result can be maximized, both sides—presuming equal participation—will profit from increased negotiation pie correspondingly. The → *orange example* illustrates the difference between interests and positions. In the example, two sisters argue over an orange. Both of them demand the whole orange (representing the position). If they negotiate according to their position, they might decide to split the orange. However, one sister only needed the juice and the other one only the peel (representing interests). Based on an interest-oriented negotiation they could have found a solution that fully satisfies both of their interests optimally.

In the course of preparations, negotiators should analyse both: (1) The interests and (2) the positions of both parties. In B2B negotiations, one usually faces a → *principal-agent-situation*. That means that a principal commissions someone to act as his/her agent; in this specific case, to negotiate and make decisions in his/her place. Under these circumstances, it might be useful to analyse the interests and positions of the negotiator himself/herself and of the company s/he is representing.

A personal → *BATNA*, i.e. the best alternative to a negotiated agreement, is essential for one's own negotiating position. By determining their own BATNA in the process of the preparations, negotiators clarify whether the specific negotiated agreement is (from a relative point of view) advantageous in comparison with other alternative actions. The individual BATNA essentially determines the own objective negotiating power. Buyers usually request offers from several sellers and compare them. In this respect, the seller's BATNA is usually harder to determine as s/he might not be able to exactly evaluate the number of other possible customers.

Since a BATNA is not immutable but rather dynamic, strengthening it during the negotiation phase—e.g. by establishing possible alternatives to the specific agreement (e.g. alternative sellers)—is essential. Negotiators should also try to establish the BATNA of their negotiation partner. Here it should be pointed out that identifying your own BATNA can already prove difficult, which is why establishing the opposing party's BATNA can be even more complicated. Even so, one should attempt to gather any kind of information that could aid identifying the other party's BATNA. It is precisely this correlation of → *negotiation power* between both parties which constitutes a key factor in the subsequent definition of the negotiation strategy and tactics which will be applied in the process of negotiations. Revealing the negotiating partner's interest can also serve as an indicator for possible objections and reservations. If these factors can be anticipated, determining an adequate response in the negotiations (i.e. anticipating objections and reservations) is a possible option. To root out these objections, it might make sense for one team member to play the devil's advocate → *advocatus diaboli* during the preparation process.

The *resistance point* (→ *deal-breaker*), i.e. the point at which the negotiations should be terminated (without reaching a result), is closely linked to one's own BATNA. If a better alternative to the current negotiation is available, negotiations should normally be terminated. The same applies to the negotiation partner. It is crucial to establish the own parties' resistance point before entering the negotiation as it provides clarity and can help avoid lengthy (hence costly) and unsuccessful negotiations. Vice versa, the expectations the own side has towards the negotiations should also be analysed beforehand. Thus, the preparation phase includes the formulation of one's own final and intermediate goals. In general, it is advisable to set concrete, ambitious targets (→ *ambitious target price setting*) since these targets act as a self-fulfilling prophecy. These goals should not only be concrete regarding their extent but should also be as specific as possible (→ *know your target*), meaning that aims are formulated regarding every single negotiation point. In this context, the → *SMART goal formulation technique* can be very useful tool. Clearly determining the goals concerning the individual negotiation points is also the basis for determining the overall goal.

The own parties'→ *resistance point* and the resistance point of the negotiation partner determine the possible bargaining range also known as the agreement zone of the negotiation parties. The area where the respective minimum targets of the parties (so called → *deal-breakers*) overlap is called → *ZOPA* (zone of possible agreement). If there is a ZOPA—in theory—the parties should be able to reach an agreement, because from a rational point of view this agreement will prove advantageous to both contracting parties. Vice versa, this implies that initiating negotiations without a ZOPA (*NOPA*—no possible agreement (→ *ZOPA*)) is not worthwhile. Oftentimes, the parties have to in the first place start to negotiate, in order to find out if there is a ZOPA. If they realise that there is no agreement zone they should terminate the negotiations, since generally negotiations are time and cost intensive. Hence, within the preparation process, it is important to at least estimate whether there is a ZOPA and if so, the respective size of it due to the fact that the ZOPA is the basis for determining possible strategies and tactics. In case there is a big ZOPA, the distribution of the negotiation pie will play a key role. In case of a small ZOPA the challenge is to reach an agreement at all.

Dealing with individual aspects also includes the consideration of lines of compromise (see for example → *non-linear compromises* and → *split the difference*) and options of action. Research shows that negotiators, who dedicate more time to this, achieve better results. Moreover, it is crucial to assess the importance of certain aspects. Regarding the ZOPA's importance for the negotiation process implementing a → *traffic light system* could be beneficial. According to this approach, single negotiations points are rated on a scale from "fully disposable" to "indispensable" using e.g. colours (red, orange, green).

Even if the negotiators prefer to remain flexible in their reactions, consideration should still be paid in advance to which strategy to pursue and which tactics, under which circumstances, could be applied. In the course of time, each negotiator develops his/her own negotiation style. In certain cases, it might be interesting to use a test (e.g. the Myers-Briggs-type indicator (MBTI) or the Thomas-Kilmann Conflict Mode Instrument[3]) to establish your own personality profile with regard to negotiations. The own personality is a significant factor that needs to be considered when

[3] Thomas and Kilmann (1974).

choosing the appropriate strategy and tactics. Particularly in the case of important and complex negotiations, it may make sense to run a simulation of negotiations in advance. Within negotiation literature, the so-called → *seven elements of negotiation* approach, developed by *Bruce Patton*, describes the main points of negotiation preparation. In case of an international negotiations with parties with different cultural backgrounds it is also important to be conscious of cultural differences (also with regard to specific negotiation habits and styles) within the process of the preparation (cf. Sect. 2.4).

2.2 The Start of Negotiations

The start of negotiations is strongly influenced by the chosen way of negotiation (→ *face-to-face*, → *e-mail* etc.), the contract's importance and other influencing factors (like → *permanent business relationship* or one-off negotiation). At this point, the characteristics of the start of negotiations during face-to-face negotiations is illustrated. However, in general there has been prior contact between the negotiation parties. The negotiation venue is the meeting point of the negotiators and agreed upon in preparation process (see Sect. 2.1). Already during the reception, a first → *impression* is established. This impression is particularly formative (as well as the last impression) due to the *confirmation bias* (→ *impression (first and last)*), i.e. the → *bias*, stating that people tend not to consider arguments that contradict their first impression. This is why it is worthwhile for the negotiator to endeavour for a positive first impression. These kind of positive impressions can be created by means of a pleasant negotiation atmosphere. Hence, it is important to make the other party feel at ease. This is usually achieved by commencing → *chit-chat*. Instead of jumping right into the core phase of the negotiation, it is generally recommendable to invest a considerable amount of time in becoming acquainted with the other party. The intensity and extent of this phase does not only depend on the individual preferences of the negotiator, but is also determined by cultural differences (see Chap. 4). It is frequently desired that negotiators become acquainted with one another during joint dinners or sports events. For the most part, negotiators with a high degree of empathy are particularly equipped to contribute to a good atmosphere between the negotiating parties.

Particularly in the starting phase of negotiations, the parties are engaged in building a harmonious relationship in order to establish negotiation trust. Trust is one key element for successful negotiations. In this context, intrapersonal (between persons) and institutional trust (within the individual organisation, e.g. a company) has to be distinguished. The starting phase of the negotiations is distinctively suitable to establish intrapersonal trust, which also helps to build institutional trust. The more important trust is for the negotiation and implementation of the contract; the more time the parties invest in building a harmonious relationship. In this context → *chit-chat* holds an important role. In many cases, the search for private similarities (→ *find something in common*, → *similar-to-me-effect*) from the outset of the negotiations can be beneficial to establishing trust. Studies show that people are more congenial towards people who are similar to them and are perceived more positively than people they do not share any similarities with.[4] In the context of building a harmonious relationship, also the expressed → *body language* is essential. The imitation of the negotiation partners' body posture (both lean forward, both cross their legs etc.) is generally regarded as a positive sign for their sympathy. People tend to trust other persons and perceive them as persuasive if they imitate their own posture (so-called *chameleon effect* (→ *body language*)).[5]

One of the most essential communicating techniques applied in this particular phase of the negotiation is → *active listening* as it helps to create a positive atmosphere of communication and encourages the other side to go on talking. Active listening can be either expressed verbally or non-verbally. A clear non-verbal sign is nodding and facing towards the negotiating partner. Verbal signs include expressions like "Yes ", "I see ", "oh ", "hmm". Not only during the starting phase of negotiations, but also in the overall negotiation process, negotiators should pay attention to listening more to what the conversation partner says than speaking themselves. This recommended ratio is emphasised by the → *70-30-rule*, even though the exact relation cannot be quantified definitely (see also Sect. 2.3).

Depending on the individual negotiation situation (e.g. imbalanced negotiation power) reversely, in this negotiation phase also power games and power demonstrations are commonly used. In this context, one of the negotiation partners often tries to impress the other one e.g. with representative buildings and pompous, big rooms (→ *big fish*). Also luxurious company cars etc. may achieve the same effect. Moreover, also company presentations are designed to impress business partners. → *Imperial gestures* are used to stress one's own high status and at the same time attribute a lower status to the other side. Imperial gestures include letting the other party wait before the meeting, positioning oneself at the head of the table or letting e-mails being answered by one's secretary. Negotiators using imperial gestures do however run the risk of struggling to sufficiently establish trust and a good rapport with the other side.

Even though the parties engage a lot in small talk, the initial phase of the negotiation can be already used to gain valuable information about the negotiation partner. The negotiator may e.g. obtain information about the person s/he is negotiating with (interests, expertise, negotiation style, personality etc.) and the organisation the negotiator is working for (organisational structure etc.). If the parties are aware of the fact that an exchange of sensitive information will take place, it is recommended to sign a non-disclosure agreement (NDA) in this initial phase of the negotiation process.

---

[4] Sears and Rowe (2003), pp. 13–24.

[5] Chartrand and Bargh (1999), pp. 893–910.

2.3 The Core Phase of the Negotiations

The core phase of the negotiations will only be presented briefly and fragmentally, since the concepts explained in the main part of the book deal comprehensively with the characteristics of this phase. According to our understanding as it is presented here, the core phase of negotiations, extends from the point of the → *first offer*, which sets the *anchor* (→ *anchoring*) for the negotiations, to the final offer (→ *BAFO*), and its acceptance or rejection by the relevant → *decision-maker*. This range encompasses the full negotiation, in which the parties strive for solutions, options, and compromises (see thematic list "solutions and compromises").

The strategies and tactics (see topic list) presented in this book can be particularly applied for the core phase of negotiations. These strategies range from a win-lose approach (→ *win-lose strategy*) to → *win-win strategies*, for example. Among the tactics presented here, a clear distinction can be drawn between aggressive tactics and those, which exploit the effects of → *behavioural economics*. Aggressive tactics, for example, aim to mislead the negotiation partner (see thematic list "deceptions"), or are based on exerting pressure and threats (see corresponding topic list). It is important to at least know those tactics and possible reactions to them, as they are used regularly.[6] Some authors even consider bluffing as a necessary skill of a negotiator.[7] In practice, negotiators often lie or overstate their own BATNA (→ *better offer*), bluff about the availability of a product (→ *tactic of small quantities*) or pretend that there are → *budget limitations* (see also → *all I've got*). Whether a negotiator wants to use those tactics, depends on his/her ethical standards. But even if one is not inclined to use those techniques it is important to at least be aware of them and have knowledge on how to prevent or respectively to react to them, if your negotiation partner makes use of them. Common tactics that include threats are: → *see you in court*, → *BAFO*, → *take it or leave it*, → *Russian front*.

Tactics which exploit the effects of → *behavioural economics* use the fact that people do not always act rationally. In fact, actions of people—and therefore also negotiators—are marked by restrictions on rationality, will power and the pursuit of self-interest. → *Biases* show the systematic distortions of perception, memory, thinking, and decision making. In negotiations, the *anchoring effect* (→ *anchoring*) is probably the most famous decision heuristic. The anchoring effect shows that a distortion can be observed into the direction of the anchor (in negotiations, often the first price offer) without the people concerned being aware of this effect. This is why it is often recommended to make the → *first offer* to use the anchoring effect for own benefits. For more tactics basing on these kinds of effect, see the corresponding thematic list ("behavioural economics – effects").

---

[6] "In the context of negotiations, bluffing is a generally accepted business practice where pretense is used to imply that one's position is stronger, more clever or more determined etc., than one's position really is." Guth (2008), p. iii.

[7] "Commercial negotiations seem to require a talent for deception." Shell (1991), p. 93; see also Lakhani (2007), p. 101.

Then again, there are tactics and techniques which encourage cooperative negotiating (see thematic list "cooperative negotiating"). Some of them have been mentioned already with regard to the start of the negotiations (see Sect. 2.2) as they are used to build rapport and mutual trust. But they are also used throughout the negotiation and are focused on equally considering the factor of → *emotions*. The tactic → *building a golden bridge* e.g., gives the other party the opportunity to agree to a proposed compromise without losing face. Cooperative tactics and techniques take into consideration that the relationship between the parties plays a particularly significant role in the negotiation itself. Depending on the nature of the contract and with a view to the implementation of the contract and potential negotiations in the future (→ *permanent business relation*), the relationship can be crucially important. Building and maintaining a good relationship and mutual trust therefore not only poses a task to be performed in the context of the initial phase of negotiations, but is also a challenge that needs to be addressed throughout all phases of the negotiation. The → *Harvard negotiation concept* generally recommends that people and arising problems need to be dealt with separately from each other. This implies that problems on the relational level should not be solved with compromises on the factual level. On the relational level → *emotions* are of outstanding importance. The → *core concerns framework*[8] identifies central aspects that are in the foreground of the negotiation. According to this concept, five basic needs of negotiators have to be addressed: (1) Appreciation, (2) affiliation, (3) autonomy, (4) status and (5) role. Contrary, however, to the initial recommendation given by the Harvard negotiation concept, some tactics deliberately aim to improve the own negotiation position by utilising emotions.

The fact as to whether there is an existing → *principal-agent-problem* within the negotiations also has a significant effect on the core phase of the negotiation. A principal-agent-problem arises when a principal commissions someone to act as his/her agent[9]; in this particular case, to negotiate and make decisions in his/her place. In this, several techniques and various specific tactics can be applied (e.g. → *calling a higher authority*, → *the missing person manoeuvre*, or the→ *entanglement tactic*) which cannot be used if the negotiator negotiates for himself/herself. Moreover, in order to ensure successful negotiations, a principal-agent-situation implies a hierarchically structured relationship between the principal and the agent. Eventually, a principal-agent-situation leads to two kinds of negotiations (1) *at the table* and (2) *behind the table* (→ *principal-agent-problem*).

In any event, the core phase of the negotiation is characterised by two phases: Expanding the negotiation pie and consequently distributing it. Ideally, the parties aim at enlarging the *negotiation pie* (*expanding the pie* (→ *negotiation pie*)) before distributing it. However, negotiators generally tend to underestimate the potential of expanding the pie. Oftentimes, they assume a *fixed pie* (→ *negotiation pie*).[10]

[8] Developed by Fisher and Shapiro (2005), p. 25 et seqq.

[9] The concept was developed in the 1970s. for basic findings cf. Jensen and Meckling (1976), pp. 305–360.

[10] Thompson and Hastie (1990), pp. 98–123; Bazerman and Neale (1983), pp. 211–228.

Achieving a mutually satisfactory result is easier if both parties value certain aspects differently. Different (but yet not opposing) preferences can help to enlarge the pie substantially. Equal interests also promote the achievement of mutually beneficial results. Expanding the pie requires the negotiators to share information in order to evaluate commonly shared or deviating interests. However, the → *negotiator's dilemma* sometimes prevents parties from cooperating. The negotiator's dilemma describes the circumstance that negotiators oftentimes fear being cheated on, if they cooperate and thus decide to negotiate competitively. A subcase of the negotiator's dilemma is the so-called *information exchange dilemma* (→ *negotiator's dilemma*), where both parties fear that the other side will withhold crucial information if oneself discloses information first. In order to overcome this impasse, it is generally recommendable to initially only disclose smaller parts of information and wait for the opposing parties' reaction. This approach is regarded to be a certain kind of → *signalling*. If the negotiation partner behaves reciprocally, i.e. there is a synallagmatic exchange of information, further information can be delivered safely. If not, one stops → *sharing information* as well, but keeps an open door to restart an information exchange at a later stage of the negotiation (→ *generous tit for tat-strategy*).

As it is crucial for the negotiators to gather information, this book includes various questioning techniques (see topic list "questioning techniques"), which are particularly suitable for gaining information. Research shows that successful negotiators ask twice as many questions as average negotiators.[11] Closely linked to these questioning techniques are the answering techniques (see topic list "answering techniques"), which, among other things, can help fend off the negotiating partners' request for information. In this context, it is essential to reiterate the importance of listening (see topic list "listening"). The → *70-30-rule* suggests that negotiators should spend 70% of their time listening to their negotiation partner and only use 30% of the time to talk themselves in order to gain more valuable information. The skill of → *active listening* encourages the negotiation partner to carry on talking, i.e. sharing more details. In the field of negotiations, special attention should also be paid to the informative value of → *body language*.

In a second step, a negotiation is a matter of distributing (→ *distributive negotiations*) the (expanded) → *negotiation pie*. In this respect, the price is oftentimes the decisive aspect. Because of the above-mentioned *anchoring effect* (→ *anchoring*), it is recommendable to propose a → *first offer* if the situation allows for it. The anchor works best if it is well-justified (see topic list "argumentation techniques") and if the negotiation partner has already rather → *low expectations*. If the counterpart made the first offer, it is key for the negotiator not to make an immediate counteroffer himself. Instead, the negotiator should try to induce his/her negotiation partner to make a better offer. Many tactics can be used in this context. The tactic → *not happy* focuses on expressing disagreement with the offer and is usually followed by the request to improve the offer. But not only words can express the refusal of an offer. → *Silence* as a reaction to an offer is usually perceived as a very negative (and

[11] Rackham and Carlisle (1978a), p. 9.

aggressive) sign. Also shaking one's head is a clear sign of a refusal (→ *wince*). *Discrediting the anchor* (→ *anchoring*) is another frequently used tactic to induce the other party to improve their offer. The negotiation partner, who is faced with those tactics has to be cautious not to fall into the trap of negotiating against him/herself. S/he should instead insist on a counteroffer. After using those tactics, the party usually sets a counter-anchor. The anchor and the counter-anchor determine the bargaining range.

Throughout the negotiation process, but particularly with regard to the specific phase where the negotiation pie is distributed, argumentation techniques have a significant role (see topic list "argumentation techniques"). These techniques primarily serve to convince the negotiating partner of the own position. In this context, it first has to be established which party carries the → *burden of justification*. The term not only refers to the requirement of justifying one's own opinion but also refers to the fact that in cases of argumentative doubt, the preferred opinion is the one, which does not require justification. In negotiations, it is preferable to shift the burden of justification onto the other party, as it is always harder for the person who is obliged to justify something. Moreover, it is generally recommendable to use rather → *fewer but convincing arguments*, because it is vice versa promising to first attack the weak arguments used by your counterpart. Common argumentation techniques include: → *conclusion by analogy* and the so-called → *floodgate argument*.

The core phase of the negotiations is a process and can be more or less time consuming, depending on the specific circumstances. Small negotiations are concluded within minutes, whereas big negotiations can take up to months or years of countless meetings. Hence, the negotiation process can also be interrupted by → *negotiation pauses* and postponement. The parties can, and in fact also should use these occurring interruptions to prepare for further negotiations e.g. by analysing new documents or working on improving one's → *BATNA*, consult with the → *decision-maker* or their → *back office* and reflect on the current stage of negotiations. If the negotiations have not been going well, → *deadlocks* can develop very quickly. It is the task of the negotiators to prevent possibly occurring deadlocks or once they occurred overcome them. Negotiators should always keep in mind, that → *time* is a key component, both, while preparing for negotiations as well as during the actual negotiations. Lengthy negotiations should be by all means avoided, since the costs they incur can be significant. The time factor must also be taken into account, since both the own sides and the negotiating partner's BATNA underlies dynamic changes over the course of time. Thus, various tactics are based on time (e.g. → *calculated delay*, → *false deadline*, → *missing person manoeuvre*). In order to comply with the given time-frame, the parties have instruments, such as a set → *agenda* or given → *deadlines*.

In the context of negotiations, it is generally advisable to record → *interim results* in writing. In this context, the person who is in charge of putting interim results to paper enjoys an advantage (known as the → *rule of pen*). Documenting interim results inter alia precludes the development of → *foggy recalls*. Foggy recall refers to situations, where an orally made agreement is written down later by one of the parties. In those situations, there is a constant risk that the written text does not exactly correspond with the before orally agreed terms.

At the end of the negotiation phase, the parties have to decide for or against the conclusion of the negotiated contract. The underlying factors for this decision are on the one hand, the own → *BATNA*, which was already identified in the preparation phase of the negotiations and has subsequently been adapted throughout the negotiation, and on the other hand the → *deal-breakers*. These factors are also the basis for assessing the negotiation result. Being in possession of a better BATNA normally leads to the discontinuation of negotiations, whereas a worse BATNA prompts the conclusion of the negotiated contract.

2.4 The Agreement

This phase of the negotiations is not the subject matter of this book. The focus of this phase is on designing the contract, i.e. how the negotiated result can be contractually specified. This is foremost a legal question on which extensive literature is available in all jurisdictions. The contract design does not chronologically follow after the negotiation, but is rather a continuous process which takes place from the preparation of negotiations (see. Sect. 2.1) throughout the actual contract negotiation (Sect. 2.3). The core phase of the negotiations usually ends once the agreement is concluded.

This book only presents a few selected key aspects of contract design. Negotiations in the B2B field commonly rely on general terms and conditions.[12] In many cases, the contract terms are pre-formulated and have been proposed by one party, thus the only factor requiring negotiation is the price. But even when contracts are negotiated more intensively, specific → *boilerplates*, i.e. standard clauses, are implemented. Among others, these can include the written form requirement, escalation clauses, → *negotiation clauses*, change order clauses or clauses defining the choice of law. In some cases, contracts also include clauses that are in practice not legally enforceable. One example of such a clause is the so-called simple effort clause (→ *empty promise*). As the name suggests, these clauses only "promise to make an effort", but in fact do not pledge to guarantee any specific result.

2.5 The Implementation of the Agreement

The importance and the procedure of the implementation of the agreement strongly depend on the nature of the contract. The implementation of the contract poses a major challenge, especially for complex, large-scale projects such as construction projects, plant construction agreements etc. In these cases, the relationship between the parties (i.e. on the relational level) is of particular importance, as the successful implementation of the contract relies on the cooperation of the parties in the

[12] With regard to the specific legal situation in Germany see Jung and Krebs (2016), p. 235 et seq.

implementation phase. Under such circumstances, the trust and rapport between the negotiating parties plays a significant role. When it comes to large-scale projects, there is a very high risk of conflict (and a potential conflict aftermath). The parties can therefore agree on ex ante provisions for possible escalations (e.g. by defining certain stages of escalation). The negotiators need to keep the implementation of the contract in mind during all preceding negotiation phases. It is particularly the → *deal-makers*, who focus on the smooth implementation of the contract and try to safeguard a trouble-free implementation by means of provisions in the contract (known as the so-called safe harbour principle). Nonetheless, not all eventualities can be dealt with ex ante (incomplete contracts). Accordingly, legal risk management comprehensively analyses all occurring legal risks, even those arising during the implementation of the contract.

The key terms described in this book are only marginally concerned with the implementation phase. One central component of this is the so-called → *claim management*. This involves recognising deviations of the actual state from the contractually agreed target state, and the enforcement of claims resulting from these deviations. Further, claim management also prevents the entitlement and enforcement of claims from the opposing party. → *Renegotiations* are also a typical element within the implementation phase. These might be legitimate, if circumstances have changed. They can even be used to enlarge the → *negotiation pie*, consequently achieving a better negotiation result for both parties. On the other hand, *opportunistic renegotiations* (→ *renegotiations*) can be rather problematic.

2.6 The Ex-Post-Phase

Above all, the ex-post-phase is a time to reflect on the negotiation and create a sustainable learning effect for future negotiations. Negotiators should ask themselves what went well (→ *WWW*) and what could be improved for future negotiations (→ *WWYDD*). Experiences are often categorized according to their situational context. In many cases, this categorisation is so narrow that it becomes more difficult to transfer the knowledge obtained to new situations. It can thus be helpful to systemize the experiences according to basic structures. So-called deal sheets, used in the course of negotiation analyses to record the main aspects of the negotiations, can help in this case. The company can subsequently systematically evaluate the deal sheets and use them to develop → *prenegotiation plans* with incorporated checklists. As already mentioned above, negotiations constitute an iterative process, which is why the ex-post-phase should not only be used to improve the preparation process, but also the other phases of negotiations such as the start of the negotiations and the core phase of negotiations. In order to make use of the ex-post-phase it is crucial to understand the structures and mechanisms of negotiations. As the negotiation itself is mentally very demanding, it is easier for negotiators to reflect on a negotiation if they went into the negotiation with two people. The other person cannot only be the → *analyst* during the negotiation, but equally a partner to reflect upon the negotiation in the ex-post-phase.

Chapter 3
Alphabetical List of Key Notions

7-38-55-rule This rule was established by *Albert Mehrabian*[1] in 1968 and refers to the effect that messages have on the conversation partner. According to this rule, how a statement is perceived depends only to 7% on the actual content of the message. The tone of voice is said to determine the effect of what is said to 38% while the decisive factor, with 55%, is → *body language*. The results of the study cannot be fully transferred to contract negotiations since only the effect of individual words was tested. However, the study reveals that body language is a significant factor which is not to be underestimated and shall also play a major role in contract negotiations.

70-30-rule This rule states that negotiators should spend 70% of their time listening and only 30% actually talking. Of course, the exact relation between listening and talking cannot be quantified. Moreover, this rule cannot apply to two negotiators at once, as the appropriate conversation portions of both negotiators need to amount to 100%. All the same, the rule illustrates how important it is to listen (carefully) to one's negotiating partner. Listening holds the opportunity of gathering important information, e.g. regarding the opposing party's interests, preferences and expectations as well as about the concrete negotiation subject. Apart from that, it helps create time windows for your own thoughts. During negotiations, negotiators should therefore be careful not to take up too much speaking time. Professional negotiators tend to exactly follow this approach. You can encourage your negotiating partner to speak by asking questions, e.g. → *open questions* and → *active listening*.

80-20-rule The 80-20-rule was developed by *Leigh L. Thompson*[2] and emphasises how important the preparation of negotiations is in relation to the other → *negotiation*

[1] Cf. Mehrabian (1971).

[2] Thompson (2014).

S. Jung, P. Krebs, *The Essentials of Contract Negotiation*,
https://doi.org/10.1007/978-3-030-12866-1_3

phases, particularly the actual negotiation. According to *Thompson*, the **preparation of the negotiation** is four times as important as the actual negotiation itself, giving rise to the 80-20-rule. Correspondingly, it is recommended that negotiators invest a considerable amount of time and energy in the preparation phase.

Even though a specific quantitative determination of the importance of preparation seems questionable, the rule certainly indicates that successful negotiations are based on intensive preparation. Frequently, negotiators do not invest a sufficient amount of preparation time. Although preparation time can vary depending on the individual case, a lack of preparation time is often devoted to the specifics of the concrete negotiation. *James A. Baker* III (formerly White House Chief of Staff, Secretary of Treasury und Secretary of State), described the importance of negotiation preparation using the notion of **5 Ps**.[3]

- ***P**rior **P**reparation **P**revents **P**oor **P**erformance.*

A study by *Rackham/Carlisle* also suggests that not only the time invested in preparation is relevant, but also what the negotiator focuses on during this preparation. The results of the study show that successful negotiators spend twice as much time simulating possible options for action and the potential results than average negotiators.[4]

A-not-A Question The A-not-A-question is a form of → *closed question*. It is a technique that serves to obtain information. Despite the (apparent) neutrality, the purpose of this type of question is generally to clarify a presumption. It is a subtype of the or-question, although unlike the normal form of the or-question, no alternative is given. Like or-questions, and unlike → *yes/no questions,* A-not-A-questions are not intended to suggest to the respondent which answer is expected. As a rule, however, the questioner will rather expect the affirmative answer—i.e. the answer that the assumption is true. This type of questioning is particularly common in the Republic of China.

Example
"Is it true that the head of your research department is moving to the competition or is it not true that he is moving?"

ACBD-Rule The ACBD-rule was established by *Fisher* and *Shapiro*[5] and is the abbreviation for the recommendation:

---

[3] Baker (2006), p. 5.

[4] Rackham and Carlisle (1978b), p. 2.

[5] Fisher and Shapiro (2005), p. 84.

- **A**lways
- **C**onsult
- **B**efore
- **D**eciding

Accordingly, the rule calls for the relevant *stakeholders* (→ *think beyond the table*) to be involved in the decision-making process in the form of a consultation prior to a decision being made. To conduct this procedure, identifying the stakeholders is essential. Within the → *core concerns framework*, this measure is intended to give stakeholders a stronger sense of involvement and thus autonomy. However, this will only be successful if the → *decision-maker* can convey stakeholders the feeling that their contributions are actually taken seriously. For the decision-maker on the other hand, the challenge is to listen to the stakeholders while not being overly influenced in his/her decision making.

Active Listening Active listening, a communication technique aimed at creating a positive atmosphere for communication, helps the negotiator to gather additional information and can be conducted by means of verbal and non-verbal signals. The speaker can be encouraged by non-verbal communication, especially signals such as nodding, facing towards the negotiating partner and maintaining direct visual contact. Active listening can also be expressed verbally, e.g. by using specific words.

Example
"Yes", "I see", "oh", "hmm"

Also, short queries signal active listening.

Example
"And then?", "Really?" "Is that what he said?"

What's more, repeating or slightly changing your negotiating partner's key sentences demonstrates that you have received as well as comprehensively understood what s/he said, although this specific type of communication is sometimes no longer perceived as active listening.

Active listening is a communication technique frequently recommended for negotiations. Although this is generally accepted, since active listening contributes to a positive and constructive negotiation atmosphere, using the active listening technique can restrict the negotiator to a certain degree as it limits his/her options for reacting to the statements of the opposing side. If the aim is to keep all available options for reaction open, it might—especially in the context of very critical questions—be better to remain silent initially, i.e. to encounter the negotiating partner with purely passive, but concentrated and attentive behaviour in reaction to the stated proposal, information or justification.

Adopt an Outsider Lens This technique recommends that negotiators should, even without calling in a third party, e.g. an expert, adopt an external objective perspective during negotiations, at least temporarily. The aim is not to assess the negotiations from the negotiating partner's perspective but rather to adopt a neutral outsider's perspective. This emotionally detached view attempts to prevent the mistakes that can arise from → *biases,* for instance. Likewise, certain thought patterns can be blanked out, allowing for the discovery of new opportunities which are much harder to detect from an internal point of view. However, if negotiators are emotionally involved in the negotiations (→ *emotions*), they will struggle to adopt this external view.

Advocatus Diaboli On the one hand, advocatus diaboli describes a technique which aims at conveying serious concerns that could offend the negotiation partner in a mild way. For this purpose, the party raising the serious concerns calls himself/herself the "advocatus diaboli" (**the devil's advocate**) in order to express that these fundamental doubts are "of course" not in line with his/her personal way of thinking. This serves to distinguish the personal relationship from the rational relationship between the negotiation parties. However, it may also be that an attack which is really meant personally is concealed behind the phrase "advocatus diaboli". In practice, the application of this technique does not necessarily require use of the phrase "the devil's advocate". For example, it would also be possible to ascribe concerns to a third party, e.g. to one's superior (then it is actually a form of the → *good cop/bad cop* tactic); or to declare it a joint task to fend off an expected offensive by a third party and to mention the possible means of attack in this context.

On the other hand, it makes particular sense to implement the advocatus diaboli technique during the preparation phase of negotiations (→ *80-20-rule*), i.e. within the company. In these situations, a negotiator of the team takes on the "role" of advocatus diaboli. In this way the negotiation team can realistically prepare for the negotiation partner's argumentation and reactions.

Agenda The agenda constitutes a technical tool with great practical relevance for the success of the negotiations. It is the agenda which determines if and what, when—and to a certain extent even how (e.g. with which → *negotiation pauses*)—a subject is discussed within the negotiation process. The agenda can facilitate a quick or slow negotiation; a trustful or confrontational negotiation. The question often arises as to whether and when problematic issues should be brought up. Concerning toxic issues, i.e. particularly problematic aspects, the general rule is to discuss these aspects neither in the early stages of the negotiation nor in the final negotiation phase. Concerning the attitude towards the agenda in the different negotiation cultures, see Chap. 4.

Based on the agenda's great importance for the negotiation success, it is generally desirable to **control the agenda**. It must be noted that proper control does not only include establishing an agenda, but also its actual implementation. In practice, the party with the greatest → *negotiation power* usually controls the agenda.

During the drafting and implementation process of the agenda it can, for instance, be useful to firstly negotiate several smaller points which are likely to be concluded successfully. This ensures a trustful basis and builds negotiating confidence before other more problematic points are tackled. This can be largely ensured by the agenda. In addition, the temporal consolidation or separation of negotiation points also influences the likelihood that these aspects can be aggregated to a package-deal (see also → *logrolling*). Sometimes even the order of negotiation points can be decisive in determining whether a subject is perceived as legitimate or illegitimate. This is due to the fact that the order of negotiation points is an integral part of → *framing*.

The time frame can influence how long and thus how thoroughly something is discussed. Usually, no particular attention is paid to aspects which were not included in the agenda from the outset. The alignment of the negotiation process with the agenda, i.e. the sequential negotiation of the individual points, is sometimes also referred to as the **one-way-street principle**.

Akerlof Market The Akerlof market is a term adopted from the field of new institutional economics and was named after its original discoverer, *George A. Akerlof*.[6] The effects occurring in this market should also be taken into consideration in contract negotiations. By using the example of the used car market, *Akerlof* proved that if quality is not transparent on the market, poor quality (lemons) will initially be preferred over good quality (peaches). This is due to the fact that buyers allow for the risk of buying goods of poor quality and are therefore not willing to pay a price that would be appropriate for the good quality on offer. Due to a lack of transparency, the quality cannot be evaluated beforehand. This constitutes a subcategory of adverse selection. The arising effect is based on **information asymmetries** in the market.

Example

A commodity is available on the market in two different grades of quality (grade A and B). Grade A is very high quality and thus also expensive. Grade B barely meets the minimum requirements and is accordingly offered at a lower price. However, the customers only perceive the difference in price and not the difference in quality, since differences in quality are not readily apparent to the buyer (information asymmetry). Demand is hence almost exclusively for the commodity with the poorer quality (B) so that the sale of the grade A product is no longer worthwhile. In the long-term, the grade A commodity will vanish from the market. If, however, information symmetry existed, those buyers willing to pay a higher price for better quality would opt for commodity A.

[6] Akerlof (1970), pp. 488–500.

Negotiators should be aware of this process, due to which no → *pareto-optimal* results can be achieved. If negotiators recognise that their product is exposed to this issue, they should take appropriate measures to overcome adverse selection. As a countermeasure, the seller can make use of → *signalling*, for example. Put simply, the seller provides the buyer with information that credibly signals the quality of the goods (e.g. by using a seal of approval or expert opinion by an independent third party or offering guarantees). Signalling is used to enable the selling party to gain distance from other sellers offering goods of poorer quality. A kind of self-selection can furthermore be achieved by offering different types of contract. Another approach is screening, which is particularly used in the field of insurance and leads to a classification of customers according to their choice of contract. Experience has shown that partial insurance is more likely to be taken out by people with a lower risk rate, whereas people with an increased risk tend to take out a full insurance, even if this is more expensive. The relationship between the negotiator and the company s/he represents is also an Akerlof-market (→ *principal-agent-problem*).

All I've Got In contract negotiations, "all I've got" refers to a tactic which involves one side stating an objective limit that, for whatever reason, should not be exceeded. The name of the tactic is derived from the formulation of this limit: "This is all I have got to offer". However, this objective limit does not always exist as claimed. It is perfectly feasible that the limit is a mere bluff. If the limit is simply alleged, information asymmetry is used to avoid giving in to the negotiation pressure exerted by the opposing side. Should the negotiator realise or suspect that the objective limit does not exist, or that it is at least negotiable, s/he will maintain the negotiating pressure. At the same time, it makes sense for the opposing party to create the opportunity for the opposing party to back down from a priorly made statement without "losing face" In the case of a bluff, the success of the tactic thus depends on its credibility, the existing information asymmetries and the fact if the parties are already negotiating within the → *ZOPA*. In the authors' view, this misleading form of the all I've got technique can be regarded as a form of → *cunning deception* and can therefore generally not be sanctioned legally. In some cases, there are in fact objective limits (e.g. such as budget limits or limits on quantity due to limited capacity). Mentioning them should either lead the negotiating partner to accept the named limits or encourage him/her to seek a common solution.

Ambitious Target Price Setting Within this tactic the primary goal is to set ambitious goal prices. Hence, it is a tactic where the negotiator puts pressures on himself/herself to achieve better negotiation results. Setting an ambitious and yet not unrealistic price is a general recommendation in the context of the *negotiation preparations* (→ *80-20-rule*).[7] In a broad sense, this also applies for the overall setting of negotiation targets (i.e. including beyond the setting of prices). The tactic of aiming

[7] For this effect cf. White and Neale (1994), pp. 303–317.

for high negotiation targets is known as **aim high**. In this context, English negotiation literature refers to a quote attributed to *Jing*, King of Zhou:

> High achievement comes from high aims.

Instead of striving for an abstract "very good" result, specific goals should be determined. These goals may inter alia be set in the form of price or percentage targets, which are determined in relation to other prices. Only if you aim high you can hope to achieve appropriate results. High aims elicit corresponding efforts and moreover establish an optimistic mind-set. A high negotiation aim functions as a self-fulfilling prophecy. Negotiators should therefore set specific, ambitious targets (**be specific**),[8] such as a 10% lower price than in previous comparable purchases and not just aim for "a good result". Specific aims generally produce good negotiation results.[9]

An ambitious goal can help to achieve better results, especially if your own → *BATNA* is not particularly promising. Without an ambitious goal, every result which appears better than the possible alternative would be perceived as positive. Moreover, specific targets help to prevent the *anchoring effect* (→ *anchoring*).[10] The more justification grounds a party can state for their own position, the less likely they are to be influenced by the opposing side's anchor. This said, ambitious aims are not without difficulty for the companies' representatives. A subjective feeling of failure can easily arise if ambitious goals are not met regularly. The situation becomes even more problematic if the results of the negotiation are compared with the previously set negotiating objective. This can potentially result in a negative evaluation within the company. If there are internal problems within the company, negotiators are tempted to avoid ambitious targets.

Furthermore, setting ambitious prices can impact the relationship between the parties as ambitious prices are often the incentive to negotiate harder. In → *permanent business relations* especially, an ambitious price setting can therefore influence the relationship between the parties negatively.[11] For this reason, in these cases it is particularly important to apply strategies which aim towards improving the relations between the parties (e.g. → *building a golden bridge*, or applying conciliatory gestures).

Analyst Better negotiation results can be achieved by means of an analyst. S/he analyses the entire negotiations, above all focussing not only on how the opposing side conducts the negotiation but also examining his/her own side's negotiation behaviour. To begin with, his/her task is to not only gather as much information as possible of contentual, argumentative, and emotional nature but also to register the

[8] Cf. Shell (2006), p. 36.

[9] Locke et al. (1981), p. 129 et seqq.

[10] Galinsky and Mussweiler (2001), pp. 657–669.

[11] Lai et al. (2013), pp. 1–12.

nuances between the individual negotiators. The analyst does this by observing the negotiations. It is then his/her responsibility to process these findings for the further course of the negotiation and provide (creative) suggestions (options for action). Ideally, there is a certain amount of emotional distance between the analyst and the negotiations, since emotional involvement can mitigate his/her competences (→ *emotions*).

The analyst should reveal → *misunderstandings* (this comprises one of the few exceptions where active intervention in the ongoing negotiations would make sense). The analyst also compiles the arguments, interests and positions presented and in this context especially attempts to analyse the opposing side's individual negotiators singly. Likewise, it is his/her task to reveal the shortcomings of his/her own side's position, thus exposing any possible vulnerabilities which are open to be the victim of exploitation by the negotiating partner. Generally speaking, the financial status of a company does often not allow to hire an analyst. Yet in a negotiation team of → *two negotiators*, the person who is currently not negotiating can adopt this role to a certain degree. This person is however emotionally involved in the negotiation. Shortly after analysing the situation, s/he will resume his/her part in the negotiations and thus the analytical result is generally considerably lower than the result provided by a professional analyst. Consciously assuming the role of an analyst in cases of emotional provocation often makes more sense than evaluating the emotional provocation from a participants' point of view as it can help maintain emotional control as well as one's own analytical ability.

Anchoring The term "anchoring" describes both a psychological-behavioural effect (known as the **anchoring effect**, **anchor heuristics**) as well as the tactical approach making use of this effect.[12]

The anchoring effect ranks among decision heuristics as it distinctly influences a person's decision. For instance, the price setting in negotiations is a particularly decisive factor. Anchor heuristics are created when the offer made by the negotiation counterparty (the anchor) affects your own counteroffer (second anchor or **counter-anchor**). Distortion can be observed in the direction of the anchor (here the first price offer) without the people concerned being aware of the effect. A possible explanation for the anchoring effect can be found in the selective availability of information.[13] Here it is presumed that the first offer influences the amount of information recalled from memory. If the offer is high, the buyer revives "justifying" recollections such as the quality, or the use of valuable materials; whereas a low offer accordingly effects connotations such as simple equipment, short period of use etc.

Anchoring within the negotiation process (also see under → *bracketing*) serves to determine an accepted starting point for the subsequent negotiations (the search for a → *reference point* serves a similar purpose and usually takes place earlier in

[12] Strack and Mussweiler (1997), pp. 437–446; Wilson et al. (1996), pp. 387–402.

[13] Strack and Mussweiler (1997), pp. 437–446.

the process). Anchor tactics aim to enforce their own demands by using the known heuristics. To put it simply, anchoring exploits the fact that in many cases there is a prevalent uncertainty about fair prices or other conditions. Moreover, generally speaking, in some cases there is no, or hardly any existing knowledge about the own sides'/or the opposing parties' → *BATNA*. Various studies have shown that even irrelevant or totally unrealistic figures can in fact influence a negotiator's perception and thus also his/her decision-making process.

Even experts are subject to the anchor effect.[14] As soon as one side names the first price, the (subjective) anchor is set. The counterbid then becomes the counter-anchor (or second-anchor). Since there is a predominate tendency to view the middle ground between two anchors as a fair compromise in the absence of conflicting information (→ *midpoint-rule*; not withstanding other practices, e.g. at a bazaar), it would seem sensible to set the (initial) anchor quite far from the actual desired target price. Anchoring raises the question of whether it is more advantageous to make the → *first offer* or let your negotiating partner go first.

Prima facie the party setting the second anchor has the advantage in that the counter-anchor determines the point midway between both anchors. What is more, it is possible that the negotiating partner will set the first anchor unfavourably for his/her own interests due to a lack of knowledge (e.g. the seller of a work of art setting a too low asking price). This underlines how advantageous it can be to set the second anchor.

However, some (second) anchors are also set too far from an actually possible negotiation result. This discourages the negotiating partner from believing an actual settlement is possible, which may lead him/her not to not start negotiations in the first place or to terminate the negotiations in progress. Moreover, the anchor's persuasive power is crucial. As the party setting the first anchor has a wider range of options available, s/he may find that employing (sound) rationale will induce his/her negotiating partner not to set the counter-anchor too far away (anchoring effect). If the party setting the second anchor (counter-anchor) chooses to do so far from the well-argued first anchor and yet for no discernible reason, it presents itself as not being willing to compromise and their negotiating partner may even regard the party as being untrustworthy. This can lower the chances of reaching an agreement or may possibly reduce the positive effect of the counter-anchor. Generally speaking, the question of the legitimacy of the anchor or counter-anchor may induce the negotiating partner to shift his/her anchor/counter-anchor, if s/he cannot find an appropriate justification for it.

On the whole, the impact of the anchor on the counter-anchor should compensate for the theoretical advantage of having a freely selectable counter-anchor. Studies suggest that negotiators who set the first offer frequently achieve economically more advantageous results.[15] Whether this result is due to the actual first-anchor or can rather be put down to a certain strength of leadership and better market

[14] Englich et al. (2006), pp. 188–200.

[15] Galinsky and Mussweiler (2001), pp. 657–669.

knowledge, still remains to be researched. Be that as it may, if someone is sufficiently confident in the content of their own anchor, it might very well be beneficial for them to set the first substantiated anchor. At the same time, it is important to ensure that this anchor does not appear to be purely subjective. You can try to raise the persuasive power of your anchor by using comparative prices which are, or appear to be, genuine, as well as other reference values, e.g. purchasing prices, which are, or appear to be, objective. However, generally speaking it should be noted that negotiators who set the first anchor tend to be subjectively less satisfied with the negotiation as a whole than negotiators who set the counter-anchor.[16] This may be due to the fact that negotiators setting the first anchor later feel regret or sense that they did not achieve or rather maximize the full potential of the negotiation. If one of the parties has no concept of what the appropriate price should be, it would be wise for them to set both a minimum (so-called → *deal-breaker*) and maximum target (→ *aspiration point*) for themselves anyhow, but to let the negotiating partner set the actual first anchor. The invitation to set the first anchor is known under the term "**you go first**" . Following this request, the negotiating partner cannot only set the counter-anchor, but can equally attempt to shift the anchor to the own favour without even setting the counter-anchor oneself. Since setting the anchor is of great importance for the overall negotiation process, it can induce the parties to approach this process extremely cautiously and slowly, consequently resulting in even slower, more time-consuming negotiations.

One special form of anchoring is the so-called **range offer**, where the anchor is determined by a specific range (e.g. we expect payments from 2500 EUR up to 3500 EUR per item). At first glance, this may seem rather unfavourable as the opposing party is sure to try to achieve a negotiation result under the midpoint (here 3000 EUR). In fact, the opposing party will usually push for the named minimum (here 2500 EUR). On the other hand, it can in fact be expedient that the negotiating partner is willing to accept the range as the basic scope for negotiations and just wants to pay less than average—or respectively a price close to the minimum. The range does generally not appear one-sided and in a sense, develops a suggestive force which prompts the partner to negotiate only within this range. If, for example, the own maximum target was 2600 EUR, setting an ambitious range offer can achieve outstanding negotiation results. When dealing with used goods or goods whose value cannot be precisely defined, setting a certain range may seem plausible and fair.

Overall, it can be said that the anchoring-tactic can certainly have a positive influence on your own negotiation result. Vice versa, it is essential to know how to counteract this effect when it is employed by the negotiating partner. The first and most important step is to be aware of this effect. From there onwards, one can specifically search for well-founded arguments against the anchor and its relevance. Likewise, setting clear objectives and focussing on these goals substantially reduces the anchoring effect. The same is true for concentrating on the opposing party's

[16] Rosette et al. (2014), pp. 629–647.

BATNA. However, the anchoring effect can only be diminished if there is sufficient relatively reliable knowledge of your partner's BATNA.[17]

In addition, there are several ways to influence the way the negotiating partner sets his/her anchor. For instance, a specific fair → *reference point* can be determined prior to the first anchoring in the negotiations. Discussing the merits of various alternative offers available on the market or thoroughly analysing the minor negative points regarding the specific conditions offered by the negotiating partner can elicit → *lower expectations* and accordingly influence the subsequent setting of the anchor. A further possible response to the negotiating partner's setting of the first-anchor is **discreditation of the anchor**. Where the aim is to achieve a result, which diverges from the midpoint of both offers (→ *midpoint-rule*), discrediting the opposing party's anchor is a widespread tactic. The anchor—the opposing party's initial demand—can be disputed as being unrealistic, forestalling the setting of a counter-anchor.

Example
"I find this offer unacceptable. The price you are asking for is way above the current market price. What changes can you make, price-wise?"

The aim of discreditation is to convince the negotiating partner to choose a different anchor before the counter-anchor is set. This can be achieved most effectively by referring to objective data or scientific expert statements. If the opposing party has completely unreasonable expectations, another tactic may be to fully ignore their set anchor. If this is the case, the negotiator should provide convincing arguments and allow the opposing party adequate time to free himself/herself from the prior offer without losing face. This procedure can prove quite challenging as the anchor always serves as an internal means of success control.

In addition to discreditation, there are other tactics for shifting an initially set anchor. To begin with, the negotiator can react by simply remaining silent (→ *silence*). This reaction generally induces the other party to at least provide further explanations and can even lead to them deviating from their starting position. This is mainly due to numerous negotiators finding silence in the course of negotiations very uncomfortable. Similarly effective as a means to having negotiators shift their initial anchors, are the negotiation tactics of → *wince* and → *not happy*.

Anchoring proves particularly problematic in constellations where one side sets a very high anchor, but the fair compromise is for instance at 1 or 2. This means that the counter-anchor cannot be placed at a sufficient distance. This phenomenon is referred to as the so called "**zero-point anchoring-problem**" and illustrates the interplay between anchoring and the → *midpoint-rule*. The problem is more frequent in negotiations which concern other aspects than the mere price. If someone is unwilling to accept a certain condition (e.g. if s/he is not willing to defer payment)

[17] Galinsky and Mussweiler (2001), pp. 657–669.

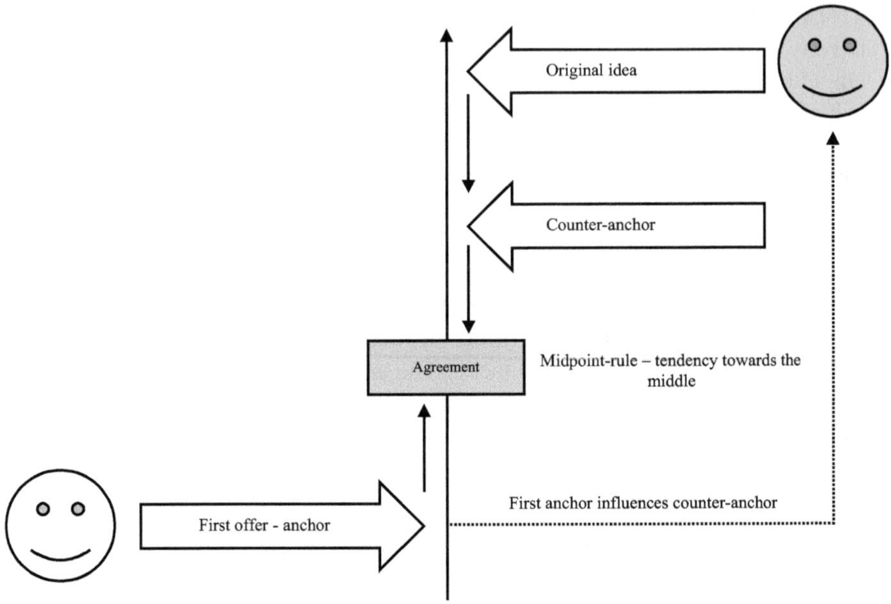

Fig. 3.1 Anchoring effect

his/her anchor is e.g. at point zero, as setting a counteroffer in the opposite direction is simply impossible. The specific issue is therefore that one party cannot maximize the distance between the set anchor and the desired target point, because setting an anchor below zero is not possible.

There are three actions which can however relativise the issue. Firstly, the parties can rely on neutral assessment criteria (→ *Harvard negotiation concept*). These criteria allow a solution which deviates from the middle point. The second option is to discredit the opposing side's anchor. Lastly, the negotiator has the option to simply refuse to negotiate this point (→ *undiscussable*). The disadvantage can also be overcome by firmly linking this negotiating point to another negotiating point, e.g. a point to which the other side can set their own zero-point anchor if necessary. The figure above illustrates the anchoring effect of the first offer (Fig. 3.1).

Annotations Annotations (further remarks on the drafts of the negotiating partner), are a technical means to support negotiations, used especially while preparing for negotiations or in between the single negotiation dates (in preparation for the next appointment). **Redlining** is closely related to annotations and refers to highlighting the clauses which are to be discussed. In major negotiations, at least one of the parties will make proposals for clauses, unless an entire corpus of clauses or even a complete draft contract (→ *single-text negotiation*) is to be negotiated. A distinction should be made between internal and external annotations: The first-mentioned are only intended for the own side, whereas external annotations are addressed to the negotiating partner himself/herself. Internal annotations on the suggestions proffered by the opposing party are made by various participants from one's own side and are meant to contribute to the preparation and support of the negotiations. Regarding the legal aspects, companies frequently consult the legal department or a law firm. Thus, legal advisors also participate indirectly in the negotiations. Internal annotations are also possible and helpful in evaluating one's own proposals, e.g. to clarify the purpose of a particular clause; why one alternative has not been accepted; or generally to discover which alternatives there are. Since internal annotations may include prime information, it is important to ensure that these are not passed on to the negotiating partner without prior reflection.

External annotations are passed on to the negotiating partner as a statement or comment and must also take tactical aspects into account. Just like clause suggestions, external annotations express a party's negotiation anchor (→ *anchoring*). In practice, it is not only common to make annotations, but also to change the respective text passages directly, rendering them visible for the negotiating partner. Changes can be made e.g. by using the modification mode (so called track change mode in a Word file) or by underlining, deleting, marking or using italics. Not highlighting changes can—depending on national law—be construed as a pre-contractual violation of duty or may render a concluded contract contestable due to fraudulent misrepresentation.

Due to the different functions of both forms of annotation, they should be strictly separated from each another.

Aspiration Point The aspiration point refers to the optimum offer pursued, i.e. the **maximum target**. It is alternatively also known under the term **aspiration level**. It is generally recommended that parties set a specific and ambitious maximum goal, since studies prove that this generally induces negotiators to strive for as well as achieve better negotiation results (→ *ambitious target price setting*). Sometimes it can be problematic that internal corporate structures do not provide the negotiators with proper incentives to set ambitious negotiation goals (→ *principal-agent-problem*). This is due to the fact that oftentimes there are (either formal or informal ways) of sanctioning the negotiator for not achieving the set goal. Accordingly, not succeeding to achieve the set negotiation target is perceived as a failure. Moreover, the goals set by the supervisor of the negotiations are oftentimes unrealistic. These unrealistic goals can result not only in the failure of the negotiations but can equally lead to results which, although matching the set goals on a pro forma basis, could only be achieved by taking considerable risks.

Instead of focusing on the concrete results of a negotiation, pre-emptive bonuses are sometimes offered for the conclusion of a contract. This can encourage negotiators to make broader price concessions than desired, in order for the contract to be concluded and the agreed-on bonus redeemed.

The maximum goal generally lies far above the → *resistance point* and thus is also located above the → *BATNA*. How the maximum goal is specifically determined depends on various criteria, inter alia the negotiating partner, the relationship towards the opposing party, the negotiation subject, the own pursued position in the negotiation, the opposing party's BATNA, as well as on the degree of information transfer (on both sides) etc. The aspiration point should not be mistaken for the → *first offer* or the *counter-anchor* (→ *anchoring*). These two factors determine the scope of negotiations.

As opposed to the *minimum goal* (→ *deal-breaker*) the maximum goal is not directly linked to a "decision" in a narrower sense. Of course, every company would be more than appreciative of an achieved result above the maximum goal. Yet, it is possible to stipulate in advance that if the maximum target is reached, the negotiators are immediately entitled to conclude the contract (negotiating proxy with power of attorney for the maximum target). For the negotiator who achieves the maximum goal, this success may be understood as a reward. The actual occurrence of such a situation is relatively rare, however, since reaching the (central) maximum goal is the exception; this does not apply to a large number of desired individual goals. Reaching the maximum target too easily and quickly is a good reason and starting point of critically re-evaluating the initial definition of the maximum target. In these cases, the assumption itself suggests that the aspiration point was set too low and that in possible follow-up negotiations in the future, the aim should be set higher.

The maximum goal should be determined prior to the starting phase of the negotiations, in order to have a formally determined benchmark for the monitoring of the achieved negotiation success and to combat the consequences of the → *anchoring effect*. Sometimes, the opposing negotiators' facial expressions as well as unexpected queries indicate that the opposing side's maximum has definitely been reached or even surpassed. Whoever made the overly favourable offer, may attempt to openly disengage from it: either by invoking a mistake (problematic from a psychological point of view) or by means of preventing an agreement of the parties on this specific point by setting additional, hardly acceptable constraints.

Example
Negotiations concern the sale of pipes. The seller's "aspiration level" is 100 EUR per unit, the "resistance point" (= BATNA) is 80 EUR per unit. The first offer (anchor) of the seller is 120 EUR. Both parties agree on 93 EUR.

Figure 3.2 shows how the relation between the resistance point (→ *deal-breaker*), → *BATNA*, → *first offer, aspiration level* (→ *aspiration point*) and eventual agreement can be designed, regarding the price in the context of a sale. In the illustrated example, the resistance point and BATNA are equal. If the offer is lower than the resistance point, it would be advisable to choose the BATNA. The first offer lies above the aspiration level and sets the anchor for the negotiations (The *counter-anchor* (→ *anchoring*) is not included in the illustration). In the example shown, the final price (agreement) lies between the aspiration level and the resistance point.

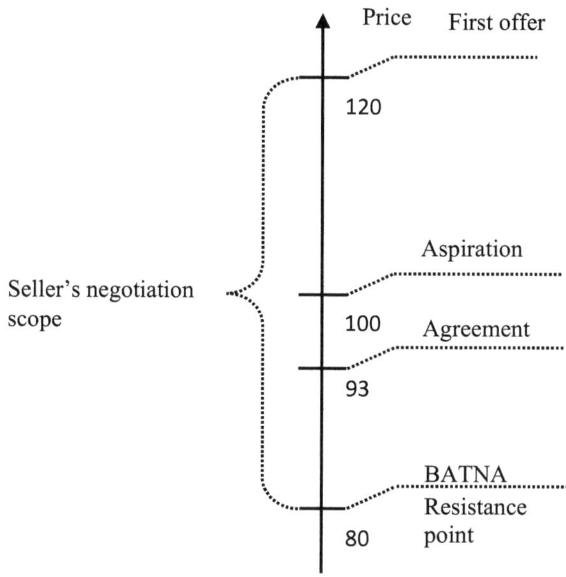

Fig. 3.2 The relation between first offer, aspiration level, BATNA and resistance point

Assertiveness Negotiation success also depends on the negotiator's psychological assertiveness in the form of mental strength. This particularly applies to negotiations between a small number of people or for → *chief negotiators* who clearly dominate the negotiations. More than that, mental strength plays a decisive role, especially if the → *BATNA* and other indications for one's own and the other party's objective negotiation power often remain at least partially ambiguous. The assertiveness level should therefore be taken into account when selecting the chief negotiator. However, a high level of assertiveness does not necessarily facilitate cooperative behaviour, since assertiveness can be associated with a tendency towards hard bargaining and may thus also increase the likelihood of a breakoff of the negotiation. Hence, the potentially greater success in negotiations is "bought" with a risk.

Auction A real auction is not a negotiation as such, but a pricing mechanism. The auction takes all sub-conditions as given and is only price-oriented. A (usually) low starting bid is intended to attract a larger number of interested parties. The counterpart to this so-called **English auction** is the reverse auction (**reversed–Dutch–auction**). This refers to an auction in which the price continuously decreases and the person making the first bid wins the auction. Although this form of auction is not very common, it is not entirely uncommon in the B2B sector. In the course of the classic (English) auction, the seller gains an excellent overview of his/her → *BATNA*, since the interested parties spur each other on. This can develop into an auction atmosphere in which the prospective buyers do not strive for a reasonable price but go all out to achieve "victory" in the auction. In addition, individual bidders do not tend to sufficiently consider potentially arising risks, based on incomplete information during the auction.

In addition, a larger number of bidders also creates bidding pressure. This is because the parties wrongly imply the adequacy of the (high) price from the large number of interested bidders (see further under → *bias*). In this case, not the market price but the bids made by others are used for price comparison and this tends to result in a higher price. To some extent this also applies to auctions with decreasing bids, well-known from the flower wholesale trade, for example. Anyone failing to propose an offer in good time does not only run the risk of paying too much, but instead jeopardise his/her overall chances of winning the auction. Accordingly, this exerts pressure to not hesitate for too long before making an offer.

If the auction has a large number of participants, it can be assumed that the auction price is generally set higher than the fair market price, which is referred to as the "**winner's curse**". This increased price depends on the specific number of bidders, whereby the price increase for each additional bidder is degressive, i.e. it decreases.

An auction is useful when the respective subject is an item that is not expected to underlie large price deviations, because although the exact value of it is unknown, the potential use, and therefore also the according value, is somewhat similar for all interested parties(so-called **common value assets**).

Example
Flower traders participating at a flower auction.

Private value assets refer to greater price deviations due to the differently intended use of the object, i.e. greater price differences can occur depending on the respective evaluation of the object.

Example
Acquisition of land as a capital investment, for residential purposes, for development with new buildings or for use in conjunction with the neighbouring plot already owned by the investor.

The auction model does not work if there is not a sufficient amount of bidders available, e.g. because there are better procurement options for them, or if sub-conditions—particularly contract conditions—have to be negotiated individually. The more specialized the good is and the more services play a role, the less suitable an auction is. However, the positive effects of an auction from the seller's point of view can also (partially) be integrated into contract negotiations (→ *negotiauctions*).

Autonomous Negotiations by Software Agents Autonomous contracts have already been concluded through software in which the software controls electronic communication and makes decisions even without (!) human supervision. If the software is complex and autodidact, not even the programmer can predict the specific conditions of each individual contract conclusion.

An autonomous contract conclusion can give rise to a variety of detrimental consequences, such as dogmatic problems regarding the attribution to the company during a scheduled course of events; dealing with potential mistakes, especially in the case of unauthorised tampering with the system, and the establishment of liability. So far, no convincing (legal) solutions to these problems have been proffered. Regarding attribution, the spectrum of suggested solutions ranges from according the software its own legal personality to fully denying the existence of this issue. Intermediate concepts between the two approaches are for instance treating the software as an envoy or granting it a status comparable to that of a representative.

However, what is missing from autonomous contracts concluded by software, are autonomous negotiations. In this respect, there is growing talk of **computer-based negotiations**. It is probably only a matter of time until software programs also take on the role of negotiators, although at first, the software will likely lack the capacity for non-verbal communication (see especially the topic list under "further communication techniques") and → *emotions*. It is not easy to imagine the principal having full confidence in the reliability of a software acting as his/her agent especially with regard to highly complex negotiations. Furthermore, creative suggestions regarding the enlargement of the → *negotiation pie* could initially be a weak point. On the other hand, the → *information procurement*, the analysis of information, calculating opportunities and risks as well as the determination of the → *BATNA* and the → *ZOPA* can be expected to be at least as efficient as performed by humans. Numerous → *mistakes* that stem from the limited cognitive performance of human negotiators or their emotional sensitivity would thus be eliminated. Additionally, exploitation of the → *principal-agent-problem* is likely to be very limited, if it is possible in the first place. Such software programmes could accordingly support rational negotiations and contract conclusions. From the perspective of negotiation tactics, these programs could help to standardise the negotiation procedure and thus reduce the transaction costs incurred. In view of these potential benefits, negotiators will have to be prepared to accept autonomous negotiations under the use of software as a common means of negotiation. However, these advantages are only open to those, who have the opportunity and sufficient financial resources to use these systems. Autonomous contract negotiations and conclusions under the use of software can therefore also cause new imbalances, especially when humans act on one side and software on the other. This effect is intensified if consumers are involved.

Availability Bias Availability bias refers to a → *bias* that impacts negotiations because it influences the decision made by the negotiators. The effect states that people tend to overestimate the probability of a relatively unlikely event if they have already experienced such events and can recall them easily.[18]

Example
The production site of the opposing side's (Party A) main supplier is in an earthquake zone. In the past, there was once a supply shortage due to a major earthquake, which caused production stoppages and bottlenecks along the whole supply chain. Party B now fears reoccurrence of this event and the effects it might have on the project currently under negotiation, even though the probability of another, very strong earthquake in the upcoming years is estimated to be extremely low.

In this example, Party B focuses too heavily on an unlikely event. Party A could address the other party's concerns by presenting alternative suppliers from "safe" areas or by keeping certain items generally in stock. Moreover, the risk could also be insured.

If one side underlies an availability bias, the other party can sell the risk that the opposing party has overestimated. If the risk lies within one's own sphere and the negotiating partner thus hesitates to sign the contract, it may be attempted to involve the negotiating partner in the costs of minimizing the risk or its effects, potentially also taking out insurance.

Back Office The back office is a technical means of providing support to the negotiations. Generally speaking, the term refers to the administrative departments of the company, i.e. those who do not come into direct contact with customers and suppliers. The term back office is used to refer to, for example, the organisation of the annual general meeting of limited stock companies which takes place in the "background". In the context of negotiations, back office often refers to the legal department, since nowadays lawyers oftentimes do not attend the actual negotiations. The negotiated compromises are then however submitted to the legal department or a law firm, which comments on the contract draft (→ *annotations*). In major negotiations, it is the back office—not necessarily the legal department—which takes on research and administrative tasks.

Backlash Effect This is an effect of → *behavioural economics*. The term backlash (= setback, counter-reaction), i.e. returning to conservative values, and with that away from progressive ideals, was linked to the so-called separation of the races in the 1950s. In the context of negotiations, the backlash effect today refers above all to the social and, in some cases, economic sanctions with which women are threatened when they display non-stereotype-compliant behaviour.[19]

---

[18] Tversky and Kahneman (1974), pp. 1124–1131.

[19] Rudman et al. (2012), pp. 165–179; Faludi (1991).

It has been observed that women who are as demanding and assertive as men when pursuing their own interests, i.e. *competitive* (→ *distributive negotiations*), are "punished" by the men in their companies. Indeed, where salary negotiations are concerned, it has been proven that men have "punished" women who attempted to negotiate higher remuneration. Accordingly, men were more willing to work with women who accepted their salary without any further negotiation.[20] A certain negative emotional reaction can even be observed in negotiations which take place outside the organisation when men initially come across women who negotiate in a highly competitive manner. This can result in negative, negotiation-threatening → *emotions*. One study has, however, shown that the risk of a backlash in company negotiations is generally lessened by habituation.[21] This is attributed to the fact that in these cases, it is no longer the social role models that act as the behavioural standard, but rather the professional experience with competitively negotiating women which is regarded as the norm. Based on the results of this study, stereotypes are beginning to return in the context of company-related negotiations, where male negotiators perceive the situation to be threatening (e.g. if major financial disadvantages are impending due to demands). Another situation where the backlash effect arises is in constellations, where women fear punishment for their non-conformity to the commonly expected role stereotype. This often leads to women behaving in conformity with their assigned "role", even though from an objective point of view (e.g. due to habituation), there is no impending danger of social sanctions. In these cases, women do not utilise their full potential to negotiate competitively based on their anticipatory anxiety.

If the backlash effect occurs during the negotiations, it can be difficult to counteract. It is therefore interesting for women to know in advance how to cope with men who display this specific attitude so that they can minimize the potential negative impact of their behaviour. When it comes to permanent contractual relations, you can expect negotiations with the same business partner to become customary after a certain period of time (lessening of the so-called type ambiguity).[22]

Rumour has it that there are also men who would find it preferable for the negotiation to fail rather than risk defeat against a female negotiator, since this would be perceived as an extraordinary loss of face.[23] One alternative possibility, at least in the context of complex negotiations, would be to take countermeasures, such as using gestures that help save face. Female negotiators could, for example, enable their male negotiating partners to achieve (seeming) success. In these situations, it is also advisable for women not to show their triumph openly (→ *hide your glee*). Such measures can at least reduce the feeling of defeat against the opposite sex.

---

[20] Bowles et al. (2007), pp. 84–103.

[21] Tinsley and Amanatullah (2008), p. 10 et seq.

[22] Bowles (2012), p. 19 et seq.

[23] Craver and Barnes (1999), pp. 299–352.

Moreover, a study has shown that the backlash effect tends to be less pronounced if women do not negotiate for themselves but on behalf of others (e.g. colleagues).[24] This can be explained by the fact that a woman's advocacy is regarded as conforming to the role, and that women do not expect a backlash effect in these negotiations and thus appear more competitive and confident. **Negotiating on behalf of others** reverses expectations in such way that sanctions are threatened if women do not negotiate competitively enough.[25] If negotiations for the company are considered to be "on behalf of others" or not is evaluated differently. For women, it can however be advantageous to emphasise that they are not negotiating for themselves but representing their company, employer, department etc. Distancing themselves from competitive demands by way of a → *good guy/bad guy* tactic could also be helpful to minimise potentially observed role breaking behaviour. In such a case, the actual or alleged bad guy making harsh demands could also hold the role of the → *decision-maker*, who is not actually present at the negotiating table.

BAFO (Best and Final Offer) The best and final offer is a tactic primarily used to bring negotiations to a close. On the basis of the BAFO, the negotiating partner should decide whether s/he wants to conclude the contract. Sometimes it is not obvious that the given offer is the final offer, which carries the risk that in extreme cases the opposing side may inadvertently fail to conclude the contract.

The BAFO is also known as the **last offer** or **very final offer**. The latter term shows that, in practice, the BAFO is not always the actual last offer. Referring to an offer as the BAFO, i.e. the last or very final offer, can therefore be a tactical means to avoid making further concessions, or at least to signal that from this point onwards, concessions will be considerably more expensive. The BAFO can accordingly serve as a defensive tactic against attempts by the negotiating partner to keep obtaining small concessions (→ *salami tactic*).

Bargaining in the Shadow of the Law This term refers to conflict negotiations that are influenced by legal circumstances. If, for example, a conflict arises while concluding the contract, the parties are free to choose whether they want to solve the dispute through negotiating or conduct litigation in court (or before an arbitration tribunal). Even if the parties choose to negotiate, the negotiations are influenced by the probable (hypothetical) outcome the dispute would have had, had it gone to court. The legal position—including the ways in which it can be enforced—has a significant impact on the → *BATNA* of both parties. Indeed, going to court is the obvious alternative to a negotiated outcome. Accordingly, the term "bargaining in the shadow of the law" does not refer to the fact that all negotiations are conducted "in the shadow (or light) of the law", namely mandatory and concessionary law.

BATNA (Best Alternative to a Negotiated Agreement) The term BATNA is used synonymously with the term "**no deal option**" in English-speaking regions. On the

[24] Paddock and Kray (2015), pp. 209–226.

[25] Cf. Amanatullah and Tinsley (2013), pp. 110–122.

one hand, BATNA is a fundamental concept in negotiation science, while on the other hand it constitutes the decisive technique for measuring negotiating power. It is thus an essential support means for making rational decisions (→ *cui bono*).

Generally speaking, the BATNA is the best possible alternative to a negotiated agreement. The sheer opposite of this is the **WATNA** (**worst alternative to a negotiated agreement**). *John Nash* had already discovered the importance of negotiation alternatives by 1950.[26] However, the term BATNA, and its importance, was essentially defined by *Fisher/Ury*.[27]

Determining one's own BATNA serves to clarify whether the concrete, negotiated conclusion of a contract makes sense compared to other possible courses of action, i.e. in relative terms. Thus, your own BATNA essentially determines your own objective negotiating power. Possible alternatives include the option of concluding an agreement (possibly only later) with the same or a different negotiating partner. Apart from that, the negotiator can also maintain the status quo (i.e. not conclude the given contract) or s/he may take actions within the company. Unlawful options for action, particularly those that could incur criminal proceedings, should not be considered when determining the own side's BATNA and are accordingly also not considered when identifying the → *ZOPA*. The BATNA is the alternative which ensures the greatest benefit for the company in case the current negotiations fail. For this reason, the BATNA and the *resistance point* (→ *deal-breaker*) are usually closely linked to one another in the course of rational and (mutual) interest-based negotiations. Compliance with legal and ethical boundaries plays an equally important role for the inclusion of alternatives. Anything beyond these limits should not be regarded as an alternative.

Determining your own BATNA can prove quite difficult since the exact conditions of the alternatives can often only be estimated roughly. At this point, the → *auction* procedure comes into play. At all events, in larger projects and longer-term relationships, the risks and opportunities regarding project execution, transaction costs for implementation, potential effects on future business relationships (including the impact on the company's reputation etc.) all play an essential role. Hence, a precise quantification is hardly possible. In addition, disparate conditions have to be weighed against each other. In this context, conditions with broad differences in many respects, not just in price, have to be assessed in-depth and evaluated according to the primary goals. Determining the own sides' BATNA therefore inevitably involves a certain residual degree of uncertainty.

It is even more difficult to determine the negotiating partner's BATNA since s/he will usually not disclose his/her alternatives openly. Furthermore, any information already disclosed is not guaranteed to be accurate; and on certain subjects, simply no information is available.

Figure 3.3 (BATNA and other alternatives) illustrates the relation of the current negotiation status as opposed to the actual BATNA and other options for action.

---

[26] Nash (1950b), pp. 155–162.

[27] Fisher and Ury (1981); new editions involving *Bruce Patton*.

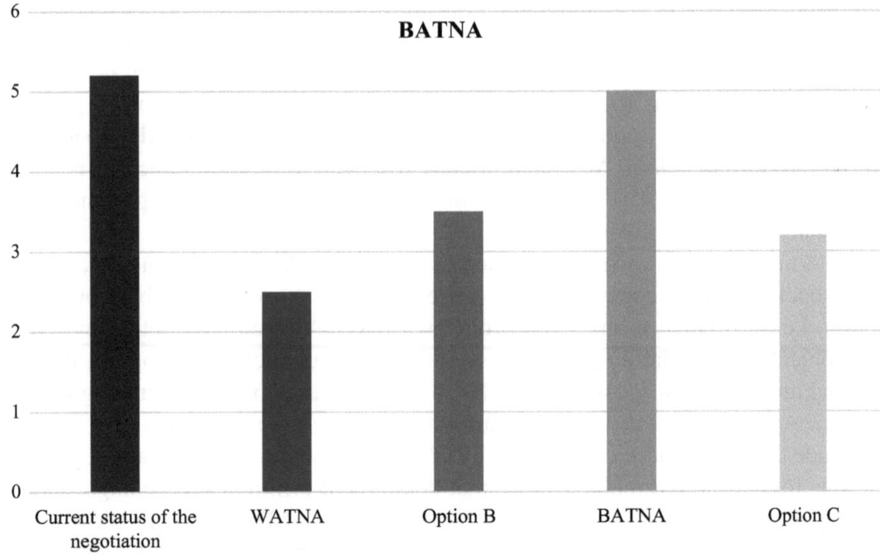

Fig. 3.3 BATNA and other alternatives

However, as the negotiating partner's BATNA is decisive for his/her objective negotiating power, it is nonetheless beneficial to obtain as much information on this subject as possible. For this purpose, it is possible to make use of general resources, informants from third-party companies or informants from the opposing party. Apart from that, asking → *open questions* during negotiations is a common means to elicit pertinent information. In most cases, conclusions about the negotiating partner's BATNA can be drawn by determining his/her main interests. If, for example, it is assumed that a very early delivery date is of key importance to the negotiating partner, deliberately setting a later delivery date can be proposed during negotiations. If this late delivery date is decidedly rejected, the desired delivery date is likely to be of great importance. Therefore, only companies that can promise to provide completion on time will be short-listed. However, the negotiating partner's BATNA can only be deduced if it is known whether competitors could also deliver on the earlier delivery date specified. Similarly, the significance of the desired qualities or requirements of technical systems can also provide valuable information about the negotiating partner's BATNA. Indeed, preferences and interests regarding technical standards are often used to deliberately worsen the negotiating partner's BATNA, by attempting to make restrictions towards a specific technical system, which is at best offered by only a few competitors. Likewise, creating a time constraint (→ *calculated delay*) for the negotiating partner may be aimed at limiting his/her BATNA, or at least shall prevent him/her from improving his/her BATNA.

A buyer's BATNA is usually not 100% certain from the outset. In some cases, the order, scope and intensity of his/her needs, interests and preferences can be influenced to a certain degree. Generally speaking, sellers often do not participate in more than one negotiation at a time, so their BATNA is often a (later) agreement with a different customer. If, however, they pressed for time (→ *deadline*) their BATNA can become significantly smaller very quickly since they have no time for future negotiations with third parties. Accordingly, delaying tactics (e.g. → *calculated delay*; missing person manoeuvre) can therefore also aim to restrict the negotiating partner's BATNA. Either way, the BATNA is heavily time-dependent and underlies a very dynamic process. As long as no cartel bans apply, it may be advisable to consult with other providers in order to limit the opposing party's BATNA. Having said this, cartel prohibitions are—at least in Europe and the US—relatively strict, and particularly prohibit collusion between competitors on price and performance. Exceptions granting leeway apply in the EU to cooperation among smaller companies—however only under the prerequisite that the cooperation of the two smaller competitors makes an economically viable offer feasible.

Taking the BATNA of both parties into account in a rational, interest-oriented negotiation indicates whether there is possible scope for agreement (→ *ZOPA*) (Fig. 3.4).

Despite all efforts, oftentimes major uncertainties remain regarding both, one's own and the opposing party's (objective) BATNA. Although, prima facie, the objective BATNA is the decisive criterion in determining whether a conclusion of the contract would make sense, the actual negotiating behaviour is more often based merely on the estimated or even felt BATNA (subjective BATNA) of both, the own and the opposing party's side. Conversely, this means that not only the actual (objective) BATNA but also the perceived (subjective) BATNA can be influenced to change the current state of the negotiations. In this context, it is common practice to bluff regarding your own alternatives (→ *better offer*). Another tactic is to try to degrade your negotiating partner's subjective BATNA by overstating certain risks.

The tendency to favour conclusion of the contract currently under negotiation even though a better alternative is available is known as "**agreement bias**". This means that under certain circumstances, negotiators tend not to fully consider their

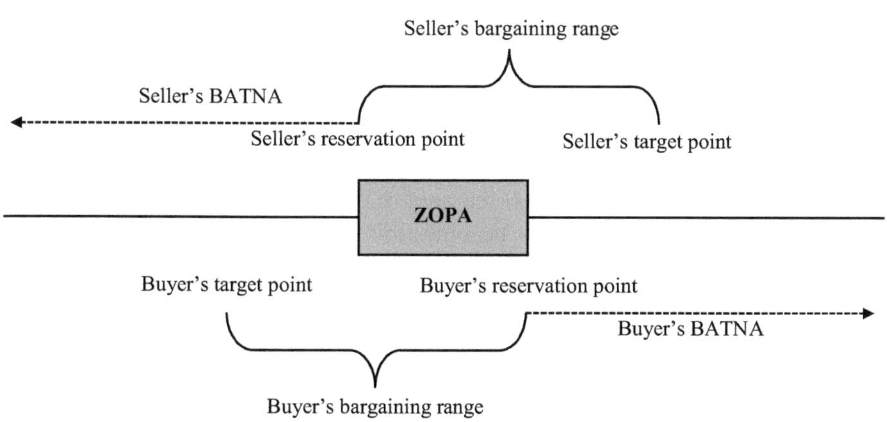

Fig. 3.4 Illustration of the relation between BATNA and ZOPA

own BATNA when concluding a contract. Another reason for this can also be the → *sunk cost bias*. This can be prevented by using two negotiators, or by submitting the final contract to review by an unbiased → *decision-maker*. Likewise, negotiators tend to not fully take into account the opposing party's BATNA, which may lead to the negotiator only asking for a small share of the → *negotiation pie*.

BATNA and the Order of Negotiations If you are negotiating with several potential partners, your own BATNA can influence the logical order in which negotiations are entered with these parties. If the intention is to conclude a contract with just one of several negotiating partners, it often more sensible to start by negotiating with the less favoured partners; i.e. the ones with whom a contract does not necessarily have to be concluded. Negotiations with the preferred contractual partner should at any rate only proceed when the other negotiations with the less preferred partners have already taken place. The advantage of this sequential approach is that the negotiator is aware of his/her alternatives and therefore his/her BATNA when negotiating with the contract partner of choice. At the same time, the preceding negotiations are ideal for gaining further negotiating experience. Therefore, this procedure is often also recommended for employees applying for jobs with various employers. Accordingly, the "preferred employer" should also be the applicant's last negotiating partner. Admittedly, this practice does incur high negotiation costs.

If a company maintains a business relationship with a number of other companies (particularly suppliers)—i.e. the aim is to conclude several contracts—a different approach with regard to the BATNA might be advisable. In this case, it could in fact be advantageous to firstly enter into negotiations with the company with which a good deal can be expected (the favourite). This strengthens the negotiator's position so that s/he can enter into negotiations with the most challenging negotiating partner much more confidently.

Bazaar Tactic The bazaar tactic is named after the negotiation behaviour of merchants at bazaars. The alternative terms **haggling** and **dickering** are also used, both of which refer to the bargaining commonly encountered at bazaars. In essence, the bazaar tactic illustrates a standard negotiation, where both sides set a specific price anchor. The, the price is negotiated in the range between both anchors (→ *bracketing*). The blockade associated with such a negotiation tactic (→ *deadlock*) is minimised by setting the anchors relatively far apart from each other and the negotiators move towards each other in rapid steps—as it were dancing. This is accordingly also referred to as the so-called negotiation dance.

The closer the parties approach the area of agreement (i.e. the → *ZOPA*) the smaller the concessions generally become (this phenomenon is known as the → *diminishing rates of concession*). The bazaar tactic offers the advantage that each side experiences a sense of achievement as the final price is significantly distant from the originally demanded/offered price. Yet, there is the disadvantage that the parties negotiate on a position-oriented basis rather than an interest-oriented one. Consequently, the negotiators often do not have the enlargement of the → *negotiation pie* in mind.

Behavioural Economics This basic concept refers to the scientific investigation of behaviour that is not purely rational in an economic context. In a different context (decision theory), it is also referred to as **behavioural decision research**. This concept is based on an image of mankind, incompatible with the image of homo oeconomicus, marked by restrictions on rationality, will power and the pursuit of self-interest. For instance, concerning their preferences, humans act inconsistently with regard to time; they do not act exclusively for their own benefit, and their decisions can be influenced by the kind of presentation (→ *framing*). These findings have a major significance for negotiations. They explain various, seemingly irrational types of behaviour, allow appropriate countermeasures or the exploitation of the negotiating partner's corresponding behaviour (→ *bias*).

Being Ready for the Negotiating Partner's Mistakes In negotiations, both parties regularly make → *mistakes*, some of which are obvious, thus detectable and may therefore prove to be serious. Such mistakes by the other side can be used in the context of so-called hard bargaining to your own advantage. Sometimes, however, negotiators are reluctant to do so; not due to severe ethical concerns, but rather because they suspect a "trap" behind the negotiating partner's (obvious) mistake (for instance a test mistake). This option should indeed be kept in mind. However, if, despite closer examination, it is not evident that the negotiating partner is using a corresponding (deceptive) tactic, the mistake can be used—in the context of hard bargaining—for one's own benefit. In many cases, mistakes in negotiations are not recognised, since negotiators generally do not expect that their partners are liable to make mistakes. In instances of hard bargaining, mistakes can therefore be consciously taken into account. In a more intense form, mistakes can even be provoked by the build-up of pressure (in the course of so-called pressure tactics, see corresponding topic list) and exploited afterwards. The negative impact on the negotiating atmosphere and the relationship between the parties should be considered beforehand. In negotiations imbued with trust, there should at least be the willingness to allow a face-saving correction of a mistake to encourage mutual trust.

Better Offer The tactic of the "better offer" (sometimes also known as the **tactic of tougher competition** or **Chinese auction**) can aim at a rational decision as well as at misleading the negotiating partner. Irrespective of the actual aim pursued, the negotiator first of all tells the opposing side that the own side has the option of a "better offer". The advantage may, but does not necessarily have to, be in terms of the price. Advantages regarding delivery conditions, quality etc. can also be mentioned.

This is first and foremost information about your own → *BATNA,* and it is intended to induce the negotiating partner to make further concessions or conclude the contract. If this information is specific and sufficiently backed up, the other party can rely on this information and react accordingly. In this case, the information encourages rational negotiations. Often, however, no specific information is disclosed to the negotiating partner in order to avoid revealing the specifics of your own BATNA. The fragmental information about the offer can also serve to make it appear more attractive than it actually is, perhaps by not mentioning unfavourable constraints or distorting conditions. In this case, it is an attempt to induce the opposing side to give in by misleading them. The reference to a better offer can also turn out to be a mere bluff, i.e. possibly there is no actual other offer. Both options can be counteracted by requesting proof, or by gathering information from third parties. Sometimes it is sufficient to put the opposing side in a predicament, by specifically asking for suspected constraints. If there really is a better offer from a third party, one can try to differentiate the own offer, i.e. offer a differently structured product, to make it more difficult to compare the offers.

Here too, the question arises as to whether applying this tactic in negotiations is within legally acceptable limits or constitutes a case of → *cunning deception*, which, according to the authors, is generally legitimate in negotiations between companies. The authors tend to assume cunning deception, since without any explicit agreements, there is not only no obligation to disclose any competing offers but the allegation of the existence of competing offers is not to be trusted and cannot be relied upon.

Better Than That This is amongst the hard-bargaining tactics, designed to nudge the outcome of the negotiations towards one's own side. To achieve this, the negotiating partner is told that s/he needs to make a better offer ("*You will have to do better than that*"). This tactic is sometimes also referred to as the **Krunch**.

On the one hand, "do better than that" clearly expresses that the other party's offer is plainly not sufficient (→ *anchor discreditation*). At the same time no *counter-anchor* (→ *anchoring*) is set, so there is no indication of a possible line of compromise. The objective is to induce the negotiating partner to further concessions without making any oneself. This means that the opposing side's anchor should be moved before setting one's own anchor. The negotiation partner is pushed to "negotiate against himself/herself". A similar situation arises when one party, given a specific price by the opposing side, does not make a counter offer but first requests an undetermined price discount. If the negotiating partner reacts to this, the new price is taken as the anchor and the according counter-anchor is set. This is one possible option to displace the anchor and is a tactic that often proves successful against service suppliers on the market. This may be due to the general existence of a certain scope for negotiation. Suppliers often find that they do not have a chance to come into play. For them, the migration of potential clients poses a very real threat. In addition, sales representatives often feel that their side's prices are quite high anyway (sometimes they even know the profit margin). What's more, the success of the sales division is often measured by the number of contracts concluded (the so-called completion rate). The negotiating partner can try to avoid this tactic by asking for the counter-offer immediately without deviating from his/her own offer.

Bias In the context of negotiations, bias refers to systematic distortions of perception, memory, thinking and decision making (**cognitive bias**). Most of these distortions are based on automatic thought processes that run unconsciously and lead to quick decisions, often even before slow, analytical thinking has commenced.[28] A standardised, automatic thought process is also known under the term of "heuristic". In the past, mankind would not have survived without the ability to think quickly and unconsciously, and would not be able to cope with many everyday situations today. Economic decisions would drag on for a very long time and would easily overwhelm those involved. The distortions which occur in quick (unconscious) thinking are the price of this ability. In negotiations, it is important to be aware of these distortions in order to avoid making bad decisions and—depending on the strategy—to potentially use the negotiating partner's distortions for your own benefit.

The tendency to prematurely draw causalities between observed facts, such as linking these to a person's behaviour and underestimating the effect of external circumstances (**correspondence bias**), are of vital importance.

The tendency to choose and assess available information in such a way that it confirms your own thoughts and behaviour (→ *impression (first and last)* (*confirmation bias*)) constitutes a further bias, while the **illusion of control** is the assumption that events, which at the very least can also be influenced by coincidence, can be controlled.

Example
In a series of six studies with 631 adults, *Ellen Langers* examined the correlation of random events and the participants' given illusion that they were capable of controlling these events.[29] As an experiment, lottery tickets were distributed in one test group while in the other group, participants were allowed to choose the lottery tickets themselves. The latter were under the impression that their choice affected their chances of winning.

Fischhoff describes the finding that the retrospective judgement of a person over a question changes once it has been answered.[30] This so-called **hindsight bias** can occur in different variations. In experiments concerning hypothetical design, probands received questions together with the correct answers. Afterwards, they were asked whether they would have given the exact same answer if they had not been told the right solution beforehand. The results proved that the probands who were given the correct solution beforehand, tended to overestimate their own ability to come up with the right answer on their own. In addition to this, there is also an experiment in the course of which the participants were asked to make a statement regarding certain questions. After a longer time-interval, they were given the "right"

[28] For basic implementations Kahneman (2011).

[29] Langers (1975), pp. 311–328.

[30] Fischhoff (1975), pp. 288–299.

answer to the question and were asked to recall their initially given answer to the question (this is known as memory design). Probands generally tended to believe their result was closer to the "right" answer than it actually was. In → *claim management*, where the predictability of the consequences of complex clauses has to be evaluated retrospectively, this bias is essential. Negotiation results are also assessed after their completion. Here, the negotiator runs the risk of being reproached with the fact that the project was doomed to failure "from the beginning". To minimalise such a risk, the negotiator should involve all the potential → *decision-makers* from the beginning, and should thoroughly document the decision-making-process.

Impact bias refers to the exaggerated depiction of the effects and duration of an imaginary, negative event. This bias can affect the contract negotiations in such a manner that clauses which (slightly) disadvantage one side are rigorously rejected by them, since they envision and exaggerate the possible negative consequences. One way to attempt to combat this would be to agree to take on part of the risk in return for certain concessions.

The **small pie bias**, i.e. the underestimation of the potential size of the → *negotiation pie* and, at the same time, also the overestimation of the own share of the negotiation pie (**large slice bias**) as well as the frequent failure to take into account the size of a problem when making decisions (**scope neglect**) are further distortions that should be borne in mind when negotiating contracts.

Example—Small Pie Bias
During the negotiation, both sides focus exclusively on the price. As a result, they overlook the fact that the → *negotiation pie* could be expanded to the advantage of both parties by means, for example, of delivery or service conditions and quality requirements.

So-called scope neglect comprises a subcategory of **extension neglect**. The missing multiplicative relation between the valuation of a problem and its magnitude is distinctive for this bias.[31]

Example
One party wants to take out insurance cover for (a) 20,000 EUR, (b) 200,000 EUR or (c) 2,000,000 EUR. They are willing to pay insurance fees of (a) 7000 EUR, (b) 10,000 EUR or (c) 11,000 EUR. This shows that an exponential increase in the scope is reflected by a degressive increase of the willingness to pay.

These examples show that these mistakes are not only based on a tendency to simplify, but often serve to maintain human self-esteem. At the same time, the **illusion of superiority** over others ("*I am good and the others are bad*"), the illusion of

[31] Kahneman and Tversky (2000), p. 708.

certainty concerning the own perception ("*I know all about it*") as well as illusory optimism ("*I will win*"), have a strengthening effect.

Big Fish With this tactic, one side tries to weaken the negotiation partner's position by convincing them of how big and powerful they are. The idea is to convince the opposing party that it is an "honour" for them to do business with this "big fish". This tactic is often referred to as the "intimidation tactic". It often begins with the negotiation partner being impressed by representative buildings and pompous, large rooms etc.; continues with complicated reception procedures or artificially prolonged waiting times (→ *imperial gestures*) and also often finds its expression in company presentations. In this context also name-dropping is applied. For this, the names of important people/companies are mentioned, with whom the company either has business relations or whom one knows personally. Although this tactic often proves successful, it may also give the partner that is in a weaker position the impression that it is impossible to conclude a fair contract with this big company. If the smaller side has a strong → *BATNA*, this can also result in a termination of the negotiations.

Blockade Strategy The blockade strategy is a subtype of the pressure strategy. Applied to a specific negotiation point, it is a pressuring tactic. It is often more difficult to influence the development of a project positively—i.e. directing it in the desired direction—than to completely block the project altogether. The blockade strategy is thus sometimes used when the blocking party can see no way of realising their interests through active negotiation. As long as the blocking party's ultimate goal is not to prevent the entire project, his/her interest often lies in making use of the annoyance value to uphold his blockade-position.

The blockade strategy is more frequently applied within organisations and in diplomatic negotiations than in the general course of business—partly due to the fact that there are more blocking positions. In addition to "buying off" the blockade position, one possible way of reacting to this strategy is to enable the blocking partner to play an active role in shaping its interests in an appropriate manner. Participation in the project can ideally lead to an attitude change.

Body Language It is not uncommon for negotiators to use various guises in the course of negotiations. These can, for example, include concealing their true attitude towards the project, to the other party's negotiators or to the individual contract clauses under discussion. It is in these cases in particular that body language—including the tone of voice and expression in the eyes—can provide important additional insight, especially into the negotiating partner's → *emotions*.

Reliable interpretation of body language can, however, be difficult to achieve. Apart from a few unambiguous cases, specific physical action can be interpreted in various ways. For instance, crossed arms are not always a sign of defensive and distant behaviour; they can also signal increased concentration. The negotiation partner's body language should therefore be observed and interpreted attentively, but with the necessary restraint. In particular, look for further signals and make a differential diagnosis. Due to the fact that certain reactions can hardly be controlled (or faked), the most meaningful reactions are: intense, spontaneous and simultaneous. The degree of their intensity and synchronicity can sometimes limit possible explanations for these physical reactions. Yet, the negotiation partner can use body language deliberately and in a controlled manner to express their approval, rejection (→ *wince*), doubts etc.

Imitating the negotiation partner's posture—i.e. if both lean forward, both cross their legs etc.—is generally judged as a positive sign of agreement. People tend to trust other people more, and perceive them as more convincing, if they imitate their own posture (so-called **chameleon effect**[32]). In order to establish a positive relationship with the negotiating partner, the mirror technique can be employed. This specific technique comprises the conscious imitation of the negotiating partner's general posture (or single aspects of it). In contrast, however, exaggerated imitation can be perceived as attempted manipulation. Imitating very individual gestures or a dialect can potentially be felt as mockery.

Body language should also be used to obtain and transfer information (approval, rejection, indecisiveness). Crossing one's arms, frowning, or hardening one's features in the middle of a negotiation which had been going well up to that point sends a clear message which in some cases can even lead to the other party changing their offer during the presentation (→ *wince*).

Boilerplates With the term boilerplates lawyers colloquially refer to commonly used **standard clauses** or text blocks which are broadly taken over into the contract without substantial changes. In this way, boilerplates rather govern the general functioning of a contract than technical or commercial details. The latter are termed as so-called operative or substantive clauses. The standard clauses generally include e.g. the written form and a clause stipulating jurisdiction. The party enforcing their boilerplates as the basis of the contract has an advantage. The occurring advantage can inter alia be explained by means of the *anchoring effect* (→ *anchoring*) and the → *status quo bias.*

Boulwarism Boulwarism is a pressure strategy which aims at bringing negotiations to a rapid close. This can of course mean the conclusion of a contract but might also be the termination of negotiations. Terminologically, the strategy is named after *Lemuel Ricketts Boulware*—a former Vice President of General Electric. *Boulware* was responsible for salary negotiations with the trade unions. His strategy was to make a fair offer to General Electric employees and to reject subsequent concessions unless any new, unrecognised information became known. Publicly announcing the offer and its non-negotiability created conscious self-commitment. In this particular case, the strategy not only focused on reaching a quick agreement but was also designed to weaken the negotiation power of the trade unions. Workers were made aware that a fair result could be achieved even without the support of trade unions. If the unions do not achieve anything for their members, then membership

[32] Cf. Chartrand and Bargh (1999), pp. 893–910.

in the trade union seems futile. The strategy chosen by *Boulware* in the course of trade union negotiations has been classed as a breach of the duty of "bargaining in good faith" by the National Labor Relations Board and the Courts (General Electric Co. 150 NLRB 192, 194-95, 57 LRRM 1491 (1964), enforced 418 F.2 d 736, 756-57 (2nd Cir. 1969)). It was therefore abandoned in this concrete form for negotiations with trade unions. This was essentially based on the fact that a general obligation to negotiate was stipulated for collective negotiations. In literature, it is up to this day still disputed whether this tactic effects a violation of the obligation to bargaining in good faith.

An alternatively used term for Boulwarism is the name **final, fair and firm**. In the general context of negotiations, the goal of this strategy is to make a final—no longer negotiable—fair and binding offer. Regarding the latter aspect, however, the differences between different jurisdictions should be taken into account: whilst U.S. law states that an offer can be freely withdrawn as long as it has not been accepted by the negotiating partner, German law states that an offer made in absence of the negotiations partner is binding—and, subject to a special agreement—its binding character remains in force until such time as acceptance can be expected at the latest. What has been said about US law does not apply, however, within the scope of the Uniform Commercial Code (UCC). Hence, in B2B-relations a written offer is in fact binding and cannot be withdrawn.

The Boulwarism or "final, fair and firm"-strategy can prove successful if the negotiating parties agree on the fairness of the offer and have no ambition to succeed on their own in the negotiation process. In this case, the negotiating partner will also not perceive this strategy as pressure either. Due to the extremely short duration of the negotiation, also negotiation costs can be reduced. Yet, the strategy also carries risks: for instance, dissatisfaction with the immobility of the negotiating partner is likely to be high since negotiators want to achieve personal success (sense of achievement) in negotiations. If the own parties' → *negotiation power* is low(er) (particularly regarding one's own → *BATNA*), i.e. if the party is depending on the negotiation to be successful, the anchoring effect (→ *anchoring*) has to be borne in mind. However, if → *renegotiations* take place, the initial—already "fair"—offer is the starting point for the additional demands made by the negotiating partner. In this case, justification for the renegotiations is required as otherwise a loss of face threatens.

The Boulwarism (or "final, fair and firm") strategy is very similar to the → *take it or leave it* tactic—the difference being that the take it or leave it tactic is not necessarily based on a fair → *first offer*. Moreover, the take it or leave it tactic is not necessarily only applied with regard to the first offer, but may also be chosen with regard to an offer in a later stage of the negotiations. That is the reason why this book categorises Boulwarism as a strategy (since it determines the overall negotiation), whereas "take it or leave it" is classified as an individually applicable tactic concerning one specific aspect of the negotiation.

Bracketing Bracketing is one of the standard tactics employed in negotiations in the context of numerically determinable values, such as the negotiated price. Both sides use → *anchoring* to set their initial offer far away from their target price, since they hope, that in this way, the price they aim for will be the result of the negotiations. They set the target "in brackets", as it were. Consequently, it is often advisable to set the *first offer* (see more in detail under → *anchoring*), which opens the "brackets". In the case at hand, the counter-offer closes the brackets. It is also recommended to only make concessions in small steps (→ *diminishing rates of concession*) and to represent your own offer firmly, and with appropriate justification. At the same time, negotiators should indicate a certain willingness to make concessions in order not to harden the mood (→ *deadlock*).

Sometimes a potential zone of agreement (→ *ZOPA*) emerges fairly quickly, e.g. in the middle between the two initial offers (→ *midpoint-rule*). However, there are also many cases with a different development, for instance if only one side is aware of the usual values and investigated his/her own BATNA. If the possible zone of agreement becomes apparent, negotiators sometimes attempt so-called **double bracketing.**

Example
If one side is discernibly aiming for 800,000 EUR and the offers are 400,000 EUR and 1,200,000 EUR respectively (bracketing), an attempt can be made to reset the brackets and thereby also the negotiation anchors. To do so, the respective side tells their negotiating partner that s/he, the seller, is obviously aiming for 800,000 EUR but that they themselves have set a maximum goal of 600,000 EUR. If an agreement is to be reached, the price to be agreed on must lie within the range of 600,000 EUR – 800,000 EUR (double bracketing).

Double bracketing shifts both anchors (brackets), yet the displacement is greater for the negotiating partner's anchor, which creates an advantage for the party making the offer.

In the example illustrated here, an agreement at the midpoint between both offers would result in a final price of 700,000 EUR instead of the initial target price of 800,000 EUR. The tactic has a chance to prove successful because the target is so firmly established in everyone's minds that there is an unconscious willingness to back the decision to shift from the target figure to the actual value of the anchor, and at first glance this change seems fair.

Double bracketing can be counteracted by preventing the change, i.e. the negotiator persists with the initial anchor.

Bracketing is also a standard technique for mediators to achieve rapprochement between the parties. If a plaintiff claims 800,000 EUR yet the defendant is only willing to pay 400,000 EUR, the mediator could ask whether the defendant would be willing to up his/her offer to 500,000 EUR, just as long as the plaintiff reduces reduce his/her claim to 700,000 EUR. Should the defendant agree, the reverse question is put to the plaintiff. If s/he also agrees, the claim is now reduced to 700,000

EUR and the offer amounts to 500,000 EUR. The positions of the parties have converged through bracketing.

Bracketing should not be confused with the brackets that are used in political negotiations. In these negotiations, brackets generally indicate that there is still a need for discussion, i.e. no agreement has been achieved. In major contract negotiations in the corporate sector, brackets can serve the same purpose. They can especially be a significant signal for the → *decision-makers* in the negotiation phase for pointing out which aspects still need to be negotiated.

Brinkmanship Brinkmanship (derived from "on the brink"—"at the edge of the abyss") describes a **bold policy** or aggressive tactic with the potential to apply very high pressure and is accordingly also associated with very high risks. The term came into being following an interview in Life Magazine given by the then US Secretary of State, *John Foster Dulles*, on January 23, 1956, in which he described "**going to the brink of the abyss**" as part of the United States' foreign policy in the Cold War. A prime example of political brinkmanship is the behaviour of the United States during the 1962 Cuban Missile Crisis, in which they accepted the risk of a possible nuclear war in order to prevent or end the stationing of Soviet nuclear missiles in Cuba.

This tactic was introduced into the economic discussion by *Thomas Schelling.*[33] Based on this tactic, the game theory developed a special game, which, after a few rounds played, regularly ends in a catastrophe. Thus, this game vividly demonstrates the danger this tactic holds. An essential part of this tactic is the element of a serious threat. In order for the threat to be taken seriously by the party threatened, a credible self-reliance regarding the central question is necessary. The other person should be convinced that the threatening party has no other choice than to comply. If the counterparty does not accept the demanded claim, the serious threat is realised. Accordingly, this negotiation tactic holds many risks and is generally only considered in emergency situations (e.g. when rescuing a company from insolvency in the event of a highly favourable contract conclusion). Even if it would make sense for the negotiating party to give in rationally, this tactic may fail since the exertion of pressure can trigger a psychological defence reaction in the opposing party's negotiator or → *decision-maker*. In particular, it should be borne in mind that the other party may not have an economically viable alternative, or that the other party's negotiator personally may not have to fear any disadvantages in the event of failure (→ *principal-agent-problem*). The tactic of brinkmanship does not only exist in the described extreme forms; it is actually more likely to be applied in less extreme forms. In these expressions it constitutes a form of self-gagging.

Budget Limitation Proposing a budget limitation during negotiations is a tactic for averting undesired claims made by the other party. Hence, this tactic is a means of withstanding the pressure applied by the negotiating partner. In this respect, the

[33] Schelling (1960).

budget limitation should be legitimised by a valid material reason, which is most importantly not only of a temporary kind.

The budget limit can correspond to the truth and in these cases the negotiator only argumentatively makes use of the actual situation. However, oftentimes the budgets are recognisably not actually limited or the limit is much higher. In this case, the tactic misleads the negotiating partner. If the negotiating partner suspects a bluff, the argumentation will not convince him. Moreover, this line of defence is very immobile, since it becomes difficult to explain plausibly why the given budget has been exceeded. The negotiator who presented the budget limit as an unsurmountable red line thus only has the option to stick to the budget limit at any cost—even at the price of the failure of the negotiations, or inadequate service in return—or has to resort to exceeding the budget limit and accordingly appears untrustworthy.

In order to maintain a certain degree of flexibility and not to appear implausible in the event of exceeding one's budget, it is advisable to first look for individual, case-related justification for overstepping the budget. Another option would be to work with an inherently fixed limit and to use the the management's authority, or that of the → *decision-maker,* to make modifications as a flexible line of defence that could potentially breach the set limit. It is precisely at this point that the negotiating partner's efforts to overcome budget constraints often also comes into play. If the opposing party's negotiator can be convinced by the proposed deal (including the above-budget price), there will often be the offer to jointly present the negotiation result to the decision-maker in order to convince him/her of the necessity of deviating from the budget limit. From the → *decision-maker's* point of view, however, it would appear more sensible to leave the offer unresponded: If rejected, it could weaken the standing of the own parties' negotiator; or, conversely, the decision-maker might only agree to overrun the budget in order to maintain the standing of the negotiator.

In the authors' opinion, deception regarding the budget limit constitutes → *cunning deception* and as such is generally not to be regarded as unlawful. The situation is aggravated if additional pressure is exerted on the negotiating partner. Apart from structural imbalances, the opposing party will probably also have to cope with additional pressure exerted, based on the impending termination of the negotiations without any remaining legal protection.

Building a Golden Bridge This tactic aims at bridging the difference between the opposing parties' and the own negotiation position. Contrary to the → *last gap* between the parties offer, here the essential difference in content is not problematic: In principle, the negotiating partner would be willing to accept the content of the proposal. The problem here is much more rooted in the fact that the opposing party has positioned itself in such a way that it apparently cannot agree to the proposed terms without losing face. This assumption concludes that building bridges is more likely to be applied successfully in position-oriented negotiations rather than in negotiations following an interest-based approach.

The bridge which is to be built should therefore allow the other party to agree without losing face. Accordingly, the first step is to recognise that an agreement would mean a potential loss of face for the negotiating partner and to understand the reasons behind this. Above that, it is essential to recognise that the fear of losing one's face is the main reason inhibiting a final agreement. If, for example, the other side has "definitively" rejected an offer, the establishment of new circumstances may allow the negotiating partner to change his/her mind (gracefully). If that is still not sufficient, or if it is simply not possible, the offers approval may well result from entirely rewording the proposal—or for numeric values, changing the method of calculation, while still obtaining the same results—and additionally linking the proposal to other negotiation points, which are seemingly beneficial for the partner. It is particularly advantageous if not only the "amended" proposal is attributed to the negotiating partner but to also present him/her as the key initiator of these changes. This does not only increase the negotiator's feeling of satisfaction but equally increases the likelihood that the decision-maker in the → *back office* will also be willing to accept the proposal.

A special need to build bridges can arise from the involvement of a rather incompetent or insufficiently prepared → *decision-maker* in the negotiations. Due to his/her power status, the negotiator will strive to enforce his/her own proposals. If none of the proposals brought forward by the decision-maker seems reasonable, it can still be advisable to accept one of these offers in order to safeguard a successful final phase of the negotiations. This offer should however only cover a side issue and, above that should not cause any significant damage to the negotiating partner. Likewise, one may also accept offers that can be adjusted subsequently. Later adjustments are either possible due to the specific structure of negotiations or by engaging other participants into the negotiations in a later stage of the negotiation. To build a bridge for the negotiating partner is also particularly important when the agreement remains to be approved by a higher instance or the negotiators of the opposing side have a significant influence on the the contract implementation.

As negotiators tend to be more satisfied with the outcome of the negotiations if they believe the opposing party is "dissatisfied" with the agreed terms, parties would be well advised not to show their opponents their pleasure in the result achieved (→ *hide your glee*). Satisfying the other parties main interests and demands should be a primary goal, especially where the proper implementation of the contract depends on the negotiation partner's willingness to cooperate, or where the own party desires to establish or maintain a → *permanent business relationship* with the other party.

Burden of Justification This term, in some cases also noted under the **burden of reasoning**, not only refers to the requirement of justifying the own opinion but likewise refers to the fact that in cases of argumentative doubt, the preferred opinion is the one which does not require further justification. This without restriction only applies to the burden of justification as a legal figure, i.e. only concerning legal balancing decisions.[34] But also for argumentation in negotiations, the burden of justification plays a key role since the person who is in charge of justifying his/her points is in a much harder, and in this way also in a weaker position. If it is therefore possible to push the own position forward as the general norm which does not require any further justification and in this way achieve to present the counter position as the exception, subject to justification, then the burden of justification lies with the opposing party. By using the argument that something was done in a certain way in the past (*"We've always done it like this"*), the burden of justification is often assigned to the negotiating partner. The other negotiator is expected to accept this past behaviour as the general rule for future business relations, and s/he should therefore provide legitimate reasons for any substantial changes. In fact, anyone who tries to reach a decision against the common rule (e.g. the usual practice) has been conferred the burden of justification. Thus, the common customs in comparable situations are of key importance. The same applies if a change in the status quo of the relationship between the parties is sought (→ *status quo bias*). This is why sometimes, by establishing an priorly uncommon rule as the future general practice (for instance by being more generous an accommodating in another negotiation point), one party attempts to create a → *precedent* for future negotiations by testing this practice in the course of small projects, where one specific rule is not as important.

The burden of justification for an opposing opinion can also be generated by means of expert opinions.

But-Yes Answer The "but-yes"-answer is a type of response and thus also a communication technique which serves to increase the other party's satisfaction and to emphasise the status of the approving person. In the context of this type of response, the concerns regarding the negotiation partner's proposal are addressed first. In the final stages of the negotiation, the respondent fully ("but yes") or partially ("but yes, maybe") accommodates the proposal. In this instance, the "but yes"-answer emphasises the concerns brought up previously more than the contradictious → *yes, but*-answer. The positive response communicated in the final result appears less obvious and is therefore perceived as particularly successful. This last point especially applies if the other party no longer expects a positive answer in view of the course of the conversation. Insofar as this positive answer only comes about following good argumentation by the respondent, the other party believes in its negotiating skills and is particularly satisfied with the achieved success. From a psychological point of view, achieving negotiation wins is of key importance for perceiving the reached agreement as satisfactory. The importance of this is demonstrated by the fact that "victories" can even be detected physiologically in the form of endorphin release. The "but-yes"-answer is therefore often directed towards making the negotiation partner more content with the result. This is especially necessary if the given approval was limited, as it allows the other party to chalk up a partial success based on their own performance in the negotiation.

[34] On this subject see further: Krebs (1995), pp. 171–211.

But-yes-answers are often used in hierarchical relationships by the higher-ranking person, since this answering technique simultaneously highlights the rank of the person who agrees after initial concerns have been addressed.

Even so, "but-yes"-answers may also seem implausible. This is particularly the case if there is an abrupt break between the concerns and the agreement then expressed. The same applies if the respondent makes frequent use of this technique. Furthermore, if the initially uttered negative statement is too intense, this can poison the whole negotiation atmosphere and inhibit the establishment of chemistry and rapport between the parties.

Example
The project you have proposed is more expensive than we had anticipated. However, based on the positive developments in this business year, we can allow ourselves a limited budget increase. As a result, we have decided to support your project despite the higher costs.

Calculated Delay The term "calculated delay" refers to delay tactics utilised in negotiations. There are various forms of calculated delay, the most important one being the delay of negotiations. Negotiations are delayed in the hope that one's own negotiation position will improve in the course of time, whether this takes the form of an improvement of your own → *BATNA* or a deterioration of your potential negotiating partner's BATNA. Particular caution should be exercised if the opposing party previously agreed to central demands very quickly and "unfortunate" circumstances now delay the conclusion of the contract.

Example
A buyer is in negotiations with two competing parties. One of the negotiations is in the final stages. In this case, the buyer can deliberately delay the advanced negotiations to await the outcome of the negotiations with the competitor. A positive negotiation result with the competitor would significantly improve the buyer's BATNA. There are two options available to the buyer's negotiating partner: Either s/he can counteract the situation by setting a → *deadline*, or s/he can put the delay to good use, i.e. improve his/her own BATNA.

One special delay tactic is the so-called missing person manoeuvre. In addition, the conclusion of a contract can also be delayed by referring to formal, in-house procedures.

As there is usually a principal-agent constellation in B2B business (→ *principal-agent-problem*), a calculated delay does not only affect the BATNA of the potential negotiating partner, but can also influence the negotiator's BATNA. If the negotiator has a tight schedule or has to fulfil given time limits imposed by his/her superior, then the negotiator can ill afford lengthy negotiation rounds. In this case, a calculated delay can induce the negotiator to grant too generous concessions or slip up and make → *mistakes* in the final, admittedly very hectic stages of the negotiation. It is not uncommon for negotiating partners to take advantage of this effect. This form of calculated delay can be countered by various measures: Reservation times, for example; the non-disclosure of the definitive, last possible return travel date; or a company culture which does not generally evaluate an inconclusive negotiation as negative at the expense of the negotiator.

Another form of a calculated delay is given if one party deliberately keeps their negotiating partner waiting. This can have the effect of demonstrating power (by so-called → *imperial gestures*) or can aim to increase the negotiating partner's interest in conclusion.

Example
Being late on purpose can have the effect that the opposing side begins to worry about the conclusion of the contract. This situation can be used to benefit negotiations. There is, however, also the risk that the negotiating partner will only be annoyed and the relationship will suffer a long-term damage.

Calling a Higher Authority If negotiations come to a halt (→ *deadlock*), there is the possibility of turning to a higher authority in cases where the highest management level did not participate in the negotiations (which are thus so-called agent-oriented negotiations) in order to find a way out of the negotiation impasse.

As a rule, negotiating parties are generally recommended to begin at the lowest level of decision-making authority—or at least at negotiation authority level—in order to retain the option of escalation. More specifically, this option can be employed not only for negotiations that have reached a → *deadlock* but potentially also to reverse concessions that were too excessive (→ *principal-agent-problem*). With respect to the latter aspect, it should however be borne in mind that overtly diverging decisions made by the higher authority could (substantially) damage the negotiator's authority and jeopardise the harmony within an organisation. This is often the reason why low-ranking negotiators are given impressive titles in international negotiations (e.g. the head of department becomes vice president). These titles do not indicate the negotiator's relatively low rank in the company. Moreover, it is generally advisable to inquire the hierarchy level of the opposing party's negotiators in advance. In negotiations between companies, it is not uncommon for the higher hierarchy level to open the negotiation together with the negotiators, but subsequently entrust the actual negotiations solely to the working plane. In this way, the people at the higher level become acquainted, which makes it easier for them to communicate with each other if necessary. Leading the negotiations from the outset at a higher level would not only mean higher costs but would needlessly let the opportunity pass to reach an agreement on a lower level. The people negotiating with each other should be of approximately equal rank in order to avoid possible changes in mood (resentment of higher ranked negotiators, feeling of inferiority among lower ranked negotiators) (→ *respect*).

The possibility of turning to a higher authority is sometimes also used as a threat. However, this tactic regularly destroys all existing mutual trust between the negotiators.

Change the Negotiator A change of negotiator during negotiations virtually allows a fresh start to the negotiations, both at confidence level, and—at least in part—at the substantive level.

A new negotiator may well have a different perspective on the issue, thus bringing new impetus to the negotiation. The change can be made to overcome a → *deadlock,* thereby potentially freeing oneself from concessions already made without a major loss of face. In addition, there are cases, where a higher escalation level is to be reached (→ *calling a higher authority*). Either way, the exchange of → *chief negotiator* entails a certain delay for the estimated negotiation time and accordingly also involves additional costs. The trust of the opposing side can often be substantially damaged by changing the negotiator and this trust needs to be regained by the new negotiator. Introducing a new negotiator generally results in the effect that his/her side is initially less predictable. Exchanging negotiators can be worthwhile, especially if the previous negotiator was strongly rejected by the opposing party on an emotional level (→ *emotions*).

Example
The resignation of the Greek finance minister, *Varoufakis*, and his subsequent withdrawal as a negotiator for Greece after the referendum and thus before the final negotiation with the European Union during the Greek financial crisis in 2015, is an illustrative example of changing the negotiator.

Changing the entire negotiation team is known as the **tag team approach**. In mentally very strenuous negotiations, however, negotiation teams cannot only be exchanged for the above mentioned reasons, but fresh negotiators can also provide physical relieve. Since there is no intention to start afresh in this case, great attention must be paid to the transfer of information concerning the negotiation progress up to this point. In these cases, it would seem better to only change parts of the negotiation team.

Change the Standards The change of standards describes a tactic, which is intended to establish a better starting position for the main negotiations. The → *Harvard negotiation concept* generally recommends the use of neutral assessment criteria. However, there often is disagreement about the neutrality of the reference points. Negotiation parties hence frequently try to establish → *reference points*, which are favourable for them. Accordingly, the evaluation criteria (if negotiable) are already part of the negotiations. In many cases, one side postulates certain assessment criteria which the other party can then try to negotiate and potentially change if they do not consider these criteria to be sufficiently neutral.

When inviting tenders for a project or service (**request for proposals (RFP)), call for tenders, bid invitation**), the standards set there and their evaluation regarding the technical system, nominal performance, quality, experience, deadlines, sustainability, social standards or the method of price calculation often determine who wins the tender. Only in very rare cases a single supplier qualifies as the best provider according to all possible criteria.

The standards also influence the negotiating partner's → *BATNA*. A commitment to short-term performance, particularly high quality or a certain technical system can quickly lead to a situation in which there are only a few potential suppliers left to meet the demand for the service. This accordingly implies that BATNA is also severely restricted. However, the standards of a call for tenders can only be influenced by law when awarding public contracts in the run-up to a call for tenders. Even when private parties invite tenders, retrospective amendment of standards is hardly possible (in most cases → *undiscussable*). The most likely approach to achieve a concretisation will be by defining standards which so far remained undefined. Often, the greatest opportunities do not lie in direct negotiation, since the opposing side's negotiators are trained to defend themselves against such attempts. Instead, conversations between the "engineers" can prove to be more advantageous as they can lead to the opposing party's technicians being convinced of a system or a certain performance standard which they subsequently enforce internally. If your own technicians propose such specifications, the potential constriction of your own BATNA should always be taken into account and the source of the "idea" behind the specifications should be checked for reliability.

Attempting to change standards has a greater chance of success if undertaken before the actual core negotiations. Changing the negotiating partner's standards within the ongoing → *negotiation process* promises less chance of success. The person aiming to change standards needs convincing arguments for the advantageousness of deviating standards (due to the prevailing → *burden of justification*). Such explanations should preferably be underpinned with neutral sources of unbiased third parties. In this context, it is favourable if the connection between the change of standard and involvement in the ongoing negotiations is as weak as possible. Furthermore, externally induced events increase the chances of the intended change of standards.

Cherry Picking The tactic of cherry picking, not to be confused with the eponymous confirmation bias (→ *impression (first and last)*), consists of choosing the best individual aspects from various offers. For this purpose, several bids are requested, with the bidders having to specify individual prices for each component, which in sum result in the total price. The buyer then reviews these offers and determines the best individual prices. The respective offerers are then contacted and asked to improve the price of certain individual items.

> **Typical Formulation**
> "Your competitors can offer us this component for 1,500 EUR. At the very least, you would have to be able to offer us the same price."

In this way, the supplier tries to optimise each individual price. If a bidder responds to this offer with a → *BAFO* (best and final offer), that indicates that this is his/her best and last bid, and that the bidder is not willing to negotiate any further in this respect. In practice, however, there is often still one very last offer, especially regarding large, lucrative orders.

Cherry picking opposes the widespread sense of justice. Even the mere attempt to cherry pick is often perceived as very unpleasant and rude and may thus endanger the confidence in the negotiation. However, if there is a strategic imbalance in negotiations, such as between the automotive industry and most of its medium-sized suppliers, cherry-picking is a tactic that can be applied successfully.

Chicken A scene from *James Dean*'s 1955 film "Rebel Without a Cause" gave this tactic its name: Two drivers are heading for a cliff. The one to brake first is the "chicken" (the coward), while the other is the "hero". The game of chicken also refers to two cars driving towards each other at high speed. The driver who swerves out of the way is the chicken.

Situation
A says: "I'm going to kill us both." B answers: "More people will come to my funeral than yours."

This tactic is based on the same idea as → *brinkmanship*: The chicken tactic also works by means of threat and blackmail to persuade the other party to give in. For example, a supplier could use the impending insolvency as a threat to obtain better conditions. The chicken tactic likewise includes the unlawful stoppage of work by a subcontractor in a major project, where both the subcontractor and client would stand to suffer high losses and claims due to late completion. In this case, the subcontractor uses the threat of insolvency as an attempt to achieve better terms and conditions. Irrespective of the fact that this behaviour may even exceed the boundaries of criminal law, applying such measures can result in an extremely negative climate for negotiations, which can in turn increase the risk of failure of business relationships.

Furthermore, considerable risks of disruption can occur during the conclusion of the contract. This is because the negotiating partner will often attempt to obtain compensation for any obligatory contract terms which were imposed in the course of contractual fulfilment (→ *claim management*). Another point of concern with threats is the fact that one must be able to enforce the threat without causing any long-term disadvantages for the own party, unless it is a deliberate bluff—a possibility which is often not taken into account. On the other hand, threats made by negotiators acting irrationally are often taken seriously, even if the realisation of the threat would result in substantially harming the side making the threat. Another point is that the person issuing the threat would lose face if the threat were not realised. As a result, realising the threat may seem rational for the individual issuing it, but certainly not for the respective company. The tactic can be further intensified if one side commits to the threat.

Example
In the case of the two cars driving towards each other, one driver tears out the steering wheel and visibly throws it out of the car window. In this manner, he has no possibility to evade his opponent.

Chief Negotiator As it is frequently necessary to deliver clear and fast decisions within the negotiation delegation, it is often sensible to determine a chief negotiator, especially if there is a greater number of negotiators on one side. Decision making should not be unnecessarily delayed, either by consulting the company with further inquiries or by discussion within the team. Likewise, the negotiating partner expects to have a chief negotiator as a contact person throughout the negotiations.

The role of chief negotiator includes various tasks. The internal chief negotiator is the person who bears responsibility for the negotiation towards his/her own company. As a general rule, s/he is also the external chief negotiator (i.e. the main contact person for the negotiating partner). If this is exceptionally not the case, one speaks of a so–called grey eminence. The chief negotiator usually also takes on the role of the → *driver*. Moreover, the chief negotiator can simultaneously be the → *decision-maker*, who can then independently decide on the conclusion of the contract. In a broader sense of the term decision-maker, every chief negotiator is also a decision-maker since s/he may at least make organisational decisions autonomously. In contrast, a negotiator oftentimes finds himself/herself in the position of the chief negotiator, yet still has to consult a decision-maker within the company for a final decision.

Oftentimes, the chief negotiator is expected to have a (high) hierarchical standing within the company. The negotiating partner takes the position of the chief negotiator within his/her own company as a signal of the esteem and respect demonstrated towards his/her own side and the overall business under negotiation. Therefore, it might be sensible to use more sonorous titles for negotiations (e.g. "vice president" instead of head of department).

Chit-chat Chit-chat (**small talk**) refers in particular but not exclusively to the preparatory "warm-up phase" prior to the actual negotiations. Even in countries such as the US and Germany where negotiation culture is seemingly very rationally based and parties get to the desired points fairly soon (see also under Sects. 4.1 and 4.3), some chit-chat or small talk before the start of the negotiation is a widespread practice. The parties mostly discuss topics that are in no way linked to the subject matter of the negotiations, such as the weather, traffic, sports or travel. The search for similarities (→ *find something in common*) uses the → *similar-to-me-effect*. Conversations may also involve talk of a common enemy, which creates a closer bond between the parties.

Caution!
It is not equally common for all cultures to make the weather the subject of small talk as it is in England or Germany. Critical issues such as politics or religion should ideally not be addressed in the context of chit-chat. Even seemingly harmless topics such as studying or children can also involve risks, e.g. if the negotiating partner did not attend university or in the worst case if his/her only child were killed in an accident. This is another reason why it makes sense that, wherever possible, information shall be gathered beforehand about the conversation partner. Furthermore, exploring social networks and general sources, such as an informal (telephone) conversation with the negotiating partner's secretary can also provide essential reference points for the upcoming chit-chat.

Small talk facilitates building an emotional relationship with the negotiating partner. In a study, it was proven that chit-chat before negotiations, via → *e-mail* between strangers, substantially increases the probability of contract conclusion and achieves a more positive mind set among the negotiators regarding the negotiations and their negotiating partner.[35] In contrast, the likelihood of negotiation failure was up to four times higher if no small talk had previously been held among the involved parties. This is likely the accumulation of several effects: A successful chit-chat, in which certain commonalities have been established, creates a positive atmosphere, builds mutual trust between the negotiating parties and, under certain circumstances, can give a sense of how the other person speaks and to some extent also indicates how s/he deals with things, and how s/he thinks. However, another study suggests that the positive effect of chit-chat may also depend on → *gender*, so that generally only men benefit from it significantly, whereas women do not reap any benefits from it. This can be explained by the fact that such communicative skills are expected of women anyway and, as opposed to male negotiators, they do not contribute any additional social investment to the negotiating relationship which could in return be rewarded as a "plus point" by their counterparts.[36]

In chit-chat, untruths are told relatively often, e.g. to highlight similarities with the other side (→ *similar-to-me effect*), because similarities encourage the development of trust. Here, deceptions are not usually causal for the conclusion or specific design of the contract. If, however, they prove to have induced the other side to conclude the contract, the question arises as to whether the deception should be evaluated as misleading, without any legal consequences (further under → *cunning*

[35] Nadler (2004), pp. 223–253.
[36] Shaughnessy et al. (2015), pp. 105–117.

deception). The authors of this work assume that, as a rule, no legal consequences are ordered, if the chit-chat is deceptive about aspects that are not directly linked to the subject matter of the contract.

Even though chit-chat is used more intensively at the beginning of negotiations, it is usually continued throughout the negotiations, e.g. during → *negotiation pauses,* and is also held up afterwards (e.g. during a joint dinner after conclusion of the contract). The aim of small talk is to convey personal appreciation to the negotiating partner (*appreciation*; → *core concerns framework*), which is particularly needed, especially after hard negotiations regarding content. In the event of a stalemate in negotiations, for instance where parties remain silent (→ *silence*), small talk is often used to try to improve personal relationships and thus favour the constructive continuation of the negotiations.

Claim (or Claims) Management Claim management fundamentally follows two strategic goals: The first is to recognise deviations between the actual state and the contractually agreed target state, in conjunction with the enforcement of claims arising from these differences; and secondly, the prevention of the emergence or the enforcement of the contractual partner's claims. The underlying objectives are consequently to defend or maximise profits on the one hand, and to minimise conflicts on the other.

A distinction is made between different claim strategies: A passive claim strategy waives all management of the claim process; a defensive claim strategy, which both fends off unjustified claims and secures the justified claims of its own side—albeit very cautiously—and an offensive or aggressive claim strategy, which aims at shifting the price-performance ratio within the context of claim management to its own advantage.

A **passive claim strategy** can only be applied if a complete submission to the negotiating partner's demands is desired or necessary. Passive claim management neither tries to promote the generation of its own claims, nor does it impede the enforcement of claims from the opposing side. Rather, the own sides claims are generally not enforced, even if they arise without one's own contribution, while the third-party claims of the negotiating partner are always fulfilled. The passive claim strategy pursues the goal of total conflict avoidance.

A **defensive claim strategy** can be applied both in the event of economic dependence on future deals with the opposing side, or if the economic advantages of trustful cooperation in the ongoing transaction are estimated to be greater than the advantages resulting from offensive (aggressive) claim-management would turn out. The defensive claim strategy seeks to balance the objectives of maximising net compensation and minimising conflict. To this end, everything possible is done to prevent the development of the own and third-party claims. However, insofar as personal claims arise, the non-enforcement of which could result in considerable disadvantages, they should be enforced, regardless of the according potential for conflict with the negotiating partner. In this context, it is essential to ensure that the appropriate framework is not exceeded. In this respect, literature speaks of "damage limitation claims". Provided that they are not justified in terms of amount or substance; third-party claims must be vigorously fended off. Conversely, legitimate third-party claims must always be met and implemented soon. Defensive claim-management consequently includes trust-building and claim-reducing measures, such as the early warning of possible damage; early notification of problems regarding deadlines or quality; the joint search for ways to mitigate damage; and fair regulations for supplements or changes to orders.

The **offensive claim strategy** is characterised by the fact that the creation of claims is actively supported, e.g. by the deliberate creation of gaps in the contract or scope for interpretation, whereby possible conflicts with the negotiating partner are accepted. This can go so far that very weakly founded claims in conjunction with high demands and the threat of work stoppage are raised at a time where the client faces the greatest possible damage. Even though this aggressive strategy partially oversteps the boundaries of criminal law, it often does not originate from a criminal attitude, but rather from economic pressure. A sufficient profit margin for the negotiating partner can thus prevent overly aggressive claim management from his/her side. The aim of the offensive claim-strategy is to maximise net compensation, i.e. your own compensation for the provision of services minus possible third-party claims and the costs of claim management. Ultimately, claim management is the attempt to change the price-performance ratio in the own favour. Consequently, even the offensive claim strategy does not rule out the strict obligation to precisely document possible misperformances on the own side as well as external mistakes in order to prevent the enforcement of third party claims as effectively as possible.

Example

Manufacturers of industrial plants are sometimes willing to submit bids under cost price in order to win the contract and then try to reach the profit zone by way of creating supplementary claims during implementation of the contract.

An offensive (aggressive) claim-strategy is more likely to be applied in the context of one off transactions, i.e. in the course of deals which are characterised by economic dependency or in the event of major economic difficulties on one side. For example, unless there is a history of long-term dependence, any customer gagging its contractor in terms of price can expect an aggressive claim strategy from the contractor.

It should be noted that the actual selection of a claim strategy involves the consideration of various criteria, such as one's own corporate culture, the possible impact of the chosen strategy on the long-term success of the company and, in particular, also the current political and economic environment in which the company operates. Due to these reasons, parties only rarely follow one of the described strategies in their pure form, but rather opt for an individual, project-specific combined approach, created on the basis of the strategy that matches the basic orientation of the company best.

Closed Questions Closed questions are not intended to collect a broad range of information but are rather aimed at determining the factual correctness/incorrectness of an assumption. The term "closed question" is a generic term that includes several variants. One form of closed question is the decision question, which can only be answered with yes or no (or, at most, with maybe). This type of question is also referred to as the → *Yes/No question.* Both control questions as well as → *a–not–a–question* are also classified as closed questions. Closed questions can further be used to determine which of several possible options is correct. Closed questions can also be used to record negotiation results.

If the negotiation partner answers open questions in an evasive or contradictory manner, closed questions may be useful to clarify important facts. Closed questions thus may also serve to exert a certain amount of pressure on the opposing party. This pressure, which depends both on the nature of the question asked previously and on the intonation of the statement, is basically intentional. However, if the situation begins to resemble an interrogation, there will most likely be objections. In these instances, the negotiating partner will then often respond with counter questions or open rejection of this questioning technique.

Example of a Decision Question
"Do you want to buy the TV in black?"

Example of an Alternative Question
"Do you want to have the coffee machine delivered or would you prefer to collect it in person?"

Example of a Closed Question That Records the Outcome of the Negotiations
"So can we agree that you will fix my car by next Tuesday?"

Columbo This term refers to Inspector Columbo, who was the leading character in a U.S. TV-series for many years. In the context of contract negotiations, the term either relates to a questioning technique or a tactic.

Concerning its application as a questioning technique, what distinguished Inspector Columbo was that he would ask suspects or witnesses simple questions during informal interviews, in the course of which he gave the deliberate impression of being slightly confused, before slipping in a final question after the interview had already supposedly ended, i.e. when leaving. In this way, Columbo took advantage of the fact that the tension and thus also the concentration and defence stance diminishes significantly when the actual questioning is over. In the context of negotiations, it is useful to bear this fact in mind, and also when obtaining information. However, using this questioning technique alone will generally not suffice to achieve approval of the demands which have already been made. Questions that are asked a little later, i.e. after the end of the negotiation, e.g. on the way to the parking lot or at dinner are particularly dangerous, since the level of concentration in these situations is relatively low. One very popular approach is to combine the Columbo-tactic with the technique of the so-called → *premise question.*

In some cases, Columbo also refers to the **Columbo tactic,** alluding to the fact that prima facie Columbo appeared to be a little slow and sometimes slightly confused from the witnesses or suspects point of view. This effect was wrought by his hesitant behaviour and his seeming to search for words, combined with rather sloppy clothing. The result was that most people often underestimated him, and hence the tactic is also discussed under the term → *play dumb.*

Conclusion by Analogy Using the results which were ascertained for one particular point to hypothesise the outcome of another, similar constellation is known as conclusion by analogy (also **argumentum a simile** or **conclusion by similarity**). It is one of the most important general figures of argumentation. Due to their professional training, lawyers are very familiar with this figure, which is why they use it frequently and deliberately. However, thanks to the persuasive power of conclusion by analogy, this form of argumentation is frequently used even by those with no educational background in the legal field. It is, after all, based on the idea of equal treatment for cases of equal status, i.e. the concept of equality. In the context of contract negotiations, the current negotiation situation would be deduced from the known result in a different situation. Since two situations are never exactly the same, i.e. not comparable at all times the potential scope of application of this conclusion is, on the one hand, very broad. On the other hand, it is often hard to decide whether there is actually sufficient similarity between the two cases, i.e. the remaining differences are so small that a different decision cannot be justified.

Above all, in the context of negotiations, conclusion by analogy does not possess the same persuasion power which it has with regard to its function of filling legislative loopholes. This is because a new contract always holds the possibility of deviating from former actions and practices. But if the opposing side decides to act differently, without any obvious reasoning, it to a certain degree displays behaviour in conflict to its prior actions. Moreover, if there were formerly no obvious problems, there is a certain assumption that in this case, under equal treatment, also no problems will arise. Based on the freedom to decide differently each time, depending on the circumstances, the conclusion by analogy only intends to put the → *burden of justification* for a desired change from the compared case, onto the opposing party. The arm's length principle follows a similar idea, although in that case the idea of a contradiction with former behaviour is not applicable.

Example
A clause is being negotiated which should contain a generous provision for the supplier. In the past, the purchaser has accepted such a clause.

Purchaser: "In its present form, this clause cannot be accepted. We cannot imagine it that way."

Supplier: "This comes as a great surprise, since in the past the supply contract XY included this clause. At the time, the clause was acceptable to you. What exactly is the problem this time?"

Considered Response Considered response is a guiding principle which serves to avoid → *mistakes*. Since information is crucial in negotiations, the negotiating partner will try to get hold of anything that could be valuable for his/her own side. Already the questioning techniques listed in this book (see corresponding topic list)—and noting that this list is by no means exhaustive—show the wide variety of question types. Behind the questioning techniques are a variety of goals, intentions and motives, which are sometimes not apparent at first glance. In negotiations, it is therefore not advisable to answer questions hastily. Instead, attention should be paid to recognising the actual meaning of the question and the underlying strategic goal before answering in a considered manner. Further inquiry can help here. If the other party's motives are ambiguous, this can lead to evasive answers. The same applies to reactions to offers and proposals made by the negotiating partner.

Core Concerns Framework The core concerns framework is an approach developed by *Fisher* and *Shapiro* and gives recommendations on how to deal with → *emotions* in negotiations.[37] The authors identify five central basic needs:

- Appreciation
- Affiliation
- Autonomy
- Status and
- Role

Appreciation plays a significant role in negotiations. No person ever likes to suffer from a lack of appreciation. Above all, this feeling can arise if one feels misunderstood and underestimated and the negotiating partner does not give the impression of listening properly, i.e. not taking his/her opponent's position seriously or acknowledging his/her achievements. Lack of appreciation frequently leads to negative → *emotions* for the negotiating partner and thus inhibits cooperative negotiations. The negotiating partner should therefore be given the feeling that his/her

[37] Fisher and Shapiro (2005), p. 25 et seq.

position is understood and a certain value of this standing has been recognised. Moreover, on a personal level, appreciation is also crucial.

The connection to the negotiating partner refers to the emotional connection between the parties. The feeling of solidarity, i.e. a good relationship between the parties, is beneficial for constructive negotiations. Establishing good negotiation relationships is hence crucial to the success of the negotiations. If, on the other hand, a feeling of emotional rejection is conveyed to the negotiating partner, this often destroys the relationship between the parties and jeopardises the conclusion of the contract.

Another central basic need is autonomy. People do not like to be restricted in their autonomy. *Fisher* and *Shapiro* also recommend → *decision-maker* to take the → *ACBD*-rule (always consult before deciding) into account before making a decision.

Likewise, status plays a significant role in negotiations. In negotiations, it is important to recognise the status of one's negotiating partner.

Experiment

In an experiment *Wilson* conducted with 110 students, one person (Mr. England) was briefly introduced by the course instructor to the students, who had been split into five groups. Mr. England's academic status varied from group to group, ranging from a student to a professor at Cambridge University. Following this short presentation, the students were asked to estimate Mr. England's height as well as the height of the course instructor, who had been standing next to Mr. England during the presentations. The course instructor had maintained the same status in each group. The results of the study show that the students estimated Mr. England to be taller in proportion to his alleged status. The estimated height of the course instructor remained constant throughout.[38]

People also play different roles in negotiations. The taken role should have a clear direction, be meaningful to the individual and consistent with the own personality in order to be perceived as positive. Furthermore, a distinction should be made between superordinate roles, e.g. the role of negotiator in negotiations, and temporary, situational roles. Examples of this are the short-term assumption of the role of problem solver, listener, or → *advocatus diaboli*. Temporary roles are sometimes taken in reaction to the behaviour of the negotiating partner and in these cases, are based less on the negotiator's autonomous decision. In negotiations, it should be reflected whether the temporary role taken is consistent with the goal of the negotiation.

Creating Facts Negotiations can be influenced by creating facts. This tactic is also referred to as **fait accompli** or **accomplished facts**. However, this tactic only

[38] Wilson (1968), pp. 97–102.

promises to be successful if these facts influence the decision-making process, i.e. if the negotiating partner does not simply avoid these facts, and if it is not possible to effectively eliminate them by legal means, e.g. because the facts were created illegally. The tactic of accomplished facts is most likely to achieve success in political negotiations or within an organisation.

This tactic is also used in B2B negotiations. Such a case occurs, for instance, when two companies are negotiating the establishment of a joint venture. At the same time, one of the companies closes preliminary contracts with one of the key potential contract partners of the joint venture. In so doing, the company brands the (not yet established) joint venture with their name, e.g. under the heading of the company's name. In this case, the preliminary agreements, i.e. the facts created, exert pressure on the negotiating partner with regards to the name of the joint venture. Unilateral announcements can have the same effect. In the case of larger service contracts, it is quite common that one side offers to start work, even though the details of the contract have not yet been agreed on. A premature commencement of work creates considerable pressure to reach an agreement. The created facts are thus generally aimed at restricting the negotiating partner's scope of action and accordingly influence his/her → *BATNA*.

Credible Threat Credible threat refers to a tactic to increase the effect of a threat. We talk about a credible threat when the person making the threat would indeed be in a better position if the threat were actually to be implemented. In this respect, not only the immediate economic consequences but also the value of the threat as a means of exerting pressure must be taken into account. The risk of losing one's reputation if the threat is not implemented must also be borne in mind, especially in the context of publicly expressed threats. In addition, there are threats which are not economical from an objective point of view, but the people involved seem so irrationally determined that the threat is subjectively perceived as credible.

Cui Bono The classic question "cui bono?" (who profits from it?) originates from Roman law and became well known when *Marcus Tullius Cicero* used it in his defensive plea for *Sextus Roscius Amerinus.* The negotiator should ask himself/herself this question for each proposed agreement, although the answer may vary depending on the various practical scenarios. In → *distributive negotiations* in particular, negotiators tend to reflexively evaluate the opposing party's proposals as negative (→ *reactive devaluation*). However, it may well be the case that the opposing party proposes a regulation which is not beneficial for them, or is least also advantageous for the own side because of common interests (→ *Harvard negotiation concept*). Conversely, the own suggestions should be considered from the "cui bono?" point of view. Yet, → *mistakes* can even occur in professionally conducted negotiations.

Cunning Deception Various negotiation tactics are based on deceiving the negotiator about a specific aspect (see topic list "competitive negotiating – deceptions").

Some of these deceptive tactics are not only very common in practise, but are also considered to be generally accepted in the business sphere:

> "In the context of negotiations, bluffing is a generally accepted business practice where pretence is used to imply that one's position is stronger, cleverer, or more determined, etc., than one's position really is."[39]

This is also confirmed by a wide-ranging international survey on the moral evaluation of individual tactical behaviour and the desired legal conditions in this respect conducted by the authors. Almost none of the respondents—neither surveyed students, professional negotiators, lawyers nor judges—saw the necessity for legal sanctions for any deliberate deception affecting the outcome of the negotiations. Participants even consider several lies to be also morally acceptable.

Concerning tactics based on bluffs, the question as to whether their use really does always constitute fraudulent deception or whether they can be classed as "cunning", arises. Hence, it is essential to answer whether the behaviour is just smart or ingenious, and shall therefore not entitle the deceived party the right to contest the contract. Claims for damages would then also be excluded. According to the authors, such cases of this → *cunning deception* do actually exist. Here it is important to determine the "rules of the game" de lege lata, and wherever necessary also by way of further developing the law.

In principle, the party which was deceived about a fact that induced the eventual conclusion of the contract, or a conclusion under different conditions, can contest the contract. The core area, in which law provisions generally protect the deceived side, comprises the cases in which the clear, normative assessment of unlawfulness can be derived from other standards. In particular, these most likely include deception about the subject matter of the contract as well as its price and the implementation of the contract.

Nonetheless, there are also cases in which no legal consequences should apply according to the idea put forward here. In the context of B2B-negotiations, there is often deception regarding such aspects as personal tastes and preferences (→ *similar-to-me-effect*). This kind of deception is quite common in negotiations and should not actually influence the outcome of a rational negotiation at all. At most this behaviour should only lead to a shift within the → *ZOPA*. Furthermore, due to the difficulty of demonstrability, legal provisions would probably prove fairly ineffective. Simultaneously, the deceived party often has relatively effective social options for reacting and later discontinuing (→ *permanent business relations*). In the authors' opinion, deceptions concerning personal preferences in B2B-relations should therefore not justify a challenge in the B2B relationship. The same should apply regarding deceptions about one's own → *negotiation power*. According to the opinion represented here, it is irrelevant whether the given statements concern exaggerations, understatements or downright lies.

[39] Guth (2008), p. iii.

Conversely, deceit regarding the availability of a limited quantity of a product (→ *tactic of small quantities*) is, for example, a borderline case. In conclusion the authors believe that deceit about own stocks should not, in B2B relations, justify challenging the contract, since by rational approach to negotiations, these statements should not influence the market price. By contrast, deceptions that affect the overall availability of a product objectively affect the value.

DAD Approach This acronym stands for "decide, announce, defend".[40] The tactical approach of the DAD approach dispenses with any involvement of potential opponents in the actual → *negotiation phase* in complex negotiating issues in which parties involved outside the direct negotiation could bring down the project (in contrast to this cf. → *think beyond the table* and → *ACBD-rule*). On the contrary: potential opponents are presented with a *fait accompli* (→ *creating facts*). In these cases, resistance will often be particularly intense due to the lack of participation and because a compromise is hardly possible. On the other hand, these opponents sometimes learn about the project at such a late point in time and would require so much preparation time that they can no longer effectively disrupt or even block (→ *blockade strategy*) the implementation of the project.

The opposite approach is the full consensus approach (→ *FC approach*) which tries to achieve full agreement between all negotiation partners in the negotiation phase. This may seem sensible for ideological reasons but rarely proves successful. A further contrast to DAD is the → *DDD approach* (dialogue, decide, deliver approach). The most promising course of action in the initial negotiation phase is to involve potential negotiation opponents who are willing to make basic compromises.

Examples of Complex Negotiation Subjects
Construction of power plants, railway stations, industrial plants.

DDD Approach The DDD approach—short for "dialogue, decide, deliver"—is a tactic closely linked to the company *Shell*. With this particular approach, *Shell* chooses to involve stakeholders (→ *think beyond the table*) in decision-making processes.[41] The DDD approach complements the → *DAD approach* and is similar to the → *FC approach*.

The obvious advantage of this approach is that there is less likelihood of late resistance in the negotiation process. Likewise, any potentially arising resistance does not stem from the main stakeholders' lack of involvement. Some potential opponents are only willing to compromise when this approach is applied.

The main disadvantage of this approach is that involving the opponent ahead of time may expedite the organisation of effective resistance at an early stage. The

[40] Cf. Susskind (1985), p. 159.

[41] Cf. Shell Quest CCS Project (2013) p. 4.

chances of stopping a project in its undeveloped stages are usually higher than at a later stage. One reason for this is that fewer stakeholders will have committed to the project at an earlier stage and thus the engagement of supporters will not yet be very substantial. Moreover, the → *sunk cost bias* plays a role in this regard.

Deadline Deadlines (time limits) can be set externally, determined mutually by both contracting parties, or set unilaterally which is probably the most frequent case. Externally determined, imperative, objective deadlines, such as the end of a tender submission period, have the strongest effect on negotiation partners and do not constitute a tactic, since they cannot be influenced by either of the involved parties. They are general framework conditions. The **time pressure** resulting from these deadlines (particularly as they draw closer) commonly influences the dynamics of the negotiation. Jointly set deadlines aid to find a solution within a reasonable time limit and thus help to control the overall incurring costs of the negotiation. A deadline set unilaterally can also have this objective. In these cases, the tacit or explicit extension of such a deadline is usually relatively unproblematic.

Nonetheless, deadlines can also be also used tactically in negotiations. By fixing deadlines, time is used as a means of exerting pressure. This pressure arises from the real consequences which threaten if the deadline should elapse (→ *credible threat*). Not complying with a deadline can for instance lead to the termination of the negotiations, or imply the loss of a compromise offer regarding a specific aspect of the negotiation. A somewhat milder form is to threaten with postponement of the negotiation. In this respect, only the current round of the negotiation will be affected by being limited in time. If the aim of this meeting had been to bring about an agreement, the negotiating partner may now face a delay. In this way, actual and artificial deadlines (→ *false deadlines*) can exert pressure on the negotiating partner. The pressure rises, if the deadline is linked to the → *tactic of small quantity*, i.e. if the buyer is persuaded that the product in question is in short supply. This combination is particularly common in B2C relations.

One exceptional form of deadline is the so-called **exploding offer**: The offer "explodes", i.e. becomes definitively void and invalid upon the expiry of a given time limit.

Building pressure in negotiations can have the purpose of deliberately provoking → *mistakes* by the negotiating partner, either because of the time constraint during the negotiation or in the course of preparing the negotiations ("*Prior preparation prevents poor performance.*" → *80-20-rule*).

Tactical deadlines serve not only to generate pressure but also to clarify certain questions or the entire contract at a fixed point in time. If used in moderation, setting fixed deadlines can in fact be legitimate, if the negotiations are otherwise likely to drag on for a disproportionate amount of time. Deadlines can thus control transaction costs. As with a threat, the consequences of failing to respond to a deadline must be thought out beforehand (and should be effective and appropriate) and must also be enforced if necessary. If the consequence is not enforced without valid justification, the deadline loses its effect as an instrument for the future. If one side threatens consequences such as the discontinuation of negotiations, they should also be prepared to follow through with it, in order to remain credible. The red line is the counterpart of a deadline, in regards to the content of a demand.

In practice, time constraints relating to a particular phase of the negotiations play a significant practical role (e.g. when the next appointment is not postponable, or there is a specifically set date for the return journey). The negotiator with the limited time frame commonly discloses this information if the unsuccessful round of negotiations does not disadvantage either him/her or his/her company. Time constraints are even more likely to be divulged if the opposing side is in urgent need of negotiation success.

Often, however, negotiators who have undertaken costly journeys and travelled a great distance are under a certain pressure to succeed in the current negotiation round. The reasons for this may perhaps be the shortage of the negotiator's free time windows; the high expenditure for the journey to the ongoing negotiation; or as well sometimes the high expectations, which some → *decision-makers* have of the negotiator. If the other party is not in the same situation, the (in this respect) weaker side—in most cases the guest—will attempt to alleviate the time pressure through reserve times. In order to make the delaying tactics more difficult for the other side, in particular in the form of a → *calculated delay*, their own deadline for this round of negotiations will not be disclosed. After all, if the other side is aware of the internal deadline, and the circumstances are such that this side has a clear interest in not being left empty-handed at the end of this negotiating round, there is a very real risk of hectic final negotiations. The side which is under time pressure may concede too much or make → *mistakes*. It would be more effective to reduce the existing pressure within the company, although in most cases this will not prove possible. One can at least try to give the impression that there is no internal pressure to succeed.

Deadlock The term deadlock describes a problematic point in negotiations at which the negotiations could potentially fail. Handling this situation requires exceptional negotiation skills. In particular, a deadlock implies that both parties disagree, but none is inclined to make any concessions or at least move or think in a different direction. A **dead point**, i.e. a deadlock, especially occurs in position-oriented negotiations, but does not necessarily justify a termination of negotiations. Particularly in position-oriented negotiations, there can still be a → *ZOPA* (zone of possible agreement), regardless of any given deadlock between the parties. In these cases, there is however a considerable risk of failure due to the impasse in which the negotiations are stalled.

A standstill is often based on negotiation → *mistakes*, which is why it is essential to take preventive measures to avoid a deadlock. If an impasse occurs, the negotiation parties have to recognise ways on how they can overcome the stalemate. Among the possible solutions for resolving this situation is, first of all and preferably, a → *negotiation pause*, which gains time for reflection and reassessment. If more time is required, the negotiations can also be postponed. In addition, it is also possible to firstly negotiate other—usually less important—points and get these out of the way, in order to allow setting the negotiation flow back in motion (Furthermore, making

→ *non-linear compromises* as well as changing to an interest-oriented negotiation can help overcome the blockade.

In terms of personnel, involving a neutral third person (such as a mediator), the addition of a creative deal-maker to the negotiation team or the exchange of negotiators (→ *change the negotiator*) could be considered. Regarding the content, the entire business could be broken down into separate tranches to enable an agreement on certain individual aspects. It would also be possible to include transactions with third parties in negotiations (→ *negotiation pie*). Furthermore, the parties could try to re-evaluate the standards against which both sides measure the outcome of the negotiations (→ *change the standards*). Finally, a negotiator could once again show himself/herself off as flexible in another, possibly already completed, point and make concessions towards the other side (**traded small movement close**). Particularly suitable for this purpose are aspects which are less important for the conceding side (**low-cost concession**), but are, however, of great importance to the opposing party.

Deal-Breaker A deal-breaker is a usually previously defined point at which, in the absence of an agreement which is profitable for the own side, the negotiations will be broken off. **Walk away term** and **resistance point** are synonyms for deal-breaker. In rational, interest-oriented negotiations, the existence of a better alternative (→ *BATNA*) is a deal-breaker. Likewise, deal-breakers can also be certain conditions that are considered indispensable for an acceptable agreement, such as specific minimum profit margin, taking over a specific risk, or compliance with certain legal or ethical boundaries. In position-oriented negotiations, these limits are often defined without considering interests, or only with a general view of interests. Deal-breakers can then obstruct interest-based solutions.

Since a deal-breaker results in discontinuation of the negotiations, defining a deal-breaker provides clarity and can help avoid lengthy and unsuccessful negotiations. Such deal-breakers often refer to isolated positions. If a deal-breaker or resistance point only concerns the price, it is also called **reservation value** or **reservation price,** and it represents the lowest value for which the seller is willing to sell. Conversely, the reservation price is the highest price the buyer would be willing to pay for a specific product. The reservation value thus reflects the own parties' → *BATNA*. Where whole negotiation packages are concerned, the reservation value should be determined not only for each individual subject, but also for the complete package. This comprehensive approach grants more scope for flexible manoeuvres in the individual negotiation points (**package reservation value**). In this way, setting below or exceeding the reservation price can be compensated for by a good compromise at another point in the negotiations.

Apart from the price there can be other deal-breakers, such as delivery dates, technical requirements, guarantees, liability clauses etc. Often, however, only a reservation price is determined, or a few deal-breakers that refer to certain positions. This approach is not unproblematic, since it may lead to a termination of negotiations being contemplated, even though the partner has proposed interesting compromises outside the mere price setting, e.g. advantageous delivery dates, or liability clauses. An isolated deal-breaker does not take sufficient account of the interaction of all the contractual provisions, which is why a deal-breaker should be determined prior to the negotiations. If, however, this point is indeed reached in the course of the negotiations, the situation should be re-evaluated in order to establish whether the discontinuation of the negotiations should actually be carried out or not. It is important that this decision is assessed not solely by the → *chief negotiator*, but also by a body not involved in the negotiations as the negotiator may be inclined to continue negotiations due to the → *sunk cost bias* (in this case with regard to the time and effort already invested), regardless of the deal-breaker (see also *agreement bias* → *BATNA*). A very broad deal-breaker might also be considered; one which takes into account the described incalculabilities, especially with regard to the interaction of the contractual provisions. This is because it can sometimes be rather difficult to break away from a point once set. In broad consideration, the deal-breaker constitutes a point at which the conclusion of a contract no longer makes sense (even taking into account potential compensation by way of other clauses). However, this also means that it may be necessary to break off negotiations before the deal-breaker is reached. That is why, in addition to defining a deal-breaker, a grey area should also be determined where a weighing of interests is decisive.

The deal-breaker(s) should be defined prior to the negotiations, in the context of *preparing the negotiations* (→ *80-20-rule*). In many cases, the deal-breaker and BATNA are largely identical. This is due to the fact that discontinuing the negotiations usually makes more sense when there is a better alternative available to the conclusion of a contract. When determining the deal-breaker and the grey area, it is advisable to use a → *traffic light system*. This signals which agreements can be assessed as unproblematic (green), which agreements could perhaps be accepted provided that they are compensated for by other points (orange or yellow) and also at which point a deal-breaker is inevitable (red). Influenced both by the negotiations and also in view of intermediate occurrences outside the scope of negotiations (e.g. changes to the BATNA), it may be necessary to adjust the defined deal-breakers. The original definition of the deal-breakers is valuable here since the → *burden of justification* for desired amendments always lies with the person proposing modification.

The deal-breakers or resistance point of both parties determine whether there is a → *ZOPA*, i.e. a possible zone in which an agreement can be achieved. Usually it is not advisable to disclose the resistance point to the negotiating partner as this would put him/her in the position of knowing how much s/he could demand at most. In the case of an agent-oriented negotiation, it is difficult to evaluate the extent to which one's own negotiator should be aware of the real deal-breakers. On the one hand, there is a danger that the opposing party would be able to deduce the resistance point (at least approximately) from the negotiator's behaviour and would accordingly be able to draw as close as possible to it. On the other hand, there is the risk that negotiators who are aware of the maximum possible discount will on average grant a higher discount than those who are not aware of it. Under these circumstances, the interest in concluding a contract could be greater than the interest in achieving an optimal negotiation result (→ *principal-agent-problem).* Consequently, it might be advisable not to inform the negotiator of the exact resistance point. Instead, the negotiator could be given a narrow framework. Any compromises going beyond this would then require the approval of a supervisor.

The resistance point (the deal-breaker) can also be the basis for deceit. One relatively subtle method is to start the gradual reduction of concessions sooner and earlier, or to reduce the concessions more quickly, so that the opposing party presumes a different resistance point (→ *diminishing rates of concession*). Parties often mislead their opponents with regard to their BATNA (→ *better offer*) and consequently also about the resistance point.

The counterpart to the deal-breaker (or minimum goal) is the maximum goal (→ *aspiration point*).

Decision-Maker The decision-maker, also known as the **decider**, is a key character in every negotiation. S/he decides whether the presented result is acceptable. In some cases, the decision-maker himself/herself is involved in negotiations while in other cases s/he sends a negotiator to the negotiations who has the authority to negotiate or with formal conclusion authorisation; but who, at the same time, has the obligation not to decide alone. This latter case gives rise to the → *principal-agent-problem.*

A differentiation can be made between the different types of decision-maker:

- Decision-makers authorised to submit proposals;
- decision-makers entitled to veto;
- active decision-makers (authorised to make decisions on their own);
- decision-makers who are part of a decision-making body (without veto authorisation);
- people who are authorised to take responsibility for decisions and
- people who are even authorised to breach or change general company policies, even if this would affect other projects.

Since the decider's decision will also depend on how it is presented to him/her, opponents should always endeavour to know the opposing party's decision-maker. This enables well-known preferences of decision-makers to be taken into account during the negotiations. For instance, a decision-maker may be particularly interested in a specific part of the contract due to his past professional activity or training.

Only those who ultimately decide on the final agreement, i.e. the conclusion of the contract, can be considered decision-makers in the narrow sense. However, this does not mean that all individual decisions should be made solely by the decision-maker. Instead, it is more advantageous to give the negotiation team or the negotiator, i.e. the person responsible for the negotiation process, a certain degree of decision-making autonomy. Thus, there may be several decision-makers for individual aspects of the negotiation.

Decision-makers are oftentimes not present at the negotiation table. This offers the advantage that the negotiation result underlies a second control. On the other hand, it also reduces the decision options to approval, rejection, and further negotiation. Medium-sized companies have profited from having the decision-maker at the negotiation table for larger projects, at least in the final negotiation round. That way, the decision-maker can form an unmediated impression of whether the full potential was maximised. They can also participate directly in the negotiations and thus influence their outcome. However, the later the decision-maker intervenes in the negotiations, the more difficult it is to deviate from the results already negotiated, especially without spoiling the relationship of trust with the negotiating partner and without undermining the negotiator's authority.

If the opposing party's decision-maker is present at the negotiation-table, it can be profitable to focus in particular on his/her reactions and his/her approval. It is not uncommon for decision-makers to open the negotiations. This way, they can get to know each other which in turn makes it easier to conduct direct negotiations in the event of complications. In rare cases, decision-makers want to participate in negotiations without being recognised. To do this, they practically take on the role of an → *analyst* and can make an informed decision without actually being involved themselves. Under certain circumstances, however, the opposing party may be able to recognise that the decision-maker is present at the negotiations—for instance, negotiators give the game away by occasionally looking enquiringly at another member of the negotiation team who was not officially presented as the decision-maker. If one negotiating member sets the tone of emotional expressions such as laughing, this can also indicate that s/he or she is responsible for making decisions.

Under certain circumstances, **opinion leaders** can be equally as important as decision-makers. They do not necessarily have to be the sole decision-making authority—or even a decision-making authority at all—but their opinion holds significant sway. Accordingly, if a decision has to be made at board level, the person who prepares or assesses the decision for the board is potentially the opinion leader.

Detection of Deception (DoD) In view of the proliferation of tactics that include elements of deception (see also topic list), the question of whether and how deceptions can be revealed is of considerable importance for negotiators (detection of deception (DoD) or **lie detection**; discovery of lies). The detection of deception can also have an impact on the dissemination of the application of appropriate tactics. Specific research into this issue focuses on statements in court and in interrogations, e.g. by police, secret services or hearings in disciplinary proceedings, since the correctness of statements is far more important there than in the context of negotiations. The transferability of these findings to the context of negotiations must always be checked critically. Criminal (interrogational) methods and technical aids such as lie detectors, voice analyses or film analyses are excluded from negotiations anyway. The uncovering of a possible deception by the deceived person could even lead to the unintentional failure of the negotiations. However important the knowledge of a deception may be, caution must be exercised in obtaining and utilizing that knowledge.

Statements should be checked for **credibility and plausibility**. These terms distinguish between the person (credibility) and the statement in question (plausibility). On an international plane, the credibility analysis is referred to as statement validity assessment (SVA) and the plausibility analysis is known as criteria-based content analysis (CBCA). While in Germany assessment reports based on these analyses are admissible as evidence in legal proceedings, this does not apply, for example, in the US. The very high degree of veracity required for juridical decisions in these assessment procedures is therefore controversial. In negotiations, however, even less reliable evidence of deception is of value as it can give rise to the need to obtain further information. At the very least it takes into account the uncertainty about the correctness of the information when making decisions.

Detecting deceptions in negotiations is complicated by various factors. Negotiations generally require extensive mental effort and are often conducted with a small number of staff (hence, no → *analyst*). In negotiations, the main issue is often not statements that are utterly false, but rather exaggerations and falsifications. Likewise, it is quite common to present circumstances as being true although the details are only known from hearsay or are only assumed to be correct in one's own view, based on other information. The according deceptions are far more difficult to detect than completely fictitious "facts". A professional negotiator handling on behalf of his/her company will usually be far less emotionally involved than s/he would be when acting from personal interest. Outward signs of emotional stress due to misleading behaviour can therefore be weaker or might not be visible at all. In negotiations with high economic relevance, the negotiators are often of considerably superior intellectual capacity. If these negotiators prepare themselves very thoroughly for deception, it will typically be extremely difficult to detect. In addition, it is also possible that a negotiator has himself/herself been misinformed by his/her own side and thus does not intentionally deceive his/her negotiating partner. In these cases, the negotiator has a clear conscience and accordingly acts unbiased. Moreover, in many cases, there are perceptual or memory mistakes. These, however, tend to favour the own side's interests (→ *foggy recall*).

The consequence of what has been said should, on the one hand, be that negotiators endeavour to verify or falsify particularly important information, even without any indication of deception (**check the facts**). In this context, it is generally recommendable to try to obtain information from at least two different and independent resources. Due to the difficulties to verify/falsify information, it is common to just subject some information to a plausibility control. On the other hand, investigating potential deceptions in negotiations should be carried out at limited effort, yet in a professional manner. In individual cases, the required effort depends heavily on the relationship between the parties and their degree of mutual trust. Any indication of deception in the negotiations should not be treated as proof of such and accordingly no premature conclusions should be drawn. Basic mistrust of the negotiating partner is detrimental to the negotiations and should therefore be avoided. Accordingly, indications of falsehood should be a reason for further research and flow into the risk assessment, if the correctness of the information cannot be clarified. Legally, there is the option to have specific statements guaranteed by the negotiating partner in the form of an explicit guarantee.

In → *permanent business relations* it can be worthwhile to keep a track record for individual negotiators from the opposing party with regard to their honesty, since the correctness or incorrectness of information often comes to light later on. Intentional deception is typically straining, both emotionally as well as intellectually. Although many negotiators can hide indications for deception well, other negotiators show clear signs of behaviour that differs from their normal behaviour. Signs of emotional stress include a high, cracking voice, redness on the throat and neck, a delay in speaking, blinking (blinking less when lying and increased blinking immediately after the lie) and dilated pupils.[42] These indications are even more significant if the negotiation situation as such would not give rise to emotional stress if the statements made were true.

Checking statements will generally decrease the risk of the negotiating partner attempting to deceive. Conducting further inquiries about important statements is advisable. The more statements that are made, the sooner the meaningful assessment of indications of deception becomes possible. Besides, → *misunderstandings* are also less likely to occur. However, inquiries should not be made in a way that suggests distrust. A study has shown that specific questions in particular can prevent deception caused by omission.[43] Unless they are questioned directly, negotiators tend not to address problems. They will, however, talk about these issues if they are explicitly asked about them. So-called test questions refer to facts that the own side is already aware of, with particular emphasis being placed on the certainty of one's own knowledge. So-called reflex questions only contain a hidden accusation from the liar's point of view. If, however, the accusation is too well disguised, not even the deceiver would notice it. If, on the other hand, the accusation is more openly expressed, a person not involved in the deceit might wrongly assume that the accusation is aimed at him/her and could conceivably be offended. Genuine (especially strong) → *emotions* are visible shortly before speaking because they trigger automatic movements of the facial muscles (so-called micro-expressions), which can only be suppressed after a delay (if at all).[44] If the emotions do not follow this rule until later, this is a sign for the artificiality of the emotion and thus equally an indication of deception. Formulaic wordings that deviate from normal speech may be an indication that these formulations were rehearsed.[45] If the exact same words and formulations are used repeatedly, this also points to a rehearsed statement. If some-

[42] DePaulo et al. (2003), pp. 74–118 for reference to a high voice; for a delay in speech cf. Harrison et al. (1978), pp. 156–161; Blinking cf. Leal and Vrij (2008), pp. 187–194; reaction of pupils cf. Strempel (2004), p. 36.

[43] Schweitzer and Croson (1999), pp. 225–248.

[44] Brewer and Williams (2007), p. 71 et seq.

[45] Adelson (2004), p. 70.

one tends to speak from the first-person perspective (formulations with "I"), yet uses a different type of speech when describing something s/he has experienced personally, this can also be an indication of deception: It is emotionally more distressing to tell falsehoods from the I-perspective.[46] Studies have also shown that liars tend to give longer answers than people telling the truth.[47] Expressing doubts about remembered details is more typical of people, who make a subjectively true statement and yet this is also behaviour which can be practiced.[48]

The intensity of emotional irritation felt about a statement being doubted is more likely to allow conclusions to be drawn about the type of person one is dealing with rather than the level of truthfulness of the statement. Mistakes of perception or memory are more likely to give rise to minor factual deviations too small to provide valuable hints for the key message. Although larger errors do not necessarily indicate deception they make the core statement more likely to be incorrect. Incorrect information regarding emotions that one supposedly felt during a certain event are not a significant indication of the inaccuracy of the core information with regard to the facts. This is because the willingness to deceive people about emotions is particularly high and, to a certain extent, even socially acceptable.

Developing the Negotiating Partner's Ideas Even if the negotiating partner's concept cannot be accepted, it should be assessed whether it contains a favourable core idea that could be further developed. Instead of criticising the shortcomings of the proposal, it is often more beneficial to develop the idea further and not to point out shortcomings too boldly or in a harsh manner, but rather to highlight the positive aspects. This approach makes sense because it allows the creativity of both sides to be exploited. Mutually found solutions create trust and are frequently regarded as a success by both sides, not least because the own contribution towards the solution is generally evaluated higher than it actually is. Since the original idea was proposed by the negotiating partner, there is also the hope that s/he will agree to the idea which has been developed further "jointly", rather than an idea developed exclusively by oneself and forced upon the opposing party (→ *reactive devaluation*).

However, it should be borne in mind that the negotiating partner can also use the outlining of an idea for tactical purposes (→ *incomplete solutions*). The aim of such an approach is to encourage the negotiating partner to think the proposal through to its conclusion. In this way, an idea which basically stems from the opposite side is accepted as one's own and is consequently scrutinised less.

Diminishing Rates of Concession Particularly regarding the price in negotiations it can be observed that the sum, which the negotiator yields diminishes with every step in the negotiation (hence the term of diminishing rates of concessions). This

[46] Newman et al. (2003), pp. 665–675.

[47] Harrison et al. (1978), pp. 156–161.

[48] Vrij and Mann (2004), p. 66.

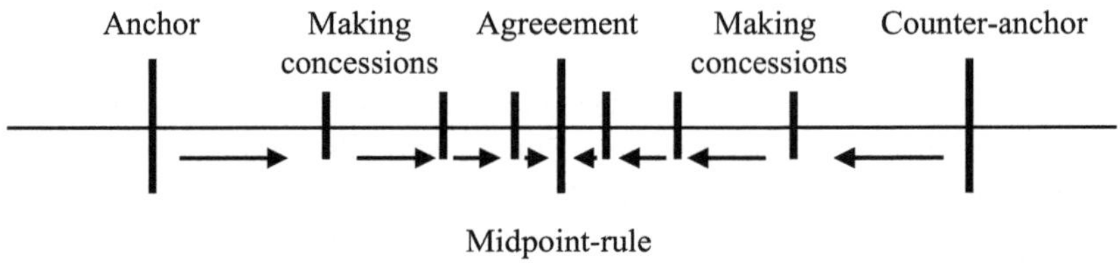

Fig. 3.5 Diminishing rates of concessions and midpoint-rule

especially applies the closer the negotiated price is to the respective maximum or minimum price → *reservation point*.[49] Further, there is a certain tendency to agree in the middle of both offers (→ *midpoint-rule*). Figure 3.5 (Diminishing rates of concession and midpoint-rule) illustrates the relation between diminishing rates of concessions and the midpoint-rule.

Professional negotiators are generally acquainted with the existence of this mechanism. Accordingly, there is a tactic to deceive the negotiation partner concerning the own marginal price, without crossing the line to committing a possibly illegal deception. In the course of this tactic the concessions made are already decreased considerably ahead the limit of the own reservation price.

Distributive Negotiations The strategy of distributive negotiations is concerned with the optimal implementation of the own negotiation position. The focus lies on the distribution of the → *negotiation pie* but not on its enlargement. The opposite are → integrative negotiations, during which the common interests of both sides and thus the enlargement of the negotiation pie are an essential part of the negotiations. The term hard bargaining is largely synonymous with distributive negotiations. In some cases, the concept of position-oriented negotiations is also regarded as being synonymous with distributive negotiations, but contrary to this assumption, distributive negotiations are also likely to be based on interests. It is generally recommendable to first enlarge the negotiation pie and only then start distributing it.

Door-in-the-Face Tactic (DITF) This tactic sometimes also referred to as the **rejection-then-retreat technique**) is based on findings from the field of → *behavioural economics* and aims at enforcing the own demands. First of all, an exaggerated demand is made, which is however quite plausible as an initial idea. It should therefore not be too extreme but leave sufficient scope for further concessions and counter-offers. The negotiating partner rejects this demand. If a second, lower demand is then made, it has a much higher chance of being accepted, since the other side would not want to be in the position of rejecting another offer. The door-in-the-face tactic is, to a certain extent, based on the *anchoring effect* (→ *anchoring*). The first, high demand sets the anchor which makes the second, lower demand seem more appropriate. The anchor is thus the → *reference point* for further considerations. In this

[49] Steedman (1987), pp. 158–159.

context, also the → *framing* effect plays a role. Moreover, *reciprocity* (→ *norm of reciprocity*) concludes that withdrawing the → *first offer* is equal to making a concession and is accordingly reciprocated with a concession from the other side.

This tactic works most efficiently if there is uncertainty about the appropriateness e.g. of the price conditions or agreed delivery times. A positive side effect of this tactic can be an increased sense of satisfaction due to reciprocity. Nonetheless, this effect is probably only of minor importance when professional negotiators are involved since not only are they familiar with it but they also already have specific ideas regarding the price etc. Above all, in these circumstances unrealistically high demands can appear dubious and can at the very least easily create an uncomfortable atmosphere for the negotiation.

Driver The term driver refers to a specific role within a negotiation team. The driver "drives" the negotiation forward (hence the name), i.e. s/he initiates a new stage of the negotiation and determines its pace and progress. The → *chief negotiator* can take on this role himself/herself, in which case there is no specific driver. It is also possible, however, for the negotiator to assign this task to a member of the negotiating team, particularly in a larger round of negotiations or where special knowledge is required. In these cases, a driver is employed alongside the chief negotiator for additional support.

EANT (Ethically Ambiguous Negotiation Tactics) Ethically ambiguous negotiation tactics include several tactics, amongst those are such that can especially be attributed to the categories of pressuring and deceptive tactics. The decision to apply such tactics in the negotiation does not solely depend on the negotiators and → *decision-makers*' idea of morality or general company guidelines and industry standards. Above these factors, there are other equally significant legal as well as non-legal risks which come along once these tactics are applied. Relevant for this is the probability of discovery, the possible social consequences (e.g. business interruption, loss of reputation with the negotiating partner and in the industry) as well as the legal consequences (e.g. rescission of the contract due to fraudulent deception; or liability) and the likelihood that the potential consequences will actually materialise.

Nonetheless, even negotiators which fundamentally refuse to apply these "ambiguous" tactics should still be aware of their existence in order to respond effectively if the negotiation partner decides to apply them during the negotiation. Due to the so-called → *fraud dilemma*, handling these tactics offers several difficulties. Effective countermeasures against unethical tactics inter alia include agreeing on common moral standards for the negotiation (concrete measures are described under the respective keywords). These agreed moral standards can either conclude a legally binding effect, or be merely designed in the form of a moral appeal to the negotiation partner. In some countries however, this kind of agreement will generally be assessed as legally binding by the parties and thus may shift the limitations of, under other circumstances legitimate actions. Yet, in practice agreements on moral standards are not very common.

Electronic Multitasking Electronic multitasking is a special form of multitasking. A study conducted by *Krishnan/Kurtzberg/Naquin* proved that the use of electronic devices influences the negotiation process.[50] A major effect can be particularly observed concerning the reading of → *e-mails* and other notifications on the smartphone or tablet. In this regard, the observed subjective effects on the negotiation partner and his/her actions must be distinguished from effects on the final objective negotiation result. Negotiators, who check his/her phone during a → *face-to-face* negotiation:

- Achieve worse results for the own side than those negotiators that do not use his/her phone during the negotiation;
- leave a more unprofessional impression on the negotiation partner and
- seem less trustworthy.

E-mail E-mails are an important means of communication. Negotiations via e-mail (e-negotiation, computer mediated communication (CMC)) are subject to own laws, adapted to the technical peculiarities. In contrast to classic written negotiations, e-mails are often not worded very carefully and the author does not usually put the draft aside to revise it again before sending it off. Conversely, e-mails are not always read carefully by the negotiating partner. This inattentiveness may be due to a lack of time. However, this phenomenon could also be due to the fact that e-mails lack the authority of a printed text. In addition to the general disadvantages of written communication—e.g. the lack of non-verbal communication, difficulties in understanding the negotiating partner on the emotional level, as well as no direct communication—there is an increased likelihood of → *mistakes*. There is a heightened risk of provoking unwanted escalations and → *misunderstandings*. In addition, the negotiators exchange fewer details than when all negotiators are present (→ *face-to-face*).

The above-mentioned increased error-rate of e-negotiations can largely be alleviated by being more diligent in the drafting and assessing of e-mails, as well as by implementing approval procedures. However, the negotiator simultaneously loses reaction speed and the effort involved increases. Ultimately this only leads to an approximation of traditional, written negotiations, which are considered to be significantly less effective than oral negotiations, especially among those present. Thus, it is generally not advisable to conclude challenging negotiations by e-mail. If, however, the negotiations are threatened by potential emotional escalation and the only available choices are to conduct negotiations by telephone or e-mail, then the latter option may offer real advantages. Although it is true that complex agreements or emotional rapprochement are seldom achieved by e-mail, escalations can be prevented much more easily than in oral negotiations, especially if the situation

---

[50] Krishnan et al. (2014), pp. 191–208.

is emotionally charged. E-mail communication allows for the content of an agreement to be ascertained reliably, in contrast to oral negotiations. Therefore, e-mails should definitely be used as an appropriate means of communication in problematic situations. As e-mails can easily be forwarded to (many) third parties, it should at any rate be borne in mind that it is important to formulate them very carefully and to be aware of the risk linked to the unlimited accessibility of e-mails.

E-mails can potentially shift the (existing) balance of negotiation power between the parties. Due to the lack of face-to-face-communication, circumstances such as age → *gender*, hierarchical position etc. are less relevant factors. Physical → *imperial gestures* no longer apply. There is no possibility to impress the negotiating partner with status symbols (e.g. expensive business premises etc.; → *big fish*). Above that, it becomes more difficult to exert *time pressure* (→ *deadlines*) with a view to concluding an agreement. The negotiator can also get help from his own side more easily (→ *back office*). E-mail negotiations provide an interesting alternative, particularly for negotiators who could be disadvantaged in the course of oral negotiations.[51]

Yet, the fact remains that it is much more difficult to have rapport with someone via e-mail, which of all things is very important, especially in → *permanent business relations*. For this reason, it is sometimes recommended to at least approach the negotiating partner by telephone before starting e-mail negotiations, and to use trust building behaviour such as → *chit-chat* to build rapport. A study has shown that in these instances, the probability of concluding a contract increases significantly.[52]

Among the various options for combining different forms of negotiations, the so-called into-the-wind-technique merits a special mention, as it combines → *face-to-face* negotiations with e-mail negotiations.

Emotions One of the fundamental recommendations of the → *Harvard negotiation concept* is to separate "people" and "content". The object of the negotiation should neither be viewed emotionally, nor should the decision to conclude a contract be merely based on the negotiators emotions. Issues on an emotional level should not be solved by making concessions in content. This is sound advice in any case, since the optimisation of one's own interests—the own company's interests—should be effected at a rational level.

On the other hand, *Roger Fisher* and *Daniel Shapiro* have also determined that it is impossible to fully suppress emotions in the course of negotiations. Hence, they recommend dealing with the so-called *core concerns* (→ *core concerns framework*).[53] In negotiations, the emotions of the opposing party should always be taken into account, especially those of the negotiator. However, the emotions of the other parties involved in the decision-making process should also be considered (→ *think*

[51] For gender differences in this context cf. Stuhlmacher et al. (2007), pp. 329–339.

[52] Nadler (2004), pp. 225–253.

[53] Fisher and Shapiro (2005).

beyond the table), since in practice, these emotions are often among the key factors when concluding a contract. Particularly, negative emotions can jeopardise or even prevent the overall conclusion of a contract. The other party's negotiators often develop negative emotions if the blame for a conflict is shifted to him/her personally, whereas from the individual negotiator's point of view, external environmental influences are the main cause of conflicts. This phenomenon is due to the negotiator's distorted perception (→ *bias*). In addition, many negotiators struggle to separate the personal level from the factual level and thus transfer conflicts from one level to the other.

On the other hand, positive emotions also have a positive impact and render the negotiating partner much more willing to conclude the contract. Positive feelings, such as a good relationship and (mutual) trust are crucial factors, especially within → *permanent business relations*. Furthermore, it should be remembered that the negotiating partner's emotions do not only influence the opposing party's behaviour but can also impact your own conduct, too, for emotions are often mirrored (see also → *norm of reciprocity*). If the behaviour of the negotiating partner signals anger, it is not uncommon for the own negotiator to react aggressively.

Negotiators also have to consider the emotions of the stakeholders (→ *think beyond the table*) on their own side. This initially requires that these emotions have been recognised and taken into account in the planning and conduct of the negotiations. Ideally, the stakeholders on the own side should be persuaded to take a decision based on rational considerations. If this is impossible—e.g. due to the rank of the person concerned—this constitutes a handicap which jeopardises, and may ultimately even entirely rule out the rationally best choice.

Finally, the negotiator's own emotions play a major role in the negotiations. Contrary to the recommendation of the Harvard negotiation concept, emotions regularly have a direct impact on the factual level and accordingly on the negotiation result. Studies prove that the negotiator's (basic) mood has an impact on the negotiations in the sense that it does not only influence his/her own behaviour[54] but also the eventual outcome of the negotiation.[55] Negotiators with a positive mind-set are said to have a tendency to negotiate less aggressively and more cooperatively. Rage and anger are assumed to have the opposite effect, which implies that such negotiators tend to negotiate more aggressively and less cooperatively. In addition, one's own emotions towards the opposing party are often, a yet to be reflected, indication of how well the cooperation will work in the implementation phase of the contract, or display how far the negotiating partner can be trusted. The chances of implementing a contract smoothly are increased if the negotiators trust each other, and if these same people are also involved in the implementation of the contract. The opposite is also true for a problematic personal relationship.

Since it is not easy to fake emotions convincingly, emotions can be an essential—although not completely reliable—source of information (→ *wince*). Lastly,

---

[54] Forgas (1998), pp. 565–577.

[55] Butt et al. (2005), pp. 681–704.

resorting to the emotional negotiation level (→ *negotiation levels*) becomes unavoidable if the opposing party does not respond to rational argumentation.

Empathy Empathy—i.e. a person's capability to relate to another person's thoughts, feelings and actions—is an essential element of emotional intelligence (EI). By means of empathy, the negotiator has the opportunity to evaluate the other party and its individual negotiators in a differentiated way; to understand their attitudes and goals, and to anticipate their intentions. Not only → *misunderstandings* and unintended conflicts can be avoided this way: If the negotiator is aware of what is important to the other party, s/he can optimise his/her own offer and the negotiation itself to not only increase the likelihood of a successful agreement but also to potentially achieve the optimisation of his/her own performance promise and consideration.

Thus, empathy can indirectly contribute to enlarging the → *negotiation pie*. It also plays an essential role within the company in avoiding conflicts and building a negotiation team that cooperates smoothly. Ideally, the → *chief negotiator* should possess a high level of empathy. Conversely, → *assertiveness* is also expected of a negotiator, and this does not often tend to coincide with a high level of empathy. In such a constellation, the → *analyst* should have a high level of empathy in order to better comprehend the line of thought, → *emotions* and actions of the opposite side, and to be able to derive recommendations from them. Another option is that the negotiation team itself represents the different strengths, equivalent to the → *good guy/bad guy tactic,* for example. In bigger negotiations, the significance of empathy for the success of the negotiations may even justify the involvement of a psychologist.

Empty Promise The empty promise tactic (also known as **reward in heaven**) refers to one side making promises for the future in the course of the negotiation—e.g. very positive scenarios—which potentially are not meant to be kept after the negotiations. The promises are often very hopeful, yet not legally enforceable. Often, **simple effort clauses** are used for any kind of supplementary performance, in case certain conditions are fulfilled. Deliberations then frequently revolve around the feasibility of the condition and not the fact that it is a mere effort clause. As the name suggests, such a clause only covers the promise to strive for something, but not the promise to achieve a certain success. A best effort would be more demanding. From the point of view of the parties involved, the negative implications of empty promises can have a greater impact on the future business relation or on one's reputation, than the question of the legal admissibility. These effects should be considered before making empty promises.

Words that indicate an empty promise are known as **weasel words**.

Examples
Trying, attempting, helping, striving, making an effort

Endowment Effect This refers to an effect thematised in behavioural economics that should be considered in contract negotiations. Anyone who owns an object generally considers it to be significantly more valuable than the person interested in buying it.[56] This can be explained by the fact that the addition is perceived as a gain, whereas handing an object over is comparable to a loss, which always feels more painful. The evaluation of an object thus depends on whether it is either seen in connection with a profit or a loss. Accordingly, the evaluation depends on the → *reference point*.

In negotiations, this effect is primarily significant if the negotiation is conducted with a person who owns the subject of the negotiation, or at least feels like the owner, e.g. when s/he is the majority shareholder. This can potentially lead to an excessive price demand, in the attempt to compensate for the suffered losses. Negotiations also often deal with a virtual or potential ownership which arises when the parties develop increasing appreciation of and attachment to a certain element of the negotiation.

Trial purchases, whereby the buyer first receives an item but the purchase contract is subject to the buyer's approval take advantage of the endowment effect. Since a feeling of ownership develops when the buyer takes possession of the item, it becomes harder for him to decide against the conclusion of the contract.

Regarding negotiations between agents, the effect only plays a role in relation to the negotiation objects which directly affect the agent personally (e.g. in negotiations regarding company cars which the agent uses himself/herself). Yet, a similar effect can also be observed if the agent or → *decision-maker* has already reported the successful conclusion of the contract within the company. The endowment effect can be mitigated by neutral evaluations that the other party can place trust in. Furthermore, the effect does not appear to be as strong in swap transactions as it is in the exchange of goods for money.

Another form of the endowment effect is the **quasi-endowment effect**, whereby one party feels like an owner without that actually being the case. This belief influences the reference point and offers are measured in comparison to the future state instead of being compared to the current status quo. The best example for this would be the → *auction*: the highest bidder already perceives himself/herself as the owner and therefore feels that any overbidding constitutes a loss. S/He is subsequently often willing to make an objectively excessive bid to avoid the loss of his/her (supposed) property. Antique dealers and other traders try to take advantage of this effect by placing the object of their customers' interest directly into their hands.

Entanglement Tactic The entanglement tactic is based on offering the other side's negotiator an individual benefit. In this regard, the acceptance of this offer would result in the negotiator acting unlawfully (in case of corruption)—or at the very least immoral or disloyal towards the company s/he represents (see further under → *principal-agent-problem*). The underlying idea of this tactic is that the opposite

[56] Cf. Kahneman et al. (1991), pp. 193–206.

side's negotiator falls into a (limited) dependence as soon as s/he decides to accept the offered advantage. During the negotiation process, this entanglement is then exploited for one's own benefit.

This tactic can even prove effective in cases where there is only the impression that the other side's negotiator has accepted a personal advantage or has taken part in unlawful actions (e.g. infringement of competition law) or other immoral behaviour. Negotiators should therefore always consider the potentially arising dependencies which can develop whenever an apparently very generous proposal has been made by the opposing side. Such dependencies are to be avoided strictly. This also goes for risky negotiation locations or situations in which even the appearance of involvement can give rise to such a precarious situation. If an entanglement occurs and the other side tries to use it for blackmail, the entanglement should be confessed to the own party. In this case, the company concerned may choose to honour this confession by (largely) waiving sanctions for the negotiator's misconduct.

The entanglement tactic itself partially fulfils criminal offences. Even the attempt to use this tactic can cause severe disruption to the negotiating parties' relationship and could potentially cause the termination of the negotiations. Companies can prevent the application of entanglement tactics by employing the → *principle of dual control*, since two people (→ *two negotiators*) are more difficult to entangle than one person alone. Concerning the acceptance of gifts, there are usually guidelines set by the company's compliance department. If there is no compliance management system (CMS) within the company, at any rate the responsible supervisor should be informed.

In a broader sense, an entanglement can also refer to situations in which the negotiator adheres to a path once embarked upon and continues to make further expenditures, although this is not backed up by rational considerations. Here, the cost-benefit considerations give way to a coercive dynamic. The reasons for this are the so-called → *sunk cost bias*, the fear of a loss of face, an illusionary optimism (→ *optimism bias*) or → *anchoring*. An effective countermeasure is a consistent focus on the future.

Exception Argument In this form of argumentation, one side concentrates on the fact that they have an exception at their disposal which is favourable to them. This is an attempt to invalidate the → *floodgate argument*. The negotiating partner is faced with the statement that s/he is not being "forced" to give up a general rule but is rather accommodating the other side by granting an exception in an unusual situation.

This form of argumentation is important as fixed rules and requirements often exist, especially in relatively large divisions of major companies. The exception argument allows the negotiator to meet the other side's demands—seemingly without breaching a fixed rule.

Face-to-Face This negotiation form, in which both parties negotiate face-to-face (FTF), is still the norm—even in this modern age of communication. It is prevalent especially in complex and large-scale contract negotiations. Despite higher cost incurrence (travel expenses, limited useable travelling time, coordination effort etc.), the advantages usually outweigh the disadvantages, particularly compared to negotiating via → *e-mail*. The direct presence of both parties is essential for getting to know each other, developing an emotional relationship and for building solid (mutual) trust. Interaction is significantly more intensive in face-to-face negotiations as compared to other communication forms. When both parties are present, compromises can be found flexibly and quickly, provided that the negotiators have comprehensive authority or the → *decision-makers* themselves are present. The amount of time, which is often limited, increases the chances of a quick agreement, which means that the transaction costs will not necessarily be much higher than those incurred by other forms of negotiation. Face-to-face negotiations are potentially more emotional than other forms of communication and allow the negotiator to apply virtually the whole canon of possible negotiation tactics. **Negotiations via video (video conferences)** are the closest thing to actual face-to-face negotiations, even though some details, such as body language, are invisible. In practice, it is not uncommon to combine face-to-face negotiations with negotiations via → *e-mail* or phone.

False Deadline With a false deadline—i.e. giving a false finishing time for the negotiations—an incorrect time limit is declared. The main aim is to build up pressure to conclude the decision-making process associated with a → *deadline*. How strong this pressure is, also depends on the consequences threatened. There is often the threat that negotiations will have to be adjourned, if, for example, no agreement can be reached within "the next half hour". In this case, the delay of the negotiations is imminent. In serious cases, one party can also threaten to terminate the negotiations. If no consequences are threatened at all, there is less pressure to reach an agreement. In this case, it is up to the negotiating partner to envisage potential consequences.

The negotiation side that creates the false deadline probably stands to benefit from the shortened time limit. The potential advantages could, for example, be due to the changing → *BATNA* of either side, or less preparation time for the negotiating partner. The side which applies the time pressure (→ *deadline*) often also desires to increase the negotiating partner's susceptibility to make → *mistakes*. A false finishing time can also be used to keep reserve time for further negotiations, or it can simply serve to reduce transaction costs resulting from the negotiation process. Oftentimes, it is not easy to convey a false deadline convincingly. If the deadline is exceeded, the side that set it may lose its credibility, if the threatened consequences are not implemented. It is therefore advisable to pre-consider a reason why the deadline could "suddenly" be exceeded without severe consequences. In agent-oriented negotiations, the deadline is often (seemingly) set by a higher authority (usually the → *decision-maker*). That way, it is possible to "convince" the (ostensible) higher authority to postpone or even cancel the deadline and at the same time, the negotiator present at the negotiating table signals his/her commitment to the contract.

False deadlines can also refer to indirectly involved parties. For example, one side can refer to an alleged deadline set by the financing bank. In this case, the false deadline combines pressure with deception. Since terminating negotiations is a general consequence of failed negotiations and can in principle be declared at any time, exerting pressure as such is not prohibited in B2B relations, unless particular circumstances apply. Especially the fact that a termination of the negotiation is always a possibility during the negotiation, is why the authors believe that misleading statements about the deadline and thus the prospect of an imminent break-off of the negotiation, is also likely to not be classified as unlawful (→ *cunning deception*).

FC Approach As the name says, the FC (full consensus) approach seeks the full consensus of all stakeholders (→ *think beyond the table*), i.e. all parties with an interest in the negotiation. The background to this approach is the fundamental idea that large-scale projects are not only about achieving a formal contractual agreement. In point of fact, the contract can also fail if there is excessive resistance from those not directly involved. Involving potential opponents early on in the negotiation process can prevent the failure of the project at a later stage. However, with regard to ideologically-oriented opponents, the FC approach often proves unsuccessful. Finding a happy medium is often sensible and more promising here, i.e. only including potential opponents who are open to compromise from the outset. If, however, a full consensus is reached yet nothing fundamental changes, the result is very stable and is accordingly accepted by conviction and not just for legal reasons. A broad consensus is therefore often sought, particularly in "non-juridified" areas, where majorities may change or the acceptance of an agreement is essential due to a lack of effective legislation in place. Agreements based on the FC approach are regularly designed to be flexible so they can be adapted to changing circumstances. In this respect, the FC approach regards the constant relationship between all involved parties.

The opposing approach is the → *DAD (decide, announce, defend)* approach; see further under (→ *DDD approach*; *dialogue, decide, deliver*). The recommendation to → *think beyond the table* is also related to the FC approach which is intended to keep all stakeholders in view. This approach, however, does not seek a full compromise but rather attempts to generate coalitions and support, aiming to divide the opposition.

Fewer, Convincing Arguments In complex questions, numerous arguments can often be found for one's own proposal. However, in negotiations it makes sense to use only a few arguments—usually up to a maximum of three—but these should be designed and formulated as strong and irrefutable as possible. For one thing, most negotiators are not receptive to a large number of arguments all at the same time. In this context, sometimes the keyword **magical number seven** is mentioned, referring to the title of an article written by *George A. Miller*.[57] In this article, *Miller* discusses the number of objects that can be stored in human short-term memory.

[57] Miller (1956), pp. 81–97.

Even though more recent studies show that it is not possible to give a specific figure for this, since it depends on several influencing factors (i.e. on what should be remembered (numbers, letters etc.)), research nonetheless proves that human capacities are limited in this respect. For this reason alone, it is advisable to focus on just a few arguments.

In addition, weaker arguments depreciate the overall value of the argumentation, since the negotiating partner will tend to focus on the weaknesses only. Although the negotiating partner may not have found any counter-arguments—at least not any convincing ones—against the main arguments put forward, his/her impression is already shaped by the inadequacies of the weak argument. Under the key word **broken record** (due to the repetition of the part before the defect on a scratched vinyl record) it is recommended to base the argumentation on a few, strong arguments and to repeat them more often.

Final Offer Arbitration (FOA) The final offer arbitration (FOA) is a problem-solving method that uses a combination of mediation and alternative arbitrational settlement. In particular, it is applied in cases where the → *last gap* between the parties is relatively small and the parties wish to reach a settlement (i.e. neither side wishes to terminate the negotiation—for example in the course of → *renegotiations*). The first step of this process is for the parties to decide on a neutral third party. This intermediary party then tries to find a solution within a kind of mediation procedure. If no solution can be found this way, the intermediary then asks both parties to make a final offer. The neutral third party, without modifying it in any way, then decides in favour of one of the two options. Since the third party always selects one of both offers, there is a certain pressure on the parties to submit the fairest and most balanced bid possible in order to increase the chances of their offer being selected.

Find Something in Common Similarities can facilitate negotiations on the *emotional level* (→ *negotiation levels*), which is why it is one of the fundamental tasks of a negotiator to search for similarities on a personal level, such as common preferences, hobbies, friends, opponents and experiences. This particularly takes place in the course of → *chit-chat,* i.e. the small talk before the negotiation and during breaks in the negotiation. Negotiators make use of the so-called → *similar-to-me-effect.*

First Offer This refers to the first offer made with regard to the subject of negotiation. In contract negotiations, there is not just one first offer. Since the negotiations are usually broken down into several individual points, a "first offer" is submitted by one of the negotiating partners with regard to each individual aspect—e.g. price, delivery date, payment date. The first offer sets the *anchor* (→ *anchoring*), the subsequent counter-offer the *counter-anchor* (→ *anchoring*). The question of whether it is advantageous to make the first offer, or to leave this to the negotiating partner is widely discussed (see also → *anchoring*). In some situations, submitting the first offer is highly recommended while in other cases it cannot be avoided, although it may not be tactically advantageous. The relevant question in this context is: "How high should the first offer be?". In that respect, *Roger Fisher/William L. Ury*[58] recommend:

> (…) the highest figure that you could justify without embarrassment.

David A. Lax and *James K. Sebenius* suggest setting an **extreme but flexible** anchor.[59] Retaining (a certain degree of) flexibility is supposed to prevent the loss of credibility and the termination of negotiations. Also mentioned is the **30-percent-rule.**[60] According to the 30-percent-rule it is generally advisable to make the first offer, which is set approximately 30% away from your own → *deal-breaker*. A buyer should therefore make a 30% lower bid and a seller should exceed his/her minimum price by 30%. However, these recommendations should be treated with caution. In some cases, the recommendations may be correct. In principle, however, the amount of the first offer must be determined in each individual case, taking into account the specific circumstances.

In relation to other important targets, the following should be emphasised: The first offer must be above one's own *resistance point* (→ *deal-breaker*) and thus also above the own → *BATNA*. It is also recommended that the first offer is above the → *aspiration point*.

Flip a Coin The **flip a coin tactic** requires the negotiating partner to flip a coin in order to choose the solution to a problem. Prima facie this idea seems strange, especially in the context of B2B-negotiations, which is precisely the reason why even the proposal alone to flip a coin might well induce the negotiating partner to make more intensive efforts to reach a rationally-oriented and content-related solution.

In the USA on the other hand, flipping a coin is more common, e.g. when the leading candidates running for presidency have exactly the same number of votes in the pre-election campaign. Flipping a coin will then decide which candidate will later represent the constituency in question. In blockade situations (see also → *deadlock*), this tactic can constitute an emergency solution in B2B negotiations, regardless of potential cultural differences.

It might even make sense to let chance decide on the distribution of opportunity or risk, especially regarding smaller contract values. Using this tactic or other closely related tactical forms, in which a game (e.g. rock paper scissors) is used to make a decision, the humoristic note may help to dissolve hardened negotiation situations. In contrast, there are also negotiators who view such proposals as proof of the untrustworthiness and lack of seriousness of their negotiation partner. In these cases, the proposal to flip a coin should be waived.

Floodgate Argument The floodgate argument (also referred to as **slippery slope,** dam break argument or "who knows where this might lead") is among the most

[58] Fisher and Ury (1981), p. 170.

[59] Lax and Sebenius (2006), p. 192.

[60] Collins (2009), p. 114.

important argumentation figures in contract negotiations that are intended to prevent the breach of previously applied standards: It is feared that if a demand is once yielded to, it will no longer be possible to maintain the previous regulation or order in the future which, in the past, was tried, tested and found to be good. To vanquish this argument therefore, the exceptional character of the demand must be emphasised. Further, it is necessary to explain why the demand does not constitute a risk, and that the previous practice is not generally jeopardised.

Alternatively, an attempt can be made to break the rule during the negotiations for an earlier, less important contract in which this detail might escape the negotiating partner or is not regarded as being of importance by him/her. In subsequent negotiations, the exception previously achieved can be cited as a convincing argument for granting the exception anew. Conversely, the underlying side of this argument explains why legal departments sometimes fight fiercely to retain certain clauses in an otherwise rather insignificant contract.

The term floodgate argument became known due to the juridical decision *Ultramares Corporation v. Touche* (174 N.E. 441 (1932)) by US-judge *Benjamin Nathan Cardozo*.

FOG Based on the general significance of information for the negotiation process, the acronym FOG (**facts**, **opinions** and **guesses**) comprises a basic classification of information which is very important for negotiators.

It is crucial for the recipient of the information to be able to assign it to a particular category so that an appropriate tactical approach can be determined in accordance with the information category in question. However, this process often proves quite difficult. Opinions and assumptions expressed not only by the negotiating partner but also by employees on the own side are often presented as facts. Opinions usually include a smidgen of fact at their core. Guesses (or assumptions) can be based on a logical conclusion of facts but they can also be purely emotion-based or even have a creative origin. These three are often combined in statements in such a way that even the person offering the information has difficulties in telling them apart. In addition, facts can have very different levels of reliability, which is why the method of transmission, the information's plausibility, and their verification are essential. In this regard, an analysis is imperative, at least for central information.

Foggy Recall Foggy recall is a negotiating tactic which is about reinterpreting an agreement which has been made orally and favours the interests of the own side. Thus, a real commitment agreed on previously can become a mere simple effort clause (→ *empty promise*), where one side only commits to strive towards a specific solution without actually promising to realise it. It is also common among negotiators to attempt presenting points as being clear and agreed on in favour of one's own side, even though an agreement might not actually have been reached. Conversely, foggy recall can also be used to negate an agreement. Thus, there is great similarity with so-called pseudo-misunderstandings. It is therefore vital to determine whether both sides or only one should draw up a protocol of the results of the specific negotiation stages or → *interim results*. Having one party in sole charge of preparing the → *protocol* harbours no opportunity for manipulation as this would be very likely discovered, endangering the conclusion of the contract. Nonetheless, this does not preclude the adaptation of small nuances of the agreement in favour of one's own interests.

Foggy recall proves particularly promising when combined with the approach of only granting limited authority. Thus, if the consent of a higher authority is needed to endorse concessions to the other side, these concessions may turn out to be somewhat smaller than originally intended. In these cases, the negotiator gains approval from the higher authority for his/her "foggy" memory of the agreement and subsequently presents this to the other side as now being successfully approved. Owing to the acknowledged difficulties in obtaining consent from a higher authority, the negotiating partner will generally not insist on renegotiating small divergences in demands as, at worst, this could possibly endanger the entire contract.

Foot-in-the-Door Technique (FITD) The foot-in-the-door technique refers to a conversation technique that—often in the form of questions—starts with a fairly small request and (quickly) increases, step by step. The aim of FITD is to obtain the other parties approval to a bigger request. This tactic has good prospects for success, since the negotiating partner may struggle to reject a very small request. By agreeing to the initial small request, a commitment or pressure towards consistent behaviour is generated, which in turn increases the chances that the negotiating partner will not reject the larger request. This effect was first observed in 1966 by *Jonathan Freedman* and *Scott Fraser*.[61] This conversation technique is based on the so-called escalation of commitment effect. Consequently, with regard to contract negotiations, the negotiating partner should be persuaded at the earliest point in the negotiation to adopt the desired position, which s/he should pursue consistently from start to finish. This effect is also associated with the **camel's nose metaphor**, in allusion to an Arabic saying: When a camel sticks its nose in a tent, its body will quickly follow—meaning that seemingly small concessions can open the door for larger—undesirable—events.[62] It is feasible that the opposing party, in response to this tactic, could demand to know the ultimate aim right away or could say no across the board (due to unfair negotiation tactics). Alternatively, the negotiating partner may become aware of the escalation of commitment effect and consistently reject the larger, subsequent request or demand an appropriate service in return.

Framing The way in which facts are presented influences the recipient's understanding and the level of agreement or disagreement and ultimately also the recipient's choice. According to the so-called **framing effect**, this applies even to statements which are logically identical. *Amos Tversky* and *Daniel Kahneman* proved and substantiated this conclusion fundamentally within the framework of the

[61] Freedman and Fraser (1966), pp. 195–202.

[62] Cf. Rizzo and Whitman (2003), pp. 539–592.

Asian disease tests which they developed in 1981.[63] Put simply, there are three forms of framing:

In **risky choice framing** (framing in risk decisions), a decision problem is presented either as a gain or a loss. Here, framing serves to influence the decision-maker's risk behaviour.

Secondly, **attribute-framing** concerns the evaluation of an object/alternative regarding its appealing effect of its fixed attributes. If a success rate is primarily mentioned, this has a positive impact on the evaluation, whereas naming the corresponding failure rate for that subject, initially has a negative influence on the evaluation.

Lastly, **goal framing** is particularly concerned with the consequences of either certain actions or their omission. The impending negative consequences following an omission have a stronger impact than the concurrent positive consequences of certain actions.

Several tactics make use of framing. The best known are the so-called gain-frame, i.e. the formulation with regard to what can be achieved by an action, and the so-called loss frame, in which the chances are formulated negatively. Both of these tactics are a particular application of risky-choice framing.

People tend to be risk-averse in the context of a positive framing, whereas their willingness to take risks increases regarding negative framings. Which formulation is more promising in each individual case depends on the specific situation. Either way, the effect of the framing should be borne in mind when drafting offers and clauses.

Fraud Dilemma The fraud dilemma occurs when one negotiating partner notices that the opposing party has deceived him/her—for instance regarding an alleged offer from the competing company (→ *better offer*)—yet, concluding the contract would still be the most favourable option. If the deceived person exposes the "fraud", s/he jeopardises the conclusion of the contract, also because the other party's negotiator could, as a result, suffer a loss of face. However, not exposing the fraud might encourage the negotiating partner to more severe fraudulent behaviour in future negotiations—although this risk is only probable if s/he has achieved a better negotiation result due to the attempted deception. Accordingly, an interim solution is to not expose the attempt to conduct a fraud (the deception), but to remain stubborn regarding the concession desired by the negotiating partner, or to point out other solution options. For example, if the negotiating partner simulates an alternative offer which is 5% cheaper, offering a best price clause would be one way of resolving the situation. The company would persist with their price with the caveat that they would be obliged to offer the lower price—possible with a lower limit—if a competing (comparable) offer can be presented in writing within a short space of time (e.g. two weeks). If the negotiating partner cannot produce such a (written) offer, it is obvious that s/he was only bluffing and is accordingly not entitled to the

[63] Tversky and Kahneman (1981), pp. 453–458.

discounted price. This behaviour can also be disguised as company policy. The opposing side does not lose face, but is aware of the fact that this method is not expedient.

Gender The negotiator's gender is a framework condition with behavioural and psychological impact that can affect the development, appropriate tactics and the result of negotiations. The starting point for looking at gender and negotiations are often the still prevalent social role models of men and women. They represent a kind of social expectation towards the genders (target state). They do not, however, make any explicit statement about the actual observed differences (actual state), which is why expectation and observation can differ. Disappointing these expectations can, however, lead to social and economic disadvantages (→ *backlash effects*), particularly for women, provided that the expectation is not overshadowed or changed by other influencing factors (see "gender in context"). There is substantial evidence which shows that there are gender-specific differences in the negotiation process—and that these are mostly only acquired stereotypes and are not based on genetic conditions. However, the mass of studies that have been carried out on this subject should be treated with caution.

Many results are fairly controversial. In the conducted studies the probands were often students or mixed groups, so the amount of propositions transferable to business negotiations is limited. Sometimes there may be several studies for the same research question, yet, they do not display disparate conclusions. Nonetheless, in the following we will try to highlight some tendencies, whereby many of the following differences are relativised over time by experience and habituation effects. Men are generally assumed to negotiate more competitively than women: They want to get every last "cent" out of the negotiation. Above that, they are more willing to take risks and thus, in comparison to women, have a greater tolerance for failure of the negotiations. In this sense, the male negotiator's attitude resembles a "low interpersonal orientation". Low "IOs" focus on maximising their results and achieving their goals.[64] However, with regard to qualified workers and executive positions, no differences in terms of the willingness to take risks between the sexes could be detected. This result is probably based on learning and habituation effects.[65] Nonetheless women are still judged by their male and female negotiating partners as being less keen to take risks.[66]

Moreover, negotiations have a significant importance in confirming the male negotiator's own ego and his status. Therefore, consequently, status-oriented power games (→ *imperial gestures*) are not uncommon, especially at the beginning of negotiations. In comparison to women, men are also more likely to negotiate in a directly aggressive manner. They try to dominate the negotiations, which is usually

[64] Cf. Rubin and Brown (1975), p. 172.

[65] Croson and Gneezy (2009), pp. 1–27.

[66] Eckel and Grossmann (2008), pp. 1–17.

expressed in a higher proportion of the overall speaking time. Moreover, men seem to interrupt their conversation partners more often than women do, although studies do not deliver entirely clear results in this point.[67] All in all, there are many studies from the field of linguistics that try to prove differences. It is repeatedly argued that women appear less assertive, since they tend to express themselves by asking questions in situations where men rather use statements.[68]

Men have aggression reducing conciliatory gestures, which are used after the conclusion of the contract as well as in → *negotiation pauses*. In comparison, women negotiate less aggressively and competitively on average. They tend to look for cooperative solutions[69] and succeed in concluding contracts more commonly than men.[70]

In this respect, women tend to have a "high interpersonal orientation", which means that they negotiate in a relationship-oriented manner, focusing on building a positive relationship with their negotiating partner. Women thus to a higher degree also consider the relational level.[71] The relation-oriented approach also concludes that women probably strive more strongly than men for a fairer distribution of the → *negotiation pie*. Such a "fair" distribution is more frequently expected of women than of men.[72]

In addition, as an advantage women are able to counteract a negative atmosphere more quickly than men. The aggressive negotiations of men often leave a long-term negative impression on women. On the other hand, there is no clear evidence that women negotiate more cooperatively in principle. However, in negotiations between mixed-sex negotiating partners, it has been observed that cooperative behaviour is favoured, whereas same-sex negotiating partners favour competitive behaviour.[73] This evidently applies equally to both male and female pair formations.

Women tend to hint at certain concerns rather than expressing them openly. Women are also particularly reluctant to negotiate on their own behalf, probably also due to the → *backlash effect,* which is considered to be one of several reasons behind pay disparities between men and women of the same hierarchical rank. Women are therefore advised to imagine that they are negotiating on behalf of

[67] Cf. Zimmermann and West (1975), p. 115 et seqq.; McMillan et al. (1977), p. 553; Campbell et al. (1992), p. 420; no differences according to Dindia (1987), p. 365; Robinson and Reis (1989), p. 149.

[68] Cf. McMillan et al. (1977), p. 554; Merchant (2012), p. 18 et seq.

[69] Cf. Walters et al. (1998), p. 14.

[70] Bowles et al. (2005), p. 958.

[71] Cf. Rubin and Brown (1975), p. 173.

[72] Cf. Solnick (2001), pp. 189–200.

[73] Cf. Sutter et al. (2008), p. 16.

someone else, e.g. family members or for the status of their department at work. This change of perspective has a far larger effect on women than on men. The so-called role of the representative (see further notes on → *backlash effects*) is known as a "gender trigger" and has shown that women achieved significantly higher salaries when negotiating on behalf of a third party, instead of for themselves.[74]

Furthermore, women are more hesitant to start negotiations.[75] Among other influences, this is partly attributed to differences in socialisation: At least on average, men more than women come into contact with sports which have a direct conflict potential, the rules and regulations of which prescribe certain direct conflict solution mechanisms (e.g. sending-off) and conciliatory gestures. Women are therefore more likely to fear that a conflict in a competitive situation, i.e. a negotiation, will automatically affect the relationship, which is why women avoid negotiations more often and accept points more quickly as being → *undiscussable*. At this point, it should be emphasised that the gender of the respective negotiating partner is of crucial importance. Women are less likely to initiate a negotiation if their counterpart is female. This, however, does not apply if the opposing partner is male.[76]

When questioning both men and women whether they, in negotiations, have ever felt discriminated against because of their gender, almost all men answer in the negative. Many women, on the other hand, have felt discriminated against at least once in negotiations based on their gender. This is usually expressed in impoliteness or not being taken seriously.[77]

Among all aspects of the gender discussion in the context of negotiations, one particular finding from recent years deserves to be emphasised and to be taken into account more specifically. The differences between male and female negotiators cannot be viewed in isolation but have to be viewed in their contextual frame (keyword: **gender in context**). The gender of a negotiator alone is not sufficient to make a reliable prediction of the his/her behaviour during a negotiation, nor of his/her expectations and possible reactions.[78] Depending on the specific conditions of the negotiation, gender stereotypes are sometimes superimposed or intensified. Studies have shown that the negotiation object can have a significant impact on the negotiation success of men and women respectively. In negotiations on cars and motorcycle headlights, which are perceived to be "male" negotiation objects, men were on average more successful than women. This, however, does not apply conversely, since

---

[74] Cf. Bowles et al. (2005), p. 959.

[75] Cf. Small et al. (2007), p. 604 et seq.; Greig (2008), p. 502; Eriksson and Sandberg (2012), p. 421.

[76] Cf. Eriksson and Sandberg (2012), p. 421.

[77] This is result of an empirical survey in the course of a master thesis at the University of Siegen at the chair for civil law and economic law of Prof. Dr. Peter Krebs.

[78] Cf. Bohnet and Bowles (2008), p. 390; cf. Paddock and Kray (2015), pp. 209–226.

men and women achieved equally good results in the case of "female" negotiation objects.[79]

It has however been proven that by preparing particularly well, woman can achieve equally good if not better results regarding "male" negotiation objects. This is especially true if women utilise the element of surprise and thus eliminate any possible preconceptions about a lack of knowledge. The transparency of the negotiation situation is another decisive factor in terms of gender in context. The more unambiguous the situation is (strong situation), the more concrete is the idea of "correct" behaviour, regardless of the gender. In ambiguous situations (weak situations), gender-specific differences and gender stereotypes play a more important role in influencing both, one's own behaviour as well as the opposing party's evaluation of this behaviour.

Particularly in first negotiations between parties, there is a risk of being judged on the basis of gender roles (type ambiguity) based on the lack of experience with the concrete negotiating partner. Due to the uncertainty regarding the attitude of the negotiating partner, the likelihood of role-conform behaviour is also increased.[80] However, habituation effects can relativise this phenomenon (cf. → *backlash effects*). In negotiating situations in which there is a general lack of information, e.g. regarding the → *ZOPA* (weak situation), women tend to achieve worse results than men. This may, among other things, be due to uncertainty about the adequacy of their own offer, since no differences between the genders could be observed in cases with insufficient information about the → *ZOPA*. The habituation effect of experienced negotiators results in a gender-independent adjustment of expectations towards the negotiator (for evidence see under → *backlash effects*).

One study has shown that the same applies to the profession or the professional status of the negotiator. Accordingly, "gender neutral" role expectations can be evoked. This e.g. applies to the profession of lawyers.[81] Above all, this effect can mitigate the dangers of negotiations with unknown negotiating partners (type ambiguity). Negotiating on behalf of others is also perceived as a factor which leads to the reassessment of the gender problem (for further notes see → *backlash effects*). Which negotiation tactic proves most successful in the medium term—i.e. taking into account implementation of the contract and follow-up negotiations—has not yet been conclusively investigated. Similarly, how male negotiators should best react to female negotiators and vice versa, where the strengths and weaknesses of mixed negotiation teams lie, has not yet been definitively clarified. However, there are indications that mixed gender negotiation teams tend to perform slightly better on average.

A more recent study conducted by *Kray, Kennedy* and *van Zant*[82] has shown that women are lied to in negotiations more often than men. The authors assume that this

79 Bear and Babcock (2012), pp. 743–744; Bear (2011), pp. 47–72.

80 Cf. Bowles (2012), pp. 1–42.

81 Schneider et al. (2010), pp. 363–384.

82 Kray et al. (2014), pp. 61–72.

is caused by the prejudice that women can be deceived more easily. In such situations, women could use this assumption to their own advantage and act skilfully and cunning, under the cover of naivety, to make use of their negotiating partner's overconfidence and thus secure advantages (unnoticed) (using the → *play dumb tactic*). The tendency to lie to women might also be due to prevalent stereotypes of men's behaviour in negotiations—which, though generally advantageous in the context of negotiations,—actually turn out to be a kind of boomerang and cause an onerous "compulsion to succeed". Male negotiators could therefore have an even greater desire to "win" against women and are accordingly more inclined to resort to deceptive measures. This is also consistent with the observation that some men would prefer the failure of a negotiation to defeat against a female negotiator, which is why particularly saving face and giving face is of major importance (also see further notes on → *backlash effects*). In many situations, it is advisable for women to use competitive elements in negotiations (especially with regards to distribution questions) and to combine these elements with positive female attributes (such as friendliness, and emphasis on a sense of togetherness) despite the possible threat of suffering disadvantages. Accordingly, one study has shown that although women's role-conform behaviour in negotiations has, in fact, led to the expansion of the → *negotiation pie*, the women involved have not been benefitting from the additional gain.[83] In this context, using female charm proved to be a promising approach, since it signals a competitive but at the same time self-interested attitude, without being perceived as a breach of roles.

All in all, it is advisable in this context to explore the negotiating partner's attitude as well as the overall negotiating situation (gender in context) in order to identify any untapped potential for a competitive negotiation or immanent risks (→ *backlash effects*) that could arise from these circumstances. Depending on the attitude of the negotiating partner, it may also be advisable for women to try separating the gender aspect from the negotiation subject and process. It has been proven that virtual negotiations via → *e-mail* or telephone establish a kind of level playing field.[84] In addition, it can also be advantageous to separate competitive demands from one's own person, so that the negotiating partner's potential negative emotions do not trigger gender-influenced reaction mechanisms (see further notes under → *backlash effects*). Emphasis on the need to negotiate such a position could also alleviate the problem (e.g. "What kind of a buyer would I be if I didn't try to get the best deal for my employer?").

Generous Tit for Tat (GTFT) Generous tit for tat is considered as the most successful negotiation strategy among the strategies that consider the negotiating partner's reaction to the other side's negotiation behaviour and especially include the relation between "fair" and "unfair" negotiations.[85]

---

[83] Kray et al. (2012), pp. 1343–1357.

[84] Stuhlmacher et al. (2007), pp. 329–339.

[85] Cf. Axelrod (2006), which was based on computer competitions and extensively studied the comparison of strategies especially within the course of a repeated negotiator's dilemma (→ *negotiator's dilemma*).

Unlike general → *tit for tat*, GTFT adds generous offers whenever negotiations have strayed from the scope of fair negotiations. Despite increasingly aggressive negotiations, the negotiator offers the other party a fresh start and signals (→ *signalling*) a concession with regard to an issue that is important to the other party—provided that the other side shows signs of moving. This reduces the risk of negotiations being bogged down due to uncooperative behaviour of both parties (→ *deadlock*) or even accelerating into a downward spiral that will eventually lead to a break-off of the negotiation. However, regarding generous tit for tat (GTFT) the principle applies that unfair behaviour should not be rewarded in order to avoid incentives for equivalent behaviour in the future (**don't reward bad behaviour**).

Go for a Walk This refers to a (longer) tactical break in negotiations (→ *negotiation pause*), which gives the parties the opportunity to fundamentally rethink and re-evaluate a → *deadlocked* situation in the negotiation. If the negotiating partner has a bad → *BATNA*, the other party can exert considerable pressure. Apart from that, there is at least enough time to contemplate alternative solution options and possibly also to let off steam while the negotiating partner is not present. In this way, the → *negotiation pause* can also help to provide emotional relief. However, this tactic can also create time pressure (→ *deadline*) for the own side. Not only the own side but also the negotiating partner can benefit from longer interruptions, since these allow to explore their BATNA extensively and accordingly reach a more favourable alternative.

Good Guy/Bad Guy The tactic of good guy/bad guy (or **good cop/bad cop** or **black hat/white hat**) is based on the division of tasks between → *two negotiators* of one negotiation side, but can also be practiced by means of an outsider (even if this third person is a fictitious one). The good guy is the person striving for the conclusion of the contract, focussing on the positive aspects of the negotiation (e.g. mutual interests). The bad guy takes on the role of the critic (and concentrates e.g. on opposing interests). In the US, the good guy/bad guy tactic is also referred to as **Mutt and Jeff**, a commonly used term for an unequal couple, based on a successful comic strip from the early twentieth century.

The bad guy is the one who makes the critical arguments and rejects certain rules. Due to the division of the two roles, the individual negotiators do not have to constantly switch between criticism and promotion of the contract project, which proves very difficult for most negotiators. Hence, the negotiators can be more convincing in their respective roles. If the good guy is responsible for the subsequent implementation of the contract, trust can be built, irrespective of the critical arguments of the bad guy. Furthermore, the bad guy's criticism or pressure can be somewhat stronger than usual, since the good guy provides a balance and prevents a negative switch of the negotiation atmosphere. If, however, the bad guy appears too strong, this can diminish the hopes of successfully concluding a contract to such an extent that the completion of the negotiation is jeopardised. If the good guy makes proposals, particularly if these are (seemingly) perceived as compromises, the risk that might result from this proposal is often underestimated and sometimes accepted without any further thought.

One variation of the good guy/bad guy tactic is dividing both roles into (1) a reasonable negotiator and (2) his/her unreasonable partner. The reasonable negotiator negotiates in a constructive manner and only makes modest demands. The unreasonable negotiator then torpedoes the negotiations and puts forward high demands, whereupon the reasonable partner tries to calm him/her down and proposes a more reasonable compromise. Often it is observed that the negotiating partner has the tendency to support the good guy in his efforts to conclude the contract. If necessary, the other party even shows willingness to accommodate the bad guy.

If lawyers are involved in negotiations as an agent, they often take the role of the bad guy, since they often have the task of gathering and formulating concerns. A single negotiator can use individual aspects of the good guy/bad guy tactic by citing third-party concerns. In this instance, the real or supposed bad guy then is a → *decision-maker* who is not present at the negotiation table.

If this tactic is generally discouraged in isolated cases, this is due to severe duress, as it is typically attributed to the "bad cop" in movies. These excesses are associated with all the disadvantages that generally go hand in hand with unlawful coercion in negotiations and are thus to be rejected. The good guy/bad guy tactics also reach their limits when the bad guy appears to be very disagreeable and the good guy's "distance" to him/her is very small: This harbours the danger that the aversion towards the bad guy will extend to the other negotiator.

Halo Effect The halo effect is a confirmation bias, i.e. a confirmation mistake and is sometimes also referred to as the **overexposure effect** or **court effect**. This effect, first observed by *Frederic L. Wells* in 1907, describes a cognitive distortion (→ *bias*) in social psychology and was firstly named "halo effect" in 1920 by *Edward Lee Thorndike*.[86] According to this effect, people are strongly guided in their assessment, not only of other people, but also regarding products and companies, by a characteristic feature of this person or their basic attitude towards this person. For example, if person A likes person B, person A will attribute positive character traits to person B, even if no guaranteed information about person B's actual character is available. A positive impression in one area is thus transferred to another, unrelated area.

This confirmation error does not only occur regarding positive features but also regarding negative features. This specific case is also known under the so-called **horns effect**. In the course of negotiations, the halo effect can have an impact at several levels. On the one hand, it can have an impact within the company. In an early study, *Thorndike* showed that the evaluation of employees—in his study, commanders who assessed soldiers—is swayed by the halo effect: If an employee is skilled in one area, his/her superiors tend to assess him/her positively in a different area.

[86] Thorndike (1920), pp. 25–29.

In contrast, the effect is also apparent in contract negotiations: It is possible to attribute positive characteristics to the negotiating partner without any actual information basis for this appraisal.

Example
The negotiating partner arrives punctually for the negotiation. This is perceived as a sign that s/he is generally trustworthy, e.g. that s/he will not use any tactics based on deception.

What is even more far-reaching is that positive characteristics pertaining to the negotiating partner will unconsciously be transferred to the company they represent. If the negotiating partner is trustworthy, reliable and qualified, there is a tendency to attribute the same qualities to the company. The other party's → *chief negotiator* is often not involved in implementing the contract, which is why his/her conduct should not be credited as a direct indication of the company.

Harvard Negotiation Concept The Harvard negotiation concept is essentially based on *Roger Fisher* and *William Ury*'s book "Getting to Yes" (new editions with the participation of Bruce Patton), which was published in 1981. The concept is also part of the large-scale Program on Negotiation (PON) the Harvard Law School.

The core title of the book "**Getting to Yes**" is synonymous with the Harvard negotiation concept. The title already reveals the main focus of the work: The authors' initial focus was not primarily recommending actions to achieve an optimal outcome, but rather on the question of how to conclude a contract in difficult situations. Hence, the book gives instructions for situations in which it is very uncertain whether an agreement is possible at all and at the same time deals with agreements of great importance, in some instances even significant for whole nations. It was originally issues arising from diplomatic negotiations, which gave rise to the concept; especially the negotiations between the U.S. and the former Soviet Union regarding nuclear disarmament and the Vietnam peace talks. These negotiations were extremely difficult due to virtually inflexible positions and → *emotions*.

Nonetheless, the Harvard negotiation concept delivers a very universal approach. It is intended to encompass a broad spectrum of negotiation types, including those within organisations, employment negotiations with employees as well as diplomatic negotiations. The specific term for the concept used by the authors in their book is **principled negotiations**. In literature, sometimes the term **negotiation of merits** is also used to categorise these negotiations. The authors use this description for the concept, as it constitutes the third path after hard bargaining and → *soft bargaining*.

The Harvard negotiation concept is based on various fundamental ideas:

- Firstly, the concept calls for a division between people and problems, which means that the personal relationship (relational level) with the negotiating partner and the relation with the concrete object of negotiation need to be considered separately. This principle is also referred to as **SOPHOP**: "soft on people, hard on points". Many negotiators sense a tension between the subject matter of negotiations and the relationship between the involved parties. The SOPHOP principle clarifies that the Harvard negotiation concept assumes a good relationship with the other side can still be maintained even in "hard" substantive negotiations. If a problem arises at the personal level, the Harvard negotiation concept recommends clarifying it at the personal level (e.g. by altering one's behaviour towards the other party). The essential aim of this division is to avoid spill over-effects of the negative effects of a strained or even a positive personal relationship on the outcome of the negotiations. Substantive concessions should not be made merely on the basis of sympathy, or with the aim of improving personal relationships with the negotiating partner. Moreover, the intention is to avert anger or other negative emotions leading to improper consideration (especially direct rejection) of the solution options.

The concept thus recommends strictly rational behaviour in the search for, and selection of, solution options. In this regard, appointing an emotionally unaffected agent in the negotiations can, under certain conditions, help to realise the division between people and problems in the specific negotiation situation.

- In addition, the Harvard negotiation concept requires a focus on **interests** rather than relying merely on the enforcement of **positions**. By focussing on interests, as opposed to positions, the parties are more likely to find common grounds. Likewise, the interest-based approach to negotiations presages that the final result will be as close as possible to the main interests of both parties to the greatest possible extent. In addition, this approach also promises the greatest possible enlargement of the → *negotiation pie* for both parties.

Excursus

In some instances, it is beneficial to classify the relationship between the interests of both parties (see Fig. 3.6 (Interests of the negotiation parties)). Firstly, there are **common interests**, the existence of which is generally underestimated by negotiators. In these instances, both parties pull together. It is essential to identify such common interests, because they often help to establish a good relationship with the negotiating partner. There are also **diverging interests**, which do not necessarily have to be opposed to each other. Parties can try to find solutions that allow the greatest possible balance of interests on both negotiating sides. In addition, there are also **opposing interests**, whereby the assertion of the interests of one side requires mirror reflection of the other side with regard to their own interests. According to the Harvard negotiating concept, it is essential to apply neutral assessment criteria regarding these critical areas in the negotiations.

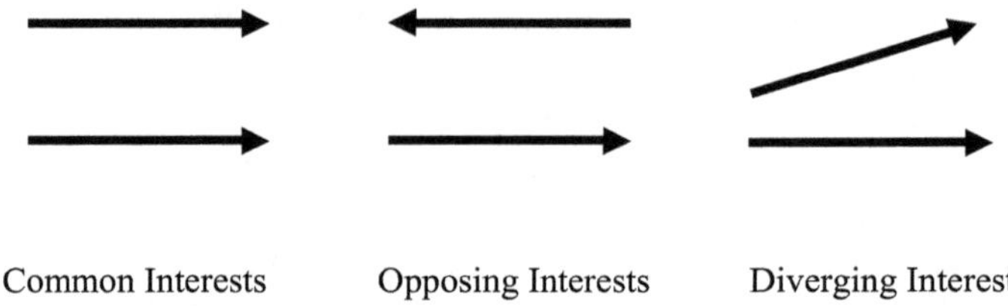

Fig. 3.6 Interests of the negotiation parties

- Furthermore, as many solution options as possible should be developed. In practice, negotiators often tend to divide the → *negotiation pie* far too quickly, instead of working out further, potentially better—agreement options. Negotiations, however, are generally all the more successful if the parties have a number of possible options for their agreement at hand. In this context, the emphasis on mutual gains (in accordance with the mutual gains approach) plays a decisive role. The search for solutions must be based on the interests of the parties involved. In particular, common interests and diverging interests (are likely to) offer the opportunity to enlarge the negotiation pie.
- In addition, the Harvard negotiation concept recommends that **neutral assessment criteria** are applied. Examples for such criteria are for instance market prices or customary contract terms. Neutral evaluation criteria are of particular importance for distribution issues (especially with regards to conflicting interests). In that sense, they are intended to help the parties to agree on a distribution that both sides consider agreeable and appropriate.
- The parties should make their final decision for or against the conclusion of a contract by taking the → *BATNA* into account. This recommendation focuses on the objective of mutual satisfaction after completion of the negotiations, which builds the basis for future cooperation or at last makes future agreements much easier.

The Harvard negotiation concept is the world's standard basic concept for contract negotiations, even if it does not take full account of certain points. However, the focus on → *win-win* for both parties has laid itself open to criticism that the concept does not sufficiently protect the parties' interests. The authors of the concept refute this decisively, pointing to the subtitle of the book—"without giving in". Yet, ulimately, the concept recommends that parties negotiate according to fair criteria and under consideration of all interests (without actually losing sight of the own BATNA). The resulting advantage of a better future relationship of the parties, as stated in the concept, seems valid regarding → *permanent business relations,* as long as there is no permanent imbalance of the negotiating power in these relations. Such an imbalance can often be observed e.g. between the automobile industry and the vast majority of its suppliers.

In other situations, such as one time businesses transactions, the "fairness", recommended by the Harvard negotiation concept is not as important. Nonetheless, its significance in view of reputation within an industry should by no means be neglected. The Harvard negotiation concept does not elaborate on diverging expectations of fairness and suitability. Concerning B2B relations, it remains to be explored in more detail how the stronger negotiating partner can be persuaded to accept common, neutral assessment criteria for the distribution of the overall negotiation pie. In practice, it would be interesting to explore the effects which would arise if only one of the parties were to follow the Harvard negotiation concept; and developing best practice recommendations on how to win the negotiating partner over, to also adopt the principles of the Harvard negotiation concept for this specific circumstance.

Even though it significantly influences negotiations in political and entrepreneurial negotiations, the Harvard negotiation concept does not discuss the significance of the → *principal-agent-problem* in greater detail. In particular, the recommendation to focus on interests rather than positions is affected by the principal-agent-problem. In an entrepreneurial context, the interests of various actors can be pursued (e.g. the → *chief negotiator*, the direct supervisor, the management board, the shareholders). In practice, it often proves problematic if, for instance the superior "corporate interests" are not communicated sufficiently to the agent in advance (or if the agent intends to pursue his/her own interests). The problem with specifications set prior to the negotiations is that they are often loaded with positional objectives. This makes it difficult for the negotiator to concentrate on interest-based solutions in the negotiation. Higher-ranking → *decision-maker* may be in the position to assess numerical targets but often do not take time to investigate the more complex situation of their business interests.

A more intensive treatment of → *emotions* within the Harvard negotiation concept would also be conceivable.[87] Positive emotions in particular hold the potential of promoting factual argumentation. The separation of people from problems is generally a worthwhile approach. In individual cases, however, a problematic personal relationship can impede future implementation of the contract to such an extent that the underlying personal issues should definitely also be taken into account on the factual level. Overall, the exceptions that deviate from the recommendations of the Harvard concept receive little attention. The Harvard negotiation concept appears to be a one-size-fits-all approach to negotiations and works towards this end, accomplishing considerable reductions in complexity. In the same way, the findings of the science of → *behavioural economics* have so far had very little input into the Harvard negotiation concept. Yet, distortions (→ *bias*), regularly influence negotiations. In this respect, the specific findings stemming from research in the field of behavioural economics could help to counteract potential negative impact on the outcome of the negotiation. Tactics based on the findings of behavioural economics (cf. corresponding topic list) also play a regular role in negotiations and could be considered in greater detail within the framework of the concept.

The Program on Negotiation (PON) of the Harvard Law School analyses the mentioned points in more detail. It would therefore be advantageous for the Harvard

[87] Fisher and Shapiro (2005).

negotiation concept to systematically integrate the results into the basic concept. In this context, Harvard's negotiation concept could also be used to differentiate between different areas of application, for instance political, entrepreneurial, private and crisis negotiations. This would make it easier to deal with the specific characteristics of each negotiation type in greater detail. Some aspects of political negotiations may not appear in this form in business or private negotiations. Even if the concept could be extended and improved by some aspects, it is important to emphasise that this concept constitutes an absolute milestone in negotiation science, the importance of which can hardly be overestimated.

Hide Your Glee Negotiators who have achieved a positive negotiation result are advised not to show their pleasure towards their negotiating partner but to rather "hide their glee". Due to the uncertainty as to when a success is really achieved (e.g. due to information asymmetries), the negotiators of the opposite side are, irrespective of the economic outcome, generally less satisfied with the result of the negotiations, if they are aware that their negotiating partner is pleased with the outcome.[88] In this respect, an additional advise would be not to accept a suggestion immediately, especially if the offered suggestion suits your expectations just fine, since a rushed acceptance is a form of showing glee. As far as the opposing party is concerned, the other party often fears that it has made too many or overly generous concessions to the negotiation partner. This can have negative effects, particularly for long-term business relations (→ *permanent business relations*).

Imperial Gestures In practice, imperial gestures take a significant role—in organisations but also in negotiations with people outside of the own company. However, men certainly tend to make more frequent use of these gestures than women. Typical imperial gestures e.g. include

- letting the negotiation partner wait in an anteroom,
- the kind of greeting, e.g. by means of a dominant touch of the arm during the handshake with the second am,
- the way the conversation partner is addressed during the negotiation,
- positioning at the head of the table,
- letting the response to an → *e-mail* be written and sent by the secretary
- not offering the conversation partner a seat so s/he has to remain standing.

Many gestures are applied unconsciously. In this regard, the person using these gestures can assume that the negotiation partner will equally unconsciously recognise the used imperial gestures and the expressed claim to power behind these gestures. Insofar imperial gestures suggest setting a non-verbal anchor. In the same way as → *anchoring*, the negotiation partner has the opportunity to set a *counter-anchor* (→ *anchoring*). In this context, the term power-posing is strongly linked to imperial gestures. According to the understanding proposed in this book power posing aims

[88] Cf. Thompson et al. (1995), pp. 467–492.

at demonstrating the own status, whereas imperial gestures are more oriented towards attributing the counterpart with a lower status.

Impression (First and Last) Since especially the first impression[89] and, with some limitations, also the last impression, is formative for the course of negotiations, it is worthwhile aiming at lasting first and last impressions on the negotiating partner. With regards to the first impression, most people unconsciously focus on evaluating the trustworthiness and competence of their counterparts, whereby trustworthiness should play a weightier role.[90] The first positive impression can be set by creating a pleasant negotiation atmosphere. In the same manner, the language, → *gender*, appearance, voice, → *body language* and scent also determine the first impression. Usual, inconspicuous business attire conveys seriousness in this respect, although uniformity makes it more difficult to stand out from the competition (e.g. in job interviews).

The search for similarities on the private level (→ *find something in common*, → *similar-to-me-effect*) before the start of negotiations can be helpful to strengthen a good first impression on the opposing party's negotiators (→ *chit-chat*)).

The first impression is important. Due to the so-called **confirmation bias** (self-confirmation of initial perception), (→ *bias*), people tend to disregard arguments that contradict their first impression. The positive last impression is not only about reconciliation gestures after what have perhaps been long, hard negotiations. It is even recommended to conclude negotiations with yielding in a side issue (→ *padding*). This allows the opposing side to end the negotiation with a sense of achievement (i.e. the concession) and thus keeps the negotiator and his company in better memory. If, however, the concession seems completely unmotivated, it can generate scepticism as to the outcome of the negotiation.

Incompatibility Bias Negotiators often mistakenly believe that their own interests will not coincide with the interests of the opposing party, but rather that their interests are diametrically opposed. This specific circumstance is referred to under the term incompatibility bias. Anyone with this fundamentally negative attitude will face greater difficulties, when attempting to increase the → *negotiation pie* and equally when attempting to achieve a successful conclusion of the eventual contract. Hence, this bias is strongly linked to the fixed pie illusion (see under → *negotiation pie*). If the parties desire a win-win strategy, it is crucial to research and evaluate the interests of the negotiating partner. Proposals made by the negotiating partner should not be rejected immediately, but rather reconciled with the own interests in the course of the negotiation. In doing so, the parties can then identify both, common as well as diverging interests (→ *Harvard negotiation concept*). In contrast to diametrically opposed interests, the latter also grant the opportunity to enlarge the negotiation pie, i.e. create an additional value for both sides.

---

[89] Hamilton et al. (1980), pp. 1050–1063.

[90] Cuddy et al. (2002), pp. 878–902.

Incomplete Solutions This is a tactic that serves to enforce the own parties expectations and aims at achieving a high degree of acceptance by the negotiating partner for the desired compromise option. In order to do so, an idea, a proposal for a solution or a compromise can only be vaguely hinted at. If the negotiating partner takes on this proposal and develops it further, seemingly only according to his own interests, this generally leads to various advantages for the side that hinted at the idea in the first place. For one thing, the negative effects of → *reactive devaluation* can be prevented, since the negotiating partner will accept the further developed proposal as his/her own. As a result, the negotiating partner is less sceptical of the proposal and also develops a certain internal acceptance towards it. This can be particularly important for a successful implementation phase for the concluded contract. Moreover, the negotiating partner's sense of accomplishment is a key factor as it is directly linked to his/her willingness to defend this solution against any potential objections, e.g. in the form of doubts expressed by superiors or impeding risks (i.e. the → *decision-maker*) (in this context also see → *principal-agent-problem*). If the negotiating partner accepts the idea as his/her own, s/he cannot expect any concessions in return.

Information Control The information flow can be subject to either full or partial control, particularly in negotiations taking place in organizations, but—as far as possible—also in contractual relationship constellations, e.g. in complex long-term contracts. The most commonly used techniques are inter alia:

- Holding back information,
- privileging individuals with information,
- filtering parts of information (deliberately leaving out single details),
- connection with other information,
- determining the point in time of the information flow,
- determining the context and the way in which information is presented, including the delivery of the information,
- *information overload*.

Information control is therefore used as a tactic. It influences the (assumed) → *BATNA* of the (active) participants in the negotiations. In the course of manipulative information control, such as an information overload, it should be borne in mind that the trustful relationship between the negotiating parties can be adversely affected in the long-term if the negotiating partner recognises the use of this tactic.

Information Procurement In rare cases, the main aim of negotiations is to collect information. It is then a question of using this information for business purposes or for facilitating another project. However, in most negotiations, the procurement of information is a central task from the outset, up until the very end of negotiations (including the implementation phase). In this regard it is essential for the success of negotiations, although it is not the primary goal. Information is crucial in contract negotiations, e.g. in order to assess the own objective → *negotiation power*, i.e. above all the own → *BATNA* and the opposing party's negotiation power, as well as to be able to recognise problems and potential solutions as well as concepts for enlarging the common → *negotiation pie*. For the latter, it is crucial to obtain information on the negotiating partners' main interests and the priority of these.

The → *information demand analysis* is an important element for the procurement of information. According to the analysis, the required information can be extracted from a variety of possible **sources of information**, including (but excluding sources for subject-specific technical information):

- Informational requests to the negotiating partner,
- Questioning former or active employees of the opposing party,
- Gathering information in the course of the negotiation,
- Existing information systems within the company,
- Individual information gathering within the own company (from colleagues, other divisions etc.),
- Obtaining information from the negotiating partner's competitors,
- Obtaining information from the negotiating partner's business partners,
- Obtaining information from the own competitors and business partners,
- Publicly accessible sources (e.g. online resources, trade registers, newspaper articles).

The central points of information should be categorised in terms of their unambiguousness (multiple meanings), timeliness, immediacy, reliability and their degree of independence from other information sources, as well as their exclusivity. In the course of the reviewing the information, it is often attempted to gather information from a variety of independent sources. The problem is that individuals often remember single facts, yet forget where, how or from whom they have received the information (**source amnesia**). The danger lies in the fact that information from unreliable sources—e.g. only unconfirmed rumours—potentially influences the decision-making process.

The actual negotiation is essential for gathering information. In the negotiation itself, questions, in connection with attentive listening (→ *70-30-rule*), are the most important means of gathering information. Comparable to a medical **anamnesis**, there is a repetitive need to gather information and ask the according questions. Hence, they can be prepared. Above that there are also questions related to specific events and moments. It may also be sensible to occasionally ask seemingly "pointless" questions or questions relating to information that is already available. This approach makes it more difficult for the negotiating partner to estimate the existing level of information, based on the questions asked. Likewise, this approach is a good way to assess the reliability of the given answers to questions, to which the according information has already been confirmed. In addition, valuable information can be obtained from the negotiating partner's statements and queries, because in return questions can equally (unintentionally) reveal the level of the questioner's information. Due to the nature of the statement, many statements contain information about feelings, undisclosed decision-making structures, premises or the opposing party's level of information and status of plans. If a negotiation party does not seem to fully grasp what has been said, the other party will often not only reformulate their statements but also provide additional explanations, which of course also contains more helpful information. Hence, in some cases pretending to non-understanding may be a tactical move. Furthermore, valuable information can also be obtained by observing the negotiating partner's non-verbal behaviour. Particularly concerning → *body language*, but also in the search for statements behind statements, being cautious is indispensable, because these conclusions are usually not very ambiguous—quite apart from bona fide cases regarding deception. Often only **informational indications** are gained here. Several independent indications without any contradicting indications can consolidate to one (derived) piece of information. To a certain degree this procedure is comparable to a differential diagnosis, known from the field of medicine, because indications are not simply added together in a numerical manner but gain their validity due to being combined in a certain way. Companies are advised to at least partially standardise their procedures of information procurement. Moreover, for complex negotiations it is beneficial to evaluate and assess the acquisition process for information.

Information Demand Analysis This is a standard business tool for planning economic decisions, which can also be applied in contract negotiations. It focuses on analysing which information is required in order to make each decision; which information is still needed; and how reliable this information needs to be. The requirement analysis makes a distinction between standard and exceptional situations. It is precisely this differentiation that can prove particularly useful in negotiations. The requirement analysis takes into account the frequency and significance of the information as well as the costs of procuring the information, and it further differentiates between early and ad hoc gathering of information, or abandoning the procurement of information. Even when the analysis suggests that the gathering of information should be waived, the information about how expensive and how fast this information could be obtained often remains.

Interim Results It is generally advisable to record all interim results of a negotiation in writing, both due to the risk of → *misunderstandings* and → *foggy recalls*, which inevitably increases with the number of details. Moreover, stating interim results in writing has a certain moral binding effect, although not expressly legally binding. The psychological bond can be strengthened by way of initialling. Interim results are often recorded as key points in the context of term sheets.

Keep Something in Reserve The tactic of "keeping something in reserve", known from the military field, also has its rightful scope of application in negotiations. This is particularly true for the notorious → *last gap* in negotiations between the different negotiating positions. It is recommended that a potential concession is kept in reserve, which is to some extent valuable to the negotiating partner but is of little consequence for the own side. Ideally, it should not be obvious to the negotiation partner that the concession is only of limited value for the own side. If there was no such reserve concession, the last gap would have to be filled with one of the items that should not be sacrificed at any price, or the negotiations would be terminated completely.

However, not only a possible concession should be kept in reserve but also demands. This is where the demands that could not be asserted in the negotiation process come into play. This reserve demand can then be used as a response to the negotiating partner's → *salami tactic*.

Knocking on the Bush This is a (misleading) tactic, which represents something as being true although it has not been verified. The intention behind this tactic is that the opposing side's reaction will give an indication of whether the assumption was correct or false. Thus, this tactic has the same objective as the → *premise question* and is closely linked to the allusions tactic. Questions of premise and allusions can be formulated a little more subtly, whereas "knocking on the bush" makes the assumption more obvious. If the assumption proves to be correct, the negotiating partner may be taken aback, since s/he cannot understand where this "knowledge" comes from (the "bush" no longer seems to be a safe hiding place).

Since "knocking on the bush" is quite an aggressive tactic, negotiating partners often react in an equally aggressive manner. This reaction alone is not proof enough to conclude whether the assumption was correct or not. In any case, applying this tactic may damage the relationship between the parties.

In negotiations, the opposing party can try to obtain more deliberation time and give a considered answer by simply ignoring a priorly made comment or applying a diversionary tactic. It is also possible to use further inquiry e.g. "what makes you think that?". This inquiry provides time and the negotiation partners immediate reaction may give an indication of whether it was just a case of "knocking on the bush". Even after a given answer, it is still possible to decide whether to admit the questioned fact or retain information. Further inquiry should also be used if the interrogator's "guesswork" was wrong because this permits the interrogator to reveal less information about their own side while simultaneously opening up the opportunity to gain information about the other side who used the tactic "knocking on the bush".

Even if this tactic is misleading in terms of existing knowledge, the authors do not believe that its application should normally have any legal consequences. Ultimately, damage to the other side can only result from the fact that it is solely responsible for disclosing information. It should therefore in general be regarded as legally acceptable → *cunning deception*.

Know Your Target The request to know the negotiation target, prima facie, seems so obvious and self-explanatory that it normally would not be worth being described in a detailed manner. However, amateurs, inexperienced negotiators and sometimes even professional negotiators—especially if there was no time to prepare for the negotiations—often only have very vague ideas about the actual negotiation target or, in lengthier negotiations, about the interim goals. For this reason alone, this recommendation is very useful. In contrast, it is not entirely unproblematic. Although a skilled negotiator should be aware of the planned negotiation goal, including the necessary interim steps, s/he should not slip into tunnel vision. The negotiator should also always "have an open eye" for opportunities for other, equally convenient goals (deals) that were not considered from the outset and perhaps could not be considered, because the opportunity was not given back then. Hence, goals must be evaluated intermediately and perhaps be supplemented or eliminated as "not achievable". In this regard, one must be aware of the fact that sometimes the red line is falsely assumed to be the target. Negotiators who know the actual lowest acceptable limit value tend to also only achieve results near the low limit. This is due to the fact that they are quite often neither personally nor professionally motivated enough to achieve results, significantly above this limit.

Last Gap The last gap is the nightmare of many negotiators, since the goal of concluding the contract seems so close, and yet everything can fail due to this last gap. Often the negotiations come to a halt at exactly this point or a → *deadlock* is reached. Moreover, a final concession can lead to one's own side being dissatisfied with the negotiator. This last gap is often very difficult to close, because several problems have accumulated. For example, if the negotiator is disappointed or even annoyed about the current progress of the negotiation process or the time and effort invested in the negotiations, s/he might see the last gap as an opportunity to take a stand against the negotiating partner. Perhaps the negotiator is also hoping to turn the negotiations in their entirety in his/her favour, or maybe re-open negotiations on certain points. This latter in particular is unlikely to work in practice, but a failure of the contract conclusion is easily possible. There are many attempts to avoid the notorious "last gap", e.g. by considering possible goal solutions early on; attempting to prevent problems from building up, by finding solutions for individual problems; or closing the last gap elegantly (→ *keep something in reserve*).

Limiting the Options Unlike the → *Russian front* tactic, the tactic of limiting options (reducing choice) is to give the negotiating partner a real choice. However, this choice is limited in such a way that none of the options are incompatible with one's own interests. In this way, two goals that are difficult to reconcile—the negotiating partner's freedom of choice and the enforcement of the own interests—can be combined. This tactic can be conducted in two ways:

The first is based on deception. The negotiating partner is shown his/her options in a seemingly objective and very persuasive way, whereby options that are contrary to the interests of the own side are simply omitted. This tactic works in part because people often focus on making the right choice between several options instead of asking themselves whether there are other potential options. This tactic makes use of the mental → *path dependency.* It can also be further enhanced by means of the → *framing* effect, in order to influence the negotiating partner's choice according to one's own interests.

The other variation of this tactic makes use of superior negotiation power, i.e. it openly reduces the options available for the negotiating partner. Yet, it is considered as "fair", since only those options are excluded that clearly contradict one's own interests. This fairness is usually emphasised to the negotiating partner in order to establish a trustful and strengthened relationship, despite a stringent enforcement of own interests. In the course of the negotiation this can subsequently be crucial for a smooth implementation of the contract. The challenge in this tactic lies in convincingly conveying this limited fairness to the negotiating partner.

Example
"The product is available in the colours blue and black. Which of these options would you prefer?"

Lock-in Tactic Within the lock-in tactic, one side deprives itself of its existing negotiation range, e.g. by making promises to their own side (or linked stakeholders) that cannot be broken without losing face. In most cases, this is done openly in front of the negotiating partner's eyes. It is a tactic often employed by trade unions in particular. In a moderated form, this tactic is reminiscent of the military tactic of the burnt ships with which, for example, *William the Conqueror* prevented his invasion troops in England from returning to France in 1066. The same was done by *Hernan Cortez* in 1519 before the conquest of the Aztec empire.

With this tactic, the negotiators put themselves under enormous pressure and hope that the opposing side will respectfully regard this action and make the according concessions. Yet, in general, the tactic can only be successful if both sides have limited courses of action and therefore necessarily aspire an agreement. One example of this tactic in use was when the new Greek government held a referendum at the beginning of 2015. The aim of this tactic is to force the opposing side to make substantial concessions. The lock-in tactic is hence a special form of the position-oriented negotiation tactic. The disadvantage of this tactic is that the solution options are limited and the risk of the failure of the negotiations is increased.

Logrolling Logrolling refers to mutual help, more specifically the term originates from the rolling of logs as part of neighbourly help in building houses in the USA. In negotiations, it refers to one partner giving way to the other on a point which is more important to the other party than to the own side. In return, the negotiating partner gives in on a different point which is less important to him. It is therefore an asymmetrical, reciprocal yielding from which both sides benefit.

The tactic was originally developed by *Lewis A. Froman* and *Michael D. Cohen*.[91] In the field of politics, it is supposed that *David Crockett*, member of the US House of Representatives, first used this term in a speech in 1835. Accordingly, the term is frequently associated with political contexts, concerning the winning of votes for legislative proposals.

[91] Froman and Cohen (1990), pp. 180–183.

Applying this tactic generally requires several negotiation points. This is because one side yields in one aspect and the other party on another point. Since logrolling is based on mutual and asymmetrical yielding, it is a principle classified within the range of → *win-win negotiations* as it is primarily concerns enlarging the → *negotiation pie*.

Low Expectations Just as happiness is described as "reality minus expectations", the perceived success of a negotiation also depends on expectations as the starting point: At best, high expectations can be entirely fulfilled and are thus not well suited to convey a sense of achievement and satisfaction. However, if expectations are low, they can be surpassed quite easily and hence create a high sense of achievement. It may therefore be reasonable to ensure that the negotiation partner only holds low expectations of the negotiation, which can then, to his/her great satisfaction and surprise, be surpassed. The fact that this principle works so well is due to the fact that the success of negotiations (e.g. taking into account the → *negotiation value*) is often not documented systematically and entirely.

It can therefore make sense for the own party to build a reputation as being a "tough cookie" for one's own → *chief negotiator* and to present him/her to the outside world as such. If this tough negotiator then makes a concession towards the opposing party, it would be more like a sense of achievement for the negotiating partner. Ultimately, inducing lower expectations for the negotiation can be categorised under the term → *framing*.

Purposely evoking low expectations in the negotiating partner is also often an attempt to induce the negotiating partner to make further concessions, such as price discounts. However, if the expectations of the opposing party are too low, it is possible that they will decide to waive negotiations altogether. As far as possible, low expectations should thus only be created immediately before the start of negotiations, only if it is certain that negotiations will take place or during the negotiations themselves. However, there is still the risk of a breaking-off of the negotiations. If the negotiating partner's expectations regarding a certain aspect, e.g. the price, are lowered before this aspect is even discussed, this can also lead the other party to set their anchor (→ *anchoring*) lower than would have been the case if the expectations had not been adapted, i.e. lowered. In this way, the initial anchor can be influenced to the own benefit even before it is set. If, however, the negotiating partner recognises the intentional use of this tactic in the course of the negotiations, it can be counteracted in the same way, i.e. like is repaid with like.

One specific tactic aimed at lowering expectations is known as the **put downs, negative qualities** or **throwing garbage at their lawn tactic.** Generally speaking, this comprises tactical behaviour during which the negotiator talks badly about the other side's goods or services in order to lower the other side's expectations of the price.

Example
"We were very upset that you did not deliver on time last time."

"To be honest, the quality of your product disappointed us a little last time."

"The last product that we bought from you is already showing signs of wear and tear."

The opposing party understands this behaviour to be a (strong) attack and thus these actions can permanently damage the parties' relationship. Besides, the criticism expressed must be true—or at least not verifiable untrue—if there is to be no risk of a bad negotiation atmosphere or even the termination of negotiations. Furthermore, the negotiating partner can "repay like with like" and start to list observed negative aspects. If it is going to be used at all, this tactic should therefore be used in moderation and the criticism should be expressed in an adequate manner. Using the → *good guy/bad guy* tactic can be useful in this context. As opposed to that, the good guy can highlight the positive aspects and the interest in concluding the contract whereas the bad guy discredits certain aspects of the offered goods or services.

In company-intern negotiations, the relationship between the involved parties is often even more important, which is why the application of this tactic requires great sensitivity.

MESO This abbreviation stands for **multiple equivalent simultaneous offers**. At the same time, this acronym corresponds with the Greek word for "middle" and "combined" solutions. This tactic of differentiated but, from the point of view of the offerer, equivalent offers (ideally three parallel offers are recommended), aims at having the negotiating partner disclose his/her interests by responding to these offers. This approach facilitates finding solution options according to mutual interests. The offerer also discloses important information, since conclusions can be drawn from the equivalence of the offers as to what his/her interests are. According to the studies of *Medvec/Leonardelli/Galinsky/Claussen-Schulz*[92] this tactic creates measurable advantages for the eventual negotiation results.

Multiple offers can particularly help to explore which one of the available offers best meets the negotiating partner's expectations. Making several offers allows the interests, preferences and wishes of the negotiating partner to be discovered. This can also be achieved by questioning (→ *questions*) and listening. Due to the → *negotiator's dilemma* of exchanging information, however, it may prove difficult to obtain the necessary information this way. Multiple offers can therefore present an alternative to other forms of information procurement. If the offers only serve the purpose of obtaining information, they do not have to be complete in the sense that they can be accepted immediately. They can also act as an indicator, pointing out

[92] Medvec et al. (2005), pp. 1–30.

different directions. This is advantageous for the offerer in that s/he is not committed definitively to the offer made.

Due to the limited receptivity of negotiators (on this specific aspect see further under → *fewer, convincing arguments*), only a limited and carefully selected number of offers should be presented at the same time. Otherwise, this can quickly overtax the negotiating partner and thus evoke a defensive stance. Most commonly two to three offers are presented.

MESO is similar to the tactics, which limit choice and those which evoke a biased choice. However, as is often the case in contract negotiations, the external appearance of a contract does not allow to draw direct conclusions about the actual purpose, because several purposes are possible. In contrast to the tactic of limiting options, MESO does not aim to restrict the negotiating partner's actual choice, neither openly nor covertly. The aim of this tactic is rather to gather information.

Meta-Anchoring Whereas → *anchoring* refers to a figure in general and in particular in the context of price negotiations, meta anchors refer to the determination of the nature of the subject matter of the contract, the nature of problems or the objectives of the contract negotiations.[93] The term is not quite precise because it focuses on the setting of framework objectives for the negotiations, which the exact wording of the term does not reveal. In any case, anchoring is presumed whenever the negotiating partner has a different idea of the framework conditions and these fundamental aspects are already being negotiated. Essentially, the significance of the proposal and the counter-proposal is governed by the general statements regarding the term → *anchoring*. In this regard. a three-step approach is recommended: (1) determining potential meta-anchors, (2) evaluating the consequences of the potential meta-anchors and (3) anticipating the opposing party's possible reactions to the stated meta-anchor and the subsequent consequences. An additional (4) fourth step, which is not usually named, is the explicit "choice" of the meta-anchor. In many cases, however, the negotiating parties agree on framework conditions, with the purpose of saving negotiation time discussing these. Accordingly, meta-anchoring is not deployed.

Midpoint-Rule The *midpoint-rule* (→ *negotiation power*) states that negotiating partners often meet about halfway between their starting points, under the prerequisite that the *negotiating power* is roughly equal (see Fig. 3.7 (Midpoint-rule)). This explains the essential importance of the starting positions in negotiations (→ *anchoring*).

Furthermore, the significance of tactics that aim to invalidate the value of an anchor (*anchor discreditation*, → *anchoring*) or attempt to shift the discussion (→ *change the standards*) derives from this. The → *Harvard negotiation concept* takes a critical view of this tendency and advocates an alignment of the negotiation with neutral assessment criteria.

[93] Terminology according to Lax and Sebenius (2006), pp. 199–201.

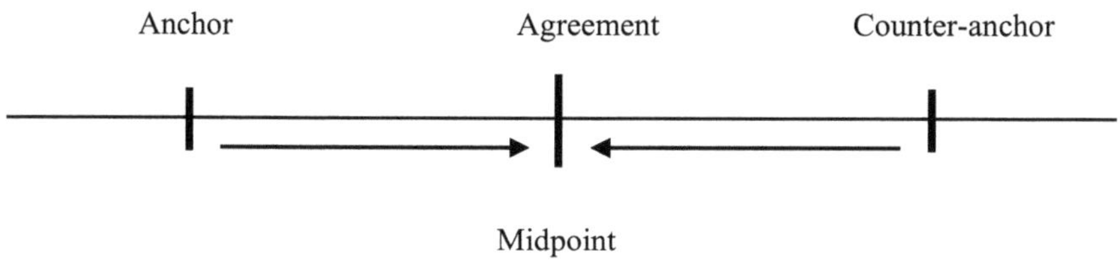

Fig. 3.7 Midpoint-rule

Missing the Big Picture In the context of complex negotiation matters, the central source of error (→ *mistakes*) lies in the fact that the negotiator "misses the big picture" or simply loses a clear overview of the key points. The results of single points of the negotiation can often not be per se categorised as specifically "good" or "bad" for one side; their evaluation rather depends on the way they are linked to other negotiation results. For instance, the Versaille peace treaty after World War I was comprised of many, separately negotiated, parts. Only after these parts were merged, it became clear that the way the clauses interlocked would constitute a very heavy burden for the economy of Germany. Economists like *John Maynard Keynes* advised to amend the treaty, unfortunately their advice came too late.

It is also possible that individual negotiation points are generally not required and distinguishing them only becomes necessary for specific results at another stage of the negotiations (e.g. the question of exceptions only arises once the general acceptance of risks is discussed; and the consequences of a breach of duty only emerge when a certain performance obligation is agreed). However, particularly in complex negotiations, the interplay of single contract clauses is often lost from sight. An overall view is essential, especially for comprehensively designed contracts, since special emphasis shall be placed on the interlocking effects between the individual clauses. This also helps to prevent contradictions and severe defects which neither benefit the own party interests, nor the negotiation partners' interests, but rather make executing the contract in mutual agreement more difficult. The risk of losing the general overview is further increased by the fact that in complex negotiations, for organisational reasons there is generally a division of tasks, whereby each person is assigned to a certain field and seemingly there is no individual, responsible for keeping track of the overall picture. This issue becomes even more prominent and complicated when → *working groups* are established.

Whenever a large number of people are involved, it can also happen that each person relies on another. This problem should not only be addressed and counterfeited by carrying out special training for all participants to maintain the overview, but—depending on the size of the negotiation—it would be even more beneficial to appoint one or more individual persons with the specific responsibility for keeping an eye on the overall picture (**person in charge of the general overview**). In most cases this task is assumed by the team leader.

Mistakes Like → *misunderstandings*, in negotiations mistakes occur very frequently. Due to the complexity of negotiations they also cannot be avoided completely. Thus, it is the task of the negotiators to at least minimise the own sides' error rate, recognise own and others' mistakes and develop effective methods for dealing with mistakes or preventing them altogether. Mistakes can happen in the course of every single task that must be handled while the negotiations are still present. Still, mistakes most often occur when:

- Information is shared,
- information is gathered,
- several negotiators have to be coordinated,
- the own behaviour is emotional,
- the own and the other sides' interests are not evaluated correctly,
- no solutions are found,
- inadequate tactics are applied and
- tactics are misapplied.

Many mistakes are not discovered and are thus also not reflected or ruled out for the sake of future negotiations. This is why oftentimes negotiators commit the same mistakes over and over. Even if the mistakes are recognised and addressed appropriately, the consequences of these mistakes cannot be resolved in the course of the ongoing negotiation. Own mistakes can be compensated by mistakes made by the other party and can in this regard also even be overcompensated. Some situations that appear to be mistakes, base on a well thought out tactic, while reversely often deliberately chosen tactical actions can be defective. Here, using an → *analyst* can be helpful. In order to learn from past mistakes an evaluation after completing the negotiation can be beneficial (→ *WWYDD*). For this the company must have a mistake culture, where single mistakes are not blamed on a single negotiator and s/he is not threatened with possible negative consequences. The focus of the failure analysis should rather be the development of future improvements.

Misunderstandings The ability to prevent or at least recognise misunderstandings and **mistakes** is a central skill for a successful negotiator. Misunderstandings concerning what the negotiation partner demands or offers, regarding the interests s/he follows, the information s/he has disclosed, how binding a formulation is or even what his/her inner attitude towards the potential closing of an agreement is are very common in negotiations. In order to avoid misunderstandings in doubtful situations, asking questions is the initial solution. In the context of information, one should generally follow the recommendation of checking the facts. In this regard. it could be reasonable to explicitly document all available information, evaluated according to relevance and reliability. Above that it is recommendable to at least also conduct a plausibility assessment of the respective information. For important information it should be attempted to find a second source (→ *information procurement*). Likewise, conclusions that are even made subconsciously should be reflected critically and reassured. As for the negotiation as such, it is reasonable to employ an → *analyst*, or rather it is important that one of the → *two negotiators*, who is not currently negotiating is very attentive in order to detect occurring misunderstandings and draws attention to these.

It is very recommendable to orally reiterate significant passages of the negotiation and set these in written form promptly after the negotiation. This approach also increases the morally binding effect of the so-far achieved interim result of the negotiation, which is important, since a legal binding effect does not (yet) exist. Due to the risk of misunderstandings prior to a possible escalation it should generally be examined whether a misunderstanding caused to commence deescalating measures. Yet, sometimes misunderstandings are also faked for tactical reasons.

Moral Hazard Moral hazard (moral risk, moral temptation) can occur whenever the agent acting on behalf of the company is not (fully) responsible for bearing the costs of the resulting consequences of their actions. This aspect is often closely linked to an information asymmetry that prevents their actions from being visible to the person (or company) who is financially liable for them (hidden actions). As opposed to adverse selection, it is neither qualities nor characteristics, but a certain behaviour that cannot be observed properly. If the party bearing the risk lacks the capacity to recognise the misconduct of their agent, the agent has incentives to behave non-cooperatively and in self-interest. This is because the individual agent in question has no personal consequences to fear.

Example
In the insurance sector, the term "moral hazard" is understood in the sense that insured persons take higher risks based on their insurance coverage and thus increase the likelihood of damage occurring (ex-ante moral hazard). A further manifestation is the lack of an incentive to reduce costs if damage has already occurred (ex-post moral hazard).

Moral hazard can play an essential role in negotiations. Companies make common use of agents to negotiate on their behalf. Consequently, the issue of the → *principal-agent-problem* arises. The negotiator has all the knowledge regarding the negotiation, as s/he is directly involved in it. On the other hand, the company usually only obtains indirect knowledge through communicating with their agent, which causes an asymmetry of information. Accordingly, the company is not always in the position to easily detect the agent's mistakes during the negotiation process (hidden actions). This could tempt the negotiator to take higher risks, since s/he does not have to (fully) bear the consequences that would arise either from, e.g. a termination of the contract agreement or completing a contract detrimental to the company's interests. Rather, s/he can attempt to justify the failure in order to escape personal consequences.

The moral hazard can be countered by the company reducing the asymmetry of information and thus diminishing the occurrence of hidden actions. As with the principal-agent-problem, the → *principle of dual control*, incentive systems and better communication can all contribute to reducing the risk of moral hazard.

Moral hazard can also occur between negotiators, as information asymmetries also exist here. Just the same as in the internal company sector, selfish and uncooperative behaviour can be facilitated if there is only a small risk of the negotiating partner noticing it. Here, not only the option to disguise or fully hide actions can cause selfish behaviour. If, for legal or contractual reasons, sanctioning this behaviour is not possible even when detected, then selfish actions become very attractive from an economic standpoint, especially in the context of one-time deals. As a preventive measure, the company can attempt to reduce the information gap here, too. However, this sometimes proves more difficult in the relationship between the negotiators, as there certainly will be some kind of information they do not want to disclose openly. In this case, clauses setting disclosure obligations can be implemented. Another option to prevent moral hazard is to contractually agree on sanctions for misconduct. Possible means are for instance, sanctioned confidentiality rules for contract negotiations, non-disclosure agreements and prohibitions of competition. The latter measures should be combined with enforceable disclosure obligations. Contractual measures can only prevent moral hazard if there is an actual possibility that misconduct is recognised and addressed by the other party. If this is not the case, the contractual instruments may only have a psychological effect.

Multi-Person BATNA It is important to note that not only the potential contract partner's → *BATNA*, but also the BATNA of both the → *chief negotiator* and the internal → *decision-maker* (due to the → *principal-agent-problem*) can play an influential role. Therefore it is advisable to identify both BATNAs and to take them into account when developing the negotiation strategy (**two-level BATNA**).

If, in contrast, many parties are at the negotiation table, for instance in political negotiations and also sometimes in B2B negotiations, it is recommendable to determine the multi-person BATNA. Determining the BATNA of each individual negotiator and (co-)decision-maker is not recommended in many cases due to the high effort that would be involved. In these cases, for example, the negotiator's BATNA or that of the entire team can be evaluated, presumed that the persons involved are pursuing similar interests. The latter is often useful, since the negotiators of a team mostly follow the same interests due to structural guidelines of the company (e.g. an increased willingness to conclude the contract, as this is the measure of their success).

Negotiation Clause A negotiation clause obliges the parties involved to firstly negotiate before they are allowed to reach the next level of escalation in the course of a conflict, e.g. referral to an arbitration tribunal, or starting legal proceedings before a court of law. A negotiation clause is a juridical instrument.

Negotiations carried out on the basis of such a negotiation clause often involve one side, which has no actual interest in the negotiation, i.e. imposedly negotiates "pro forma". In order to demonstrate a serious will in negotiating, this party can make concessions in unimportant side issues, but remain firm in all other negotiation points. As long as the conduct otherwise complies with normal negotiation demeanour, violation of the obligation to negotiate can hardly be proven with substantial evidence, which is why the efficiency of such negotiation clauses is not without controversy. In favour of this clause, it can be stated it at any rate guarantees a potential agreement period and the necessity to negotiate. Consequently, this may create a real willingness to negotiate, smoothing the way for a solution of the conflict.

Negotiation Levels Negotiation theory relies on the fact that negotiators are assumed to follow logical and interest-driven structures during negotiations and that negotiators weigh the advantages and disadvantages for their business and themselves rationally. This is accordingly referred to as the **rational level of negotiation**. Particularly in the business sector—specifically in B2B-negotiations—the rational negotiation level dominates. However, human actions are not solely based on economic objectives—mankind can simply not be described as a pure form of homo oeconomicus, as his/her → *emotions* cannot be disregarded. There is therefore always an **emotional level of negotiation**, which encompasses the feelings of both sides. Even if agreement is reached and accordingly the contract is concluded at the rational level of negotiation, it can still be worthwhile to invest additional time in further developing a positive relationship on the "emotional level". If agreement between the negotiators can also be attained on an emotional level, the likelihood is far greater that the agreement will be "lived"—i.e. that both sides will behave constructively in potential conflict situations and comply with agreed deescalating measures.

The third level is the so-called "identity level", which concerns the personal involvement of the negotiator. Hence, this level deals with the honour and appreciation of the individual negotiator. One possible tactic which relates to this level is, for instance giving the negotiation partner face.

Negotiation Pause Breaks in negotiations (**take a break!**) are exceptionally valuable. In long negotiations, negotiators can recover during these breaks and also exchange both information and impressions as well as preparing for the upcoming stages of negotiation. Breaks are particularly important if an → *analyst* is involved, or a third party who at least temporarily holds the role of analyst. The analyst can then, in a constructive and analytic manner, outline his/her impressions during the negotiation pauses. Depending on the negotiation situation, plans, and tactics can be modified during the break. Likewise, information can be exchanged with the → *back office* or the → *decision-maker* in the background. However, many breaks do not offer the negotiating partner the opportunity to temporarily seclude himself/herself from the negotiations. Rather, breaks are spent together with the negotiating partner, e.g. at joint lunchs. This often creates the opportunity for informal conversations that provide for further information and mutually beneficial options. During a break spent together, often only single negotiators can excuse themselves for a brief period of time, e.g. to consult with the decision-maker by telephone. If there is however a need for a (detailed) discussion within the negotiation team, it may make sense to postpone certain points of the negotiation until the next round of negotiations.

In complex negotiations, particularly in the political field, the negotiations that take place during the breaks (i.e. off the records) are often decisive for the eventual achievement of a compromise.

In addition to that, a negotiation pause can be used for the purpose of emotionally "cooling-off" if, for example, the negotiations reached an emotional peak. On the whole, negotiators can strive for a good negotiation climate and positive personal atmosphere between the parties, especially during the breaks between negotiations. These breaks are also generally used for → *chit-chat*.

If the other side is in flow, pausing the negotiation can—as in sports—be used to interrupt the flow and raise the morale of the own negotiators; in this case, the negotiation pause is a tactical instrument within the negotiation process (**tactical pause**). Nonetheless, in the same manner also actively preventing a break can be a tactic with the aim that the negotiating partner cannot reap benefits from the break. In some cases, the aim is hence to "overload" the negotiator, either with emotions or with information. Refusing a negotiation pause is sometimes achieved by presenting fake and surprising *time pressure* (→ *deadline*). Often a subsequent appointment is used for justifying the supposed time pressure. Conversely, the extension of a break can also be an attempt to further build up time pressure.

Negotiation Phases Negotiations can be categorised into different phases. Neither the number of phases nor the terms used to describe them are uniform in literature. Nonetheless, the most important steps encompass:

- preparation for the negotiation
- initiating the negotiation
- core phase of the negotiation
- agreement
- implementation of agreement
- ex-post-phase

Each of the negotiation phases faces individual challenges. The preparation stage of the negotiation plays a significant role for the success of the negotiation; see also → *80-20-rule*. Among other things, in this phase the negotiation goals are elaborated; the own and the other party's → *BATNA* is determined, and the negotiation strategy and tactics to be implemented are established. The initiation phase of a negotiation is characterised by the negotiating partners getting acquainted with each other (when new negotiation partners meet, the → *first impression* is very important), building a positive relationship and gathering information, particularly with regard to preferences, wishes, goals and ideas. Especially the clever use of questioning techniques (see topic list) can help to gather additional information.

This phase is followed by the core phase of the negotiation, in which the individual aspects are negotiated, and solutions and compromises must be found. This is the exact moment, where the negotiation strategy (cf. topic lists), which has been decided on previously, as well as most of the chosen tactics, are put into practice. Quite often there are further subdivided phases. Within a first subphase parties may primarily search and deal with negotiation points where they can most likely agree on and then unfold and compile open points, where no instant agreement is possible. In a second subphase these open points are then discussed in-depth and (hopefully) solved for the most part. Lastly, the third subphase attempts to fill in the last gaps.

If the negotiation is successful, the parties agree to conclude a binding contract. However, it may also be the case that the parties terminate the negotiations if one or both parties have a better alternative available. If a contract is concluded, the subject matter agreed upon is implemented. Especially in projects where cooperation between the parties is decisive, a good relationship between the parties is important. The ex-post phase, i.e. the phase after the implementation of the agreed contract, is sometimes used within the framework of → *claim management* to enforce claims and demands. This is an attempt to influence the result once again. Moreover, this phase also serves to reflect on the development of the negotiation.

Negotiation Pie The term negotiation pie refers to the total value of the negotiations, in the sense of the sum of advantages and disadvantages that can be achieved within the negotiation process. Negotiations can either induce an increase of the negotiation pie, or cause shrinking or stagnation of such. These options are discussed respectively under different keywords.

If it is possible to maximise the net profit of both parties in total, both parties will benefit equally from the negotiations—assuming the sides were involved equally in the negotiation. This is a desirable negotiation outcome, and conforms with the → *win-win strategy*. In this respect literature speaks of "**expanding the pie**" or "**maximising the total pie**". The outermost limit of the created value is known as the **efficient frontier**. According to the *small pie bias* (→ *bias*), negotiators generally tend to underestimate the potential size of the negotiation pie. When enlarging the pie, the general limitations of the prohibition of cartels (in Europe e.g. Art. 101 TFEU), which prohibit anticompetitive agreements, apply. For an efficient increase of size, negotiators should move away from the idea of merely focusing on the price aspect, and rather opt for integrating other conditions into the negotiations, such as delivery terms, quality requirements, additional services, financing, contractual relationship, and liability risks.

Achieving a mutually satisfactory result is even easier if both parties value certain aspects differently. Different preferences can help to enlarge the pie substantially. Equal interests also promote the achievement of mutually beneficial results.

Example

The seller wants to deliver quickly in order to have more storage space and the buyer wants a fast delivery in order to be able to use the item.

Possibilities to enlarge the negotiation pie:

- Different value assessment, different resources, different capabilities;
- different preferences regarding time limits;
- varying estimates regarding future developments;
- different risk structures;
- expanding/shifting the deal by same parties;
- involvement of a third party on the supply/demand side and
- in a broad sense, the pie could also be enlarged by finding new, creative solution mechanisms that satisfy the parties' interests even better.

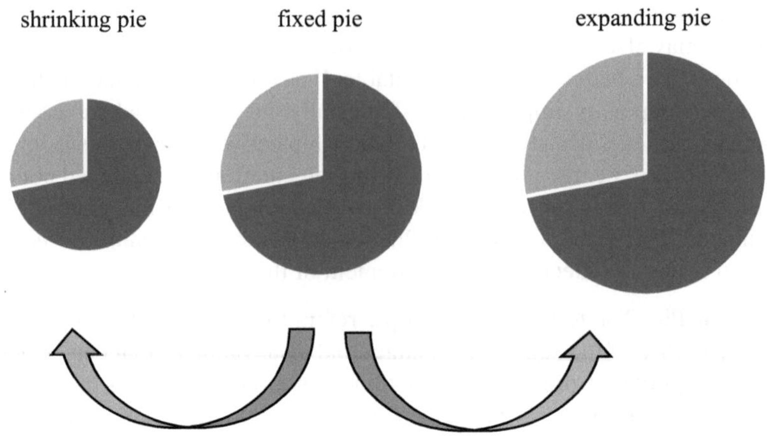

Fig. 3.8 Illustration of the fixed, shrinking and expanding pie

The possibility to increase the pie is more common than negotiators would assume. This is because they are generally subject to → *incompatibility bias*, the distorted perception of non-compatibility, also known as the **illusion of conflict**. As a result, negotiators proceed on the assumption of a fixed pie. This phenomenon is also referred to as **fixed pie illusion** or **fixed pie bias**.[94] In → *distributive negotiations* a fixed pie is generally assumed, meaning that the parties presume they can only gain an advantage at the expense of the opposing party (→ *win-lose strategy*).

Even though negotiations have the primary objective of increasing the size of the pie for distribution between the parties, or alternatively to divide the "fixed" pie, there are many cases in which the negotiation pie even shrinks during negotiations (for instance due to negotiation costs, newly arising competitors, rising project costs etc.). This phenomenon is discussed under the term **shrinking pie.** It is a possibility which must be kept in mind during negotiations and must be taken into particular account under the consideration of the pace of the negotiations. Mutually agreed → *deadlines* can help to regulate an efficient negotiation pace and thus also the transaction costs (Fig. 3.8).

Negotiation Power Negotiation power is not to be confused with negotiation authority, which is used to describe negotiators who negotiate but are not allowed to conclude contracts. Negotiation power refers to the power of a negotiator in negotiations. The own power position includes: (1) the → *BATNA*, (2) the influence on future developments, particularly concerning organisations (**role power**), and (3) the element of psychological negotiation power. The term "role power" primarily refers to the power associated with the position held by the negotiator (e.g. → *chief negotiator* or managing director of one of the contracting parties). The first two characteristics are objective, whereas psychological negotiating power is a subjec-

[94] Cf. Thompson and Hastie (1990), pp. 98–123; Bazerman and Neale (1983), pp. 211–228.

tive element. Psychological negotiation power can be influenced before a negotiation by the negotiator evoking situations in which s/he felt powerful in the past (in negotiations). → *Imperial gestures* can also help the negotiator to feel more confident and powerful.

This threefold division, which is very common in negotiation literature, is complemented by negotiation competence as a power factor. The entirety of the competences thematised in this book concerning the procurement of power, prevention of mistakes, techniques, tactics, strategies as well as the cooperation between the negotiators etc. can have a significant impact on the final negotiation result. The power of this factor depends not only on the corresponding competence of the opposing party but also on the complexity of the specific negotiation. The more complex the negotiation subject and the negotiations in general are, the more important the negotiation competencies as a factor of power become.

Negotiation power is the lynchpin of negotiations. Since it is often difficult not only to determine the concrete strength of one's own negotiating power, but also the opposing party's negotiating power, in practice, the "felt" negotiating power is of great importance.

Negotiation Value How high the negotiation value is, i.e. how much the negotiation result is worth (negotiation value), depends not only on the concrete results but also on the negotiating standard against which the results are measured. These standards are also called benchmarks or **acceptance criteria**, and they should be both objective and measurable. Furthermore, they should be functionally related to the company's objectives and, in order to prevent manipulation, they should be determined before the parties engage in negotiations.

It is common practice to determine the net value of the negotiation result using the BATNA. The net worth then illustrates what value was created for the own side compared to the BATNA. It is calculated as shown below (Fig. 3.9).

In practice, however, the net value of the negotiation result is rarely documented. This may partly be due to the fact that it is sometimes difficult to determine the own BATNA with sufficient accuracy. Even though the negotiation value is linked to the success of the negotiation, it is not necessarily decisive for the negotiators' satisfaction with the outcome. Negotiators often do not measure the success of negotiations by objective factors, but rather rely on their subjective feelings.

net worth of the concluded deal

− net worth of the BATNA

= net worth of the negotiation result

Fig. 3.9 Negotiation value calculation

Negotiator's Dilemma The **negotiator's dilemma** is a version of the game theoretical prisoner's dilemma.

Excursus
Police suspect that two prisoners have cooperated in a crime and interrogate them both separately. The punishment of the two depends on whether both remain silent, only one remains silent while the other admits the crime or both admit committing the crime. If only one of the prisoners confesses, s/he will receive a shortened sentence of one year in prison as a principal witness, whereas the other offender will be sentenced to seven years. If they both remain silent they cannot be sentenced for lack of evidence. If both suspects admit the crime, they will each receive a five-year prison sentence. The prisoners are thus faced with the dilemma of either confessing to the crime or remaining silent, without knowing how the other prisoner will behave. In the end, it would be best for both prisoners to remain silent. To do this, however, they would have to trust each other. If they do not, they will admit to the crime since this is the best solution from an individual point of view, unless they are sure that the other will remain silent.

Applied to the negotiation situation, this implies that the negotiating parties would oftentimes benefit from cooperating, but sometimes they shy away from it in fear of being taken advantage of and, thus decide to negotiate competitively. The negotiator's dilemma was first described and analysed by *David A. Lax* and *James K. Sebenius*.[95] Potential countermeasures to overcome the negotiator's dilemma are trust-building measures and the (long-term) establishment of parallel interests.

A subset of the negotiator's dilemma is the **information exchange dilemma**. Here too, negotiators would benefit from an exchange of information, but do not act accordingly as they fear the negotiation partner will not behave in a reciprocal manner. Unlike the prisoners' dilemma, the information exchange dilemma is an ongoing process, i.e. information is not exchanged just once (similarly, the prisoner's dilemma can be played several times (finitely and infinitely)). With regard to the exchange of information, it is often recommended that only partial information be disclosed initially, while awaiting the opposing party's reaction. This approach is regarded as a kind of → *signalling*. If the negotiation partner behaves reciprocally, i.e. offers information in return, then further information can be delivered safely.

Hence the exchange of information can be organised in the style of the *generous tit for tat – strategy*. As a matter of principle, even during the preparation for the negotiation it is advisable to start thinking about which information can be exchanged and which information the own side wants to withhold—or at least only disclose under certain conditions during the negotiation. In many cases, it is often more problematic to disclose the intensity of one's own interests rather than disclosing the

[95] Lax and Sebenius (1986), pp. 154 et seqq.

actual interests themselves. Even the announcement of one's own interests can be used by the negotiating partner, should s/he be employing tactics of hard bargaining. However, in order to enlarge the → *negotiation pie,* the exchange of information is essential, since only in this way can the negotiation's full potential be realised.

Negotiauction The term "negotiauction" was invented by *Guhan Subramanian*[96] to describe the fusion of negotiation and → *auction.* The starting point for the development of this strategy was an observation made by *Subramanian* during an experimental negotiation. Contrary to the rules set out in this experiment, the participating students incorporated typical auction elements in two-person negotiations as well as typical negotiation-specific elements in auctions. The main finding is that, in addition to negotiations and auctions, mixed forms are a noteworthy option and thus deserve consideration. In this finding, *Subramanian* above all promotes an extension of the options for action and thus more available options to reach an ideal result. In addition, mixed forms are common in company sales and for the allocation of orders for industrial plants in cases in which the vendor hopes to achieve a better → *BATNA,* to shorten the sales process and to create the type of bidding pressure typically found at auctions. A simple auction is usually out of the question in these cases due to the importance of the contractual conditions to be negotiated. Thus, the seller's first step is to negotiate with several interested parties at the same time, similar to an auction, as to who offers the most, or is willing to supply the good for the lowest possible price. The second step is either a negotiation with the company that submitted the best bid (at least partially implemented in company acquisitions) or a parallel negotiation in the case of several similarly good offers. The starting point for company sales is therefore a low minimum bid instead of starting off with a high demand anchor. Aggressive cherry picking can be frequently observed during the second step.

From time to time, practises comparable to negotiauctions can also be observed in the sale of desirable properties. A potential bidder should demand clear rules, not least so that s/he can influence the performance parameters for his/her own benefit and gain knowledge about the competitors and their strategies. Thorough preparation and a set limit, inter alia based on one's own BATNA, are essential in order not to fall for the so-called "**curse of the winner**".

Non-linear Compromises Negotiators often have the task of achieving a certain goal (e.g. regarding the price). The pressure in this direction is particularly strong if the results of the negotiation are to be published (at least partially), even if only in internal company publications; or if bonuses within the company depend on the goal (regarding the consequential issues also see → *principal-agent-problem*). From the negotiator's point of view, non-linear compromises provide a good alternative here. This implies that the sensitive figures (prices) are relativised by other values that determine the relationship between price and performance. In the following, a non-linear compromise is illustrated by means of differentiated periods of time in wage negotiations:

[96] Cf. Subramanian (2010).

Example
If wages are increased by 3% for the period of 15 months, the trade unions see the important number "3" before the decimal point. However, the effective wage increase calculated for the period of 1 year is under 3%.

The success of this kind of compromise is based on the fact that clients usually only take into account whether or not their target has been met, instead of paying attention to the fulfilment of their interests. Even if the client sees through this mechanism (e.g. in the company), the terms will still often be accepted if the overall result is justifiable because the client is under observation regarding their goals and their achievement. In this way the people involved save their own face, which is particularly relevant if extensive expectations have been raised by stakeholders on one side (→ *think beyond the table*), e.g. trade unions towards their members. The disadvantage of non-linear compromises lies within the position-orientation instead of interest-orientation, the increased complexity of the contract content and the consequential higher costs of the contract implementation.

Norm of Reciprocity Reciprocity is a general psychological principle which also plays a role in the context of negotiations. It means that people tend to reflect the behaviour of the opposite side, regardless of whether the behaviour is positive or negative. Mirror behaviour can accordingly be observed for concessions concerning certain aspects, but as well for → *emotions*, threats help, the exchange of information and → *body language*. It is also irrelevant whether a favour is unsolicited or solicited. If a favour is granted that had previously not been requested, it often happens that more is returned than was received. This secures the balance of debt and particularly emphasised the voluntary nature of giving, since an equal return may seem forced. The fact that even unsolicited favours are subject to the norm of reciprocity implies that the person granting a favour can, at least to a certain extent, determine who owes him/her something, while the recipient's ability to prevent this is limited.

If understood as equal treatment, reciprocity is also a fundamental principle of justice that influences negotiations (**anticipation of reciprocity**). Specifically with regard to negotiations, the expectation of reciprocity leads to the assumption that the negotiating partner will accommodate his/her negotiating partner to the same extent as s/he was accommodated. Hence, it is no coincidence that even in the case of a legally unambiguous situation in favour of one side, legal settlement proposals still include a more than symbolic concession in favour of the losing side. Also the → *midpoint-rule* can be at least partly explained by the norm of reciprocity.

Situations can occur, where both parties consider that they are making "fair" or "justified" demands, and yet no agreement can be achieved. In these instances, it can be helpful to apply the so-called **test of reciprocity**: One has to ask oneself if the own proposal would still be considered as fair and equitable even if one were in the position of the negotiating partner. The point here is to assume the role of the opposing negotiator.

Not Happy Anyone who responds to the negotiating partner's proposal saying s/he is not happy expresses a clear rejection. This tactic consists of signalling one's rejection in a way that is at once not aggressive and yet unmistakable (thus the tone of voice is also essential). The effectiveness of this statement is achieved by directly addressing the → *emotions* of the negotiating partners and by not being formulated as a direct attack (because it is a so-called "I-message"). Ideally, this induces the negotiating partner to make concessions towards the "unhappy" partner. In other words, the tactic is aimed at shifting the anchor (→ *anchoring*), without simultaneously setting a counter-anchor. Even if this is not successful, there is at least the hope that the negotiating partner will explain why s/he considers the proposal to be appropriate. In this way, the negotiator can at least obtain some information. It is, however, right that the opposing party should first of all inquire why the proposal is not pleasing enough and may possibly ask for a counter-proposal (counter-anchor), as long as the justification for the objection cannot be invalidated.

One of the more aggressive tactics aimed at shifting the anchor is remaining silent (→ *silence*).

Open Questions The knowledge obtained about the opposing party is crucial for the success of a negotiation. This refers to information about their aims, interests, preferences and → *negotiation power*. Thus → *questions* are essential in negotiations and influence their eventual success. Open questions—e.g. who, what, when, where, how much, why—are considered to be particularly promising in this respect. This type of question is also referred to as an **open–ended question**. Open questions are so effective because the answer often goes far beyond the actual question. In this way, the negotiator gives away valuable additional information. A key factor here is the negotiator's ability to listen attentively. However, questions which inquire into the conversation partner's attitude (why-questions) are controversial as the other party could interpret these questions as an attack. In some cultures, an excessive number of questions can evoke the impression of a very tactical approach to negotiation, which tends to be answered with rejection. Intensive questions can also be perceived as aggressive. Open questions are not only employed during negotiations to gather information. They are often used in the preceding small talk (→ *chit-chat*) phase as well, in order to positively stimulate the conversation.

Optimism Bias Optimism bias describes over-optimism with regard to the successful outcome of a project, negotiation etc. It is closely linked to the overconfidence bias, which refers to a person's individual capabilities. As risks lie in the future and are probable rather than definite, there is a certain propensity to value risks less than their actual likelihood. This gives rise to over-optimism, which can particularly be observed among business-oriented people. If this were not so, then there would be no trading at all due to risk aversion, which is often encountered.

Orange Example The → *Harvard negotiation concept*'s famous orange example serves to illustrate the differences between position-oriented and interest-oriented negotiation solutions: In the example, two sisters argue over an orange. In the course of a position-oriented agreement, each sister would ask for and possibly receive one half of the orange. However, since one sister needed the juice and the other the peel, an interest-oriented agreement could be designed so that one sister would get all the juice and the other would get all the peel. In this way the interests of both sisters would be satisfied, whereas in the position-oriented negotiation the result would satisfy neither party. A solution in line with the interests of both parties would therefore be clearly superior and preferable to a position-oriented solution.

Organiser For negotiations, it is often recommended to assign the role of organiser to one of the participants on the own side. This seems convincing since the organisational tasks within contract negotiations should not be neglected. Organisational tasks can also be distributed among team members, particularly if the negotiation team is experienced. This then eliminates the need for a special organiser.

Ostensible Connexity It is not uncommon for negotiation points to be combined in such a way that they appear as a unit. It would appear that the only alternative is either to agree to the package or reject it. In contrast to the **package deal**, in which the parties are aware of the fact that different negotiation points are under discussion, the tactic of the ostensible connexity aims at presenting several points as an "inseparable" unit. This is especially the case when one partial aspect seems to be hardly rejectable. The so called → *halo effect* has an impact here, since the arguments in favour of this partial aspect overshadow everything else. It is therefore not obvious that these arguments cannot justify the entire complex encompassed in the negotiation object. It is the negotiating partner's task to identify whether points that are presented as an inseparable unit in the argumentation actually form an authentic unit, or whether a differentiated view is required.

Example

The negotiating partner offers a more generous guarantee than usual, but only under the condition that maintenance is carried out by the supplier in a shorter period of time than usual; this is adequately reflected in the pricing. Maintenance and service are usually only side conditions when purchasing industrial goods, so the buyer will not let these points cause the contract to fail. In this instance, however, it would be more favourable for the buyer to undertake the maintenance himself/herself since the machine is on site and s/he can thus determine the maintenance requirements directly. Furthermore, the buyer can consciously choose a service provider on the basis of certain criteria, or potentially change the provider if necessary, whereas under the circumstance of "ostensible connexity", the buyer would be bound to the supplier's maintenance team.

Padding Padding describes a tactic in which unimportant things are presented as being important in order to subsequently give in to the negotiating partner and be able to grant corresponding concessions. Hence there is deceit regarding one's own preferences and evaluations, although this only constitutes a case of → *cunning deception*. In this way, the own offer is presented as being more attractive; it is "padded", so to speak. It gives the opposing party the feeling of having achieved a major success in the negotiations. This is important since the negotiating partner's satisfaction with the result also influences the relationship between the parties. In contrast to the bogey tactic, padding, as described here, does not require immediate consideration for the granted concession. It is therefore not a question of enforcing one's own demands, but rather of upgrading the own offer and/or improving the relationship with the negotiating partner. If, towards the end of the negotiation, one side grants a concession to the negotiating partner without expecting any concessions in return, this is known as the so-called **delight factor**. In this way, the negotiating partner leaves the negotiations with a sense of achievement, thus retaining a positive last *impression of the negotiations* (→ *impression* (*first and last*)).

Sometimes padding is also used as a synonym for **bogey**. Then it concerns to obtain the greatest possible concession of the negotiating partner for yielding to an unimportant point. Since the evaluation of many aspects is highly subjective and the negotiation partner has also no protection-worthy interest to learn the value, according to opinion of the authors this is a case of → *cunning deception*.

Pareto Optimum This term, named after *Vilfredo Pareto*, represents both a general economic concept as well as a concept for solution optimisation. According to the Pareto optimum, a solution is optimal if there is no other combination of results where one side is in a better position and the other side is not simultaneously placed in a worse position. The search for the Pareto optimum thus describes the search for an optimum solution. Figure 3.10 (The Pareto optimum) illustrates Pareto–optimal solutions and those that are not Pareto optimal.

A Starting point for both negotiators

B Inefficient point: Here negotiator 1 is in a worse position

C Pareto improvement: Both are brought into a more favourable position than in point **A**

D Inefficient point: Both are in a worse position than in point **A**

E Pareto optimum: There is no possible improvement, without putting the other negotiator into a worse position

F Also a pareto-optimal point

G Another Pareto optimum

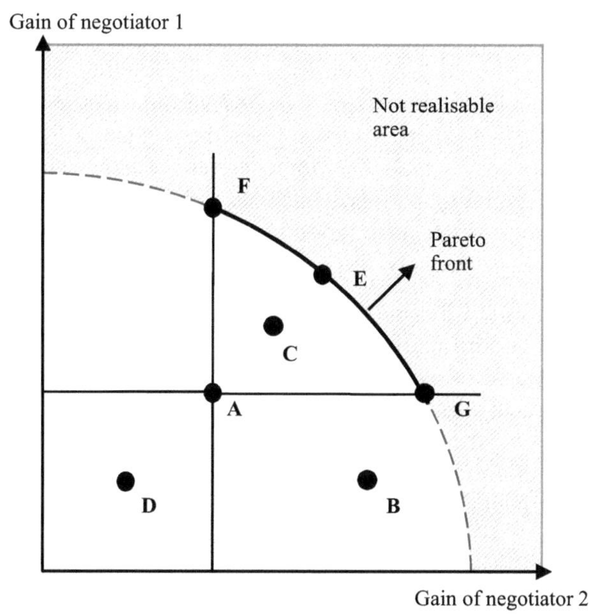

Fig. 3.10 The Pareto optimum

Path Dependency Path dependency is a concept used in the field of social sciences. On the one hand, it can simply refer to the fact that past events have an impact on future events due to causalities (**history matters**). However, the concept is more comprehensive. At the same time, it describes that decisions are influenced by past events, even when they are no longer relevant. Small, random events can consequently have disproportionate implications on future developments. Originally the theory was primarily related to the development of technical standards. In these cases, path dependency is usually based on **network effects** and the *bandwagon effect* (→ *tactic of small quantities*). In this context, path dependency contributed to explain phenomena such as the implementation of the QWERTY-keyboard. What is more problematic is the fact that lock-in effects occur (→ *lock-in tactic*). This means that it is very difficult for participants to abandon or modify existing practice, even in the face of a marked disadvantage.[97]

Within companies and in negotiations, path dependency has the effect that once a path has been chosen, it is often not abandoned for a long time. If the standard practice of the contract negotiations, drafting of contracts and their consequent implementation is to be altered this requires thorough preparation. Hiding the intended change behind a complex construction often proves unsuccessful. On the contrary, due to its complexity this is usually associated with serious disadvantages. The simplest way would be to first find a justification for why, in this case, an exception to usual standard practice should be made (→ *exception argument*). At the same time, it should be by no means disclosed that in fact a general deviation is being pursued, because it is precisely in these instances that alterations are countered with the floodgate argument (→ *floodgate argument*).

Patience Contract negotiations require patience. This applies to the application of tactics as well as to protracted decision-making processes. Patience is worthwhile, especially if the own side's → *BATNA* improves in the course of time and an agreement is not urgent. Patience gives the negotiator the opportunity to overthink difficult and new situations. Moreover, only patience affords enough time to understand the negotiating partner's interests and preferences. Accordingly, patience can contribute to better negotiation results. Patience is closely linked to negotiators' self-control (conversely, there are actions which allow letting-off-steam).

Permanent Business Relations Ongoing business relations are a crucial framework condition of negotiations. In an ongoing business relationship, the negotiation parties assume that there will be further negotiations in future and that more contracts will be concluded. The counterpart to this is one-time negotiations. In the context of ongoing business relations, the parties' relationship is of significant importance. In the long-term, negotiators who maintain a good rapport with their negotiating partners achieve better negotiation results. Accordingly, it is

[97] Sydow et al. (2009), pp. 689–702.

essential to build rapport and confidence in the negotiation. The subjective feelings of the parties regarding success are also essential. One scientific study suggests that this subjective feeling is conducive to future cooperation, regardless of whether the negotiations were successful or not from an objective point of view.[98]

Play Dumb The play dumb negotiation tactic is based on the concept that the negotiating partner will not put much effort into negotiating with a "dumb" or "naïve" negotiating partner as it doesn't seem necessary to do so. At the same time, a clever move made by the seemingly dumb partner is often not discovered because the negotiating partner will assume it is a "dumb" or "naïve" move. The tactic is thus deliberately based on being (severely) underestimated by the other party.

However, it is difficult to play dumb throughout the entire negotiation process; naivety can possibly be faked a little more easily. To simulate this kind of behaviour requires not only acting skills but also a high degree of intellectual modesty.

Moreover, it can happen that the negotiating partner tries to take advantage of the other partner's "stupidity", if it is assumed. At that point at the latest, the seemingly stupid partner has to reveal his/her intelligence. In these cases, in particular, there is a risk that the conclusion of the contract will fail as there will then often be mistrust on both sides. Hence a mitigated form of this tactic may prove more promising regarding results. Playing a (reasonably) "intelligent" partner who just does not always act carefully down to the last detail and who occasionally overlooks points, requires less acting ability and also runs a much smaller risk of the negotiating partner trying to take full advantage of him. Nonetheless, this seemingly occasional inattentiveness can conceal a clever and far-reaching plan (also see under → *Columbo*). It would be worth considering whether a **smart guy/dumb guy-tactic** along the lines of → *good guy/bad guy* might be possible and, above all, sensible. The "dumb" partner could make far-reaching proposals in his/her naivety, and also freely address problematic points with the freedom of a "fool", which could otherwise only be expressed for the other side with loss of face.

Precedent Concerning previous cases, two tactics can be differentiated: the first tactic (**no precedent**) is aimed at blocking the negotiating partner's request. For this purpose, one side points out that nothing like this has ever been done before, which is why this tactic is also known as "**we have never done that before**" or "**that would set a precedent**". In order to emphasise the fact that it is not possible to make concessions in this way, the argument is often made that these conditions would then have to be granted to all customers (→ *floodgate argument*) and thus is not feasible. The conversation partner can attempt to counter these arguments with an → *exception argument* which accordingly places the own position in a broader

[98] Cf. Curhan et al. (2010), pp. 690–709.

context. Sometimes the opposing partner's demands are also blocked by referring to company policy. The rejection of the demand is justified with → *path dependency*, which ensures that not only people but organisations as well rarely leave paths once entered.

Conversely, there is also the tactic of the precedence, which aims at setting a successful precedent as the future rule for these cases. Since the opposing party already accepted the desired compromise once, it is more difficult to reject it when it is requested again. The precedent case can therefore have the effect of shifting the → *burden of justification*.

Premise Question Premise questions can be described as questions that assume a premise—hence also called subordination questions—that the questioner is not (yet) entirely sure of and is therefore followed up by a subsequent question. The person answering the question is often unaware that the answer confirms the premise that the questioner had previously only suspected.

Example
Customer: "How do you intend to compensate for the departure of your best engineer X?" (premise to be verified: departure of engineer X).

Contractor: "There is nothing to worry about. We have already found an extremely skilled replacement for X. She will take over from X in March" (Contractor thus confirms premise).

The information gain is achieved by the fact that the opposite side does not regard the premise as the subject of a question and, due to the wording of the question, often assumes that the questioner is already in possession of this information. Moreover, coping with the premise question often proves difficult, which is why most of the energy of the person answering is invested in giving a tactically skilful answer to the follow-up question—without realising that the premise itself is the hidden object of the question. This questioning technique may be combined with the *Columbo tactic* (→ *Columbo*) or can be used in other situations, wherever possible taking advantage of the opposing party's lack of attention. The technique → *knocking on the bush* follows a very similar direction.

Prenegotiation Plan A prenegotiation plan is a guideline for the preparation of contract negotiations. The prenegotiation plan and contract checklists can be integrated to ensure comprehensive negotiation preparation (according to the → *80-20-rule*). A prenegotiation plan could for example be designed as follows:

1. Identification of the relevant parties and actors,
2. Definition of key issues and aspects,
3. Determining the necessary information (→ *information demand analysis*),
4. Information procurement,

5. Determining the own interests,
6. Determining the negotiating partner's interests,
7. Determining one's own → *BATNA* (including possible improvements of one's own BATNA as well as risks which might lead to a deterioration of the BATNA, i.e. a dynamic view of the BATNA),
8. Determining the negotiating partner's BATNA (also based on a dynamic view),
9. Formulation of objectives,
10. Interim goals,
11. Options for action in order to achieve the objectives, including interim goals,
12. Contract preparation,
13. Determining a strategy and corresponding tactics,
14. Developing an → *agenda*, if this task has not been taken over by the negotiating partner, also see fallacy, formal control and
15. Further organisational tasks (determining the negotiation venue, the negotiation timeframe etc.).

The plan needs to be adapted to each individual negotiation as many points depend on the respective framework conditions (are the negotiations a single text procedure? If so, who is providing the text? Are the negotiations held within an → *permanent business relation*? Or is it a one-time negotiation? etc.). Hence, a company may have different prenegotiation plans for different circumstances. Further structuring the priorly mentioned steps, such as determining the negotiation partners' BATNA, may be useful, for instance this could comprise conducting a specific information demand analysis.

Presenting a False Legal Opinion The deliberate assertion of a false legal opinion was already mentioned in *Arthur Schopenhauer's* manuscript (Eristic Dialectic) ca.1830 as stratagem 28, described as **argumentum ad auditores**. For legal questions, there is a wide margin of justification and also room for purely subjective opinions (e.g. "in my view, this is not legally acceptable"). This can also be used tactically, but it is not legally relevant. The other side cannot derive any information from such statements. There is, however, also the intentional presentation of a false legal view as a deceptive tactic. In negotiations, this deceptive tactic is mostly used to represent something as being illegal or at least legally risky (**unfounded, legal objections**) and thus fend it off. Much less frequently, something is presented as being lawful that is in fact not permissible. In this instance, one is more aware of the legal consequences, so therefore more indirect statements are common, e.g. a seller describes the possible uses of a device, which indirectly implies from the other side's view that these uses are also legal. The deceptive tactic of putting forward a false legal view is particularly common if the other party's negotiator is not in a position to assess the incorrectness and there is a fairly low risk that this legal position will be further questioned due to e.g. time pressure, cost reasons etc. Even when there is a not insignificant likelihood of a legal review, this tactic is still frequently used because its intention can hardly be verified. Often, however, no unjustifiable legal view is expressed, but rather views that are legally justifiable—which, however, will and should be understood differently by the other side. It should however be borne in mind that such behaviour can endanger the contractual relationship, since lies and pretension are considered immoral, at least by some negotiators.

Should the opposing parties' negotiator normally be able to judge this legal question according to his/her own self-image, but in the concrete situation is not capable of doing so, the deception is often formulated using the phrase: "as you know".

Example
"As you know, there are serious concerns in legal literature against such a clause. I don't think we should risk the invalidity of this clause".

In order not to disclose his/her ignorance, the negotiating partner may not object and may even waive a further examination. With this deceptive tactic, the question arises as to whether negligence (at least existing) or the intent of the person expressing the false legal opinion can give rise to reason damage claims at all, i.e. the question is whether this deception is unlawful. In the sense of the concept of → *cunning deception* depicted in this book, this is a borderline case which is difficult to assess.

Principal-Agent-Problem A principal-agent-problem, in some instances also known as **agency dilemma** or **agency theory**, arises when a principal commissions someone to act as his/her agent; here, to negotiate and make decisions in his/her place. This constellation is problematic, since the principal and agent generally possess neither the same degree of knowledge, nor do they necessarily pursue the same interests. This theory was developed in the 1970s without direct reference to contract negotiations.[99] Accordingly, this theory finds application not only in the field of economic sciences, but also in the context of social and political science. Its importance for contractual negotiations follows from the fact that the actual → *decision-makers* do not attend the negotiations themselves in most cases, but rather instruct negotiators to act on their behalf. However, even if a decision-maker negotiates on his own behalf, the issue of the agency dilemma cannot be entirely ruled out. This is due to the fact that only in very rare cases the decision-maker is also the actual owner of the company s/he represents. Due to multiple hierarchy levels within the company, a so-called "multilevel agency dilemma" arises.

The first difficulty of the principal-agent-situation lies with the initial selection of the agent. In some circumstances, the principal may not know the agent and his/her characteristics and attributes (**hidden characteristics**) which may lead to the problem of adverse selection. The advantage of company negotiations is that in many cases, the decision-maker has been working with the agent for a sufficient amount of time and is therefore often able to assess the agent and his/her negotiation abilities quite well.

[99] Based on Jensen and Meckling (1976), pp. 305–360.

A second issue of the principal-agent-situation refers to information asymmetry. On the one hand, representatives (agents) of lower hierarchy levels usually possess more detailed (specialist) information due to having direct contact with the negotiating partner. This puts them in the position of having an informational advantage (**hidden knowledge**). Conversely, however, oftentimes the representative's superiors do not provide the full information. Hence, the agent cannot fully deduce the actual interests of the company s/he is to represent. The representative is therefore often not made aware of strategic interests of the represented company because, from the point of view of the company's management, there is a need for confidentiality. Not being aware of these interests however, the agent cannot take them into account and represent them. **Hidden actions** are also possible, because the decision-maker is not sitting at the negotiating table and therefore cannot observe all the representative's actions. This problematic situation can give rise to → *moral hazard,* an issue which is essential in the context of the principal-agent issue.

Representatives (agents) certainly have their own interests that do not necessarily reflect those of the principal. These interests can arise in particular from reward or penalty systems used within the represented company. Individual interests arise strikingly often with regard to premium systems that pay a flat rate for the successful conclusion of contracts. In this way, they may create an individual incentive to conclude contracts even in cases where it would not be advisable for the company to do so. Developing incentive-compatible reward systems is therefore a highly demanding task, especially since the company's interests are often not rigid, but are rather determined within a dynamic process. Reward systems should comply dynamically, corresponding to the company's changing requirements. Even without reward systems, the prospect of approval or criticism, promotion or the end of a career, can substantially influence the negotiator's interests. Negotiators thus perhaps do not always represent the true interests of the company in the required manner (**hidden intentions**). In practice, some agents attempt to take advantage of these circumstances by aiming at agent oriented negotiations. In contractual negotiations this involves the so-called **trust dilemma.**[100] The more an agent is trusted and thus granted real freedom of decision, the better the agent can use the freedom to create advantages in cooperation with the opposing side, i.e. to increase the → *negotiation pie* in the interest of both parties. In contrast, these possibilities for intensive cooperation also increase the risk of potential abuse. Companies frequently attempt to limit the risks for their own negotiator, e.g. by implementing the → *principle of dual control.* If two negotiators have been instructed, it becomes more difficult for the individual negotiators to achieve individual motives and interests that disagree with the company interests in the negotiations. In order for this control mechanism to work, both negotiators need to be interested and determined in fulfilling this specific "control" function. If, however both negotiators collusively follow the same hidden intentions, the control mechanism will prove futile. In order

[100] Cutcher-Gershenfeld and Watkins (1999), p. 35 et seqq.

to safeguard the company's interests, representatives from the highest levels of hierarchy need to attend important negotiation rounds.

Closely linked to the trust dilemma, is the so-called **flexibility dilemma**. When principals and agents reach clear agreements to combat the risks of the principal-agent-problem, this is inevitably to the detriment of flexibility during negotiations. Clear guidelines can, however, also help the negotiator to defend himself/herself against the aggressive negotiating tactics of the other side as s/he can then point out the strict instructions s/he has been given governing room for negotiation. The other side of the coin also concludes that the negotiator usually does not have the leeway to develop alternative solutions that would serve the interests of the company best. Establishing a high level of trust and the implementation of a reasonable reward system can provide efficient alternatives to pre-setting strict negotiation guidelines, which may inhibit the level of flexibility in the negotiation.

Another problematic aspect is the **transformation dilemma**. On the one hand, companies appreciate the negotiator's effort to transform the interests of the company into creative solutions in order to maximise the benefits deriving from the negotiation. On the other hand, deviating from instructions which ultimately also have a positional element, or deviating from the norm as a rule can often have a negative impact for the negotiator. In some instances, creating individual solutions is not rewarded but sometimes even sanctioned. Any negotiator deviating from the usual or specific orders s/he has been given is thus liable to justify his/her actions to the company, even if the negotiators motivation to do so was to benefit the company.

In addition to the danger that the innovation is generally not advantageous, or contradicts the strategic interests of the company (that are not known to the negotiator), there is a further risk that the innovation will not be understood, e.g. due to a lack of willingness to accept it from the company's management. The transformation dilemma could be diminished if the companies implemented a suggestion scheme for contractual improvements, comparable to those already in place for technical or administrative procedures.

With the principal-agent-problem, two areas of negotiation emerge: One being the negotiations between the agent and the actual negotiating partner (**negotiations at the table**) and the other being the internal negotiations, as between the agent and his/her principal (**negotiations "behind the table"**) (the keyword → *think beyond the table* not only addresses negotiations between the agent and the principal but has a considerably broader scope for various constellations). In practice, this often leads for instance to negotiations between a seller and a buyer. Desired clauses brought forward by the negotiator at the table must first be internally agreed with the head of the responsible department as well as with the legal department in the → *back office*. This shows that, in companies, there is often more than one principal within the company with whom the contract terms have to be agreed. In the same manner, several agents can act for one or more principals simultaneously. This is often the case particularly in contract negotiations, since in practice teams of two negotiators regularly act for one company (→ *principle of dual control*, → *two negotiators*).

In order to reduce the negative effects associated with the principal-agent-problem in contract negotiations, the company has various measures at its disposal (some of which have already been addressed):

First of all, the company can implement incentive systems, which allow the agent to act in the interests of the principal. Developing an appropriate corporate culture can also serve the same purpose. The pursuance of exact content guidelines is a further effective means. The four-eye principle is a control mechanism whereby negotiators exercise mutual control. Further controls can be structured according to the company hierarchy. In principle, it is possible to overcome information asymmetries by improving the flow of information. Communication between the different hierarchy levels is one of the key factors here, regarding both directions (**downward communication** as well as **bottom-up communication**).

The result from the principal's point of view is that appointing an agent leads to costs (**agency costs**). These include the costs for measures to combat the principal-agent-problem, as well as costs deriving from the potential negative effect of the agent's hidden intentions and hidden knowledge etc. (Fig. 3.11).

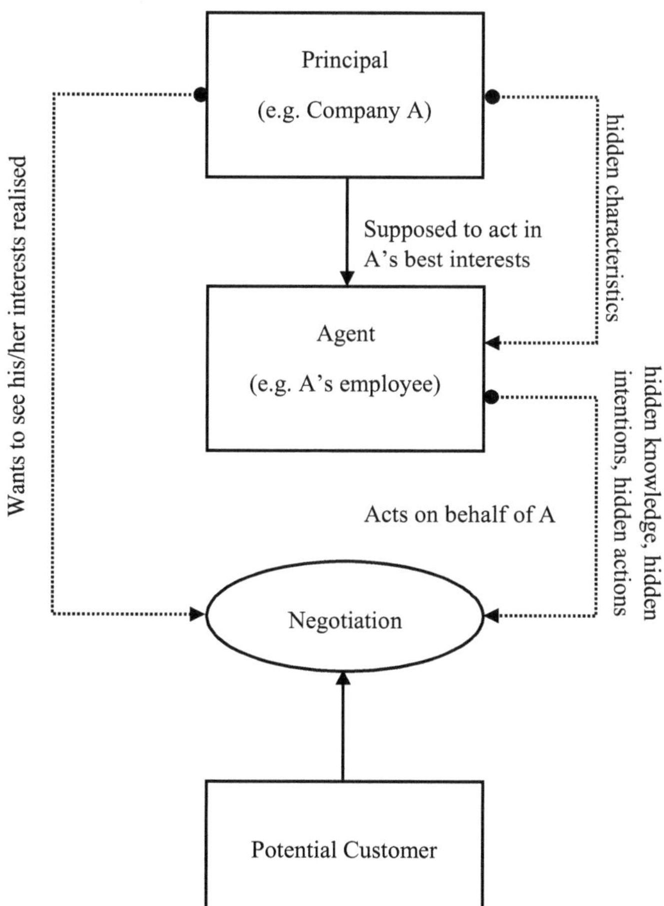

Fig. 3.11 The principal-agent-situation and the resulting problems thereof

Principle of Dual Control Also known as the **two-men rule**, this is a control mechanism. Decisions made by one single individual are prone to mistakes and abuse. Two people can check each other and thus prevent → *mistakes* and abuse. There is also the option of variation in the negotiation, for example by subject area (so called **zone defence**), whereby the person currently not negotiating can assume the role of → *analyst*. The principle of dual control can also help to overcome the → *principal-agent-problem*. In order for the four-eye principle to work properly, there can be no relation of dependency between the people involved. Given the size of the team, the coordination effort is still fairly low yet the benefits are relatively high.

The four-eye principle is not to be confused with negotiating under four eyes, in which two negotiators negotiate together, one on one. In particularly sensitive situations, e.g. when starting a trial balloon, it may be advisable to negotiate under four eyes, even if negotiations otherwise involve a whole team.

In practice, the four-eye principle is a frequently occurring example of the so-called **multiple-eye-check**, because even larger groups consisting of 3 or 4 people also exercise mutual control. The size of a negotiation team depends on the task at hand and other framework conditions. Bigger negotiation teams have certain advantages to the extent that the negotiators' specific competencies can be pooled and used in combination. At the same time, however, the problem arises of coordinating the negotiators on the own side. Bigger teams are thus generally more cumbersome and sometimes also less effective. Even in large negotiations it is therefore often advisable not to exceed a team size of six negotiators. Nonetheless, some negotiations cannot avoid bigger negotiation teams due to the complexity of the negotiation process.

The general authority of representation implements the four-eye principle with regards to the negotiators' authority to conclude the contract. General representative authority requires that two agents jointly act on behalf of the represented person to effectively conclude the contract. For example, managing directors and other directors can be granted joint authority of representation.

Protect Your BATNA Time and again, the negotiating partners tactics focus on weakening their opponent's → *BATNA*, e.g. exclusive negotiations, delaying (→ *calculated delay*) or accelerating negotiations, limitations to technical systems (→ *change the standards*) by means of a small first deal and required preliminary work (cf. → *renegotiations*). It is the negotiator's task to examine the consequences for the own BATNA at every step of the way and to prevent or counteract any deterioration of the own BATNA. Protect your BATNA!

Protocols Negotiation protocols are a means to summarise the (interim) results of negotiations. There are different kinds of protocols. On the one hand, it is possible to distinguish protocols according to the person who is in charge of writing them. Frequently, the two negotiating parties jointly determine someone to take the minutes and keep track of the negotiation results (see further under → *rule of pen*).

By logging the negotiation progress → *misunderstandings* between the negotiating parties can be prevented and—though the negotiation as such has no legally binding effect—a certain pressure of justification arises if one side wants to deviate from the previously recorded (interim) results (→ *interim results*). This usually even applies when negotiations are conducted according to the principle "nothing is agreed until everything is agreed". Often, each side also records the results of the negotiation for themselves, i.e. each party has appointed a minute-taker. This inter alia serves to provide information for people on the own side who are not present at the table (e.g. the → *decision-maker*). The binding pressure created by this recording is clearly less intense than with a jointly created protocol.

Above that, protocols can be distinguished according to their content. Protocols, only documenting results are short result protocols (→ *interim results*). Progress protocols however, document exactly who said what. The latter are rarely used in economic negotiations, since they are very laborious and prone to cause conflicts, but do not imply a particular benefit. The opposite is true for the area of political negotiations. These negotiations are structured into several negotiation rounds, where in some rounds no actual content is negotiated further, but the negotiators rather present already prepared statements "for the record". These statements are then oftentimes recorded "word-for-word". The party writing the protocol can claim a certain advantage (see under → *rule of pen*).

Put Your Money Where Your Mouth Is Manufacturers often have the problem to convince customers of the higher quality of their products in comparison to competing products. The phrase "Put your money where your mouth is!" is meant to indicate that the manufacturer should signal the quality of his/her products by, for example, granting a guarantee for the measurable difference in quality. If the product really is better, competitors will not be able to offer the same guarantee.

Questions Questions are a key component of negotiations. They primarily serve the purpose of gathering information (→ *open questions*, but also → *premise questions*). However, → *closed questions* (→ *Yes/No questions* and → *A-not-A-questions*) in particular disclose the existing level of information on the own side to the conversation partner. It is also not uncommon to ask something which is already known to the person asking. This is done to test the honesty of the other side (test-questions). Questions can also urge the other party to make a final decision, or they can be a means of argumentation disguised as a question. Questions can also be used to formulate an otherwise firm rejection less severely. Moreover, questions can buy time to think through a problem or deliberately delay the negotiation. The aim of a particular question depends on the nature of the negotiation. Within the framework of → *win-lose strategies,* questions often aim at obtaining pieces of information that support the own argumentation, or that can be used as a counter-argument against the other party's argumentation. The latter often induces negotiators to refrain from → *sharing information*, in order to reduce the risk of information being used to the detriment of the own side. If the parties are striving for a win-win solution (→ *win-win strategy*), questions primarily serve to find out the interests and preferences in order to enlarge the → *negotiation pie*. According to a study carried out by *Neil Rackham* and *John Carlisle*,[101] successful negotiators invest 20% of their total speaking time in questions as opposed to the 10% spent by negotiators whose results are average. A successful negotiator thus spends twice as much time asking questions as an average negotiator. For further information on the different questioning techniques see the respective topic lists in the appendix.

Reactive Devaluation This term refers to the effect of reflexive devaluation, i.e. a *cognitive bias* (→ *bias*) within the field of → *behavioural economics,* first described by *Lee Ross* and *Constance Stillinger*.[102] According to this effect, the evaluation of a proposal also specifically depends on the person who submits it. If the proposal is presented by an opponent, it will be deemed worse than if it came from a neutral third party, or from someone in the own negotiation team. This effect can also be observed during negotiations, presumably because the other party is often not perceived as a negotiating "partner" but rather as an opponent. Concessions made by the opposing side are thus often rated as less valuable than they actually are. It may therefore be advisable to just hint at a compromise, so that the negotiating partner can develop it further (→ *incomplete solutions*). This induces the suggestion that the proposal comes from the negotiating partner. Engaging a neutral third party (such as a notary) can also prevent the occurrence of reactive devaluation.

Reference Point The evaluation of a solution or condition is usually not possible in an absolute sense. The relation to other situations is often decisive. How people evaluate something thus depends on the reference point they use: Depending on the reference point, a solution is regarded as good or bad, or as a profit or loss for the own side. Ultimately, this process can be categorised as → *framing*. Other, similar situations are the respective reference points against which the current situation is compared. Hence, reference points are essential for the negotiation process. They decide whether a result is perceived as fair or unfair. Therefore, it is important to discover and enforce reference points that are advantageous for the own side.

In 1981, *Tversky* and *Kahneman* conducted a study to examine the significance of reference points, i.e. the importance of *framing*.[103] It makes practical sense to first communicate a common → *reference point* and then find a common result based on the → *anchoring*.

---

[101] Rackham and Carlisle (1978a), pp. 6, 9.

[102] Ross and Stillinger (1991), pp. 389–404.

[103] Tversky and Kahneman (1981), esp. p. 457.

Study
The probands were asked to imagine that they are in the process of buying a calculator for 15 $ when the salesman approaches and tells them that the exact same calculator is in a clearance sale in a different subsidiary, a twenty-minute drive away. The majority of the participants (68%) said they would buy the calculator in the other shop if it meant they could save 5 $.

Another test group was asked the same question, except that this time the price of the calculator was 125 $. In this case, only 29% of respondents said they were willing to drive to the other store for a 5 $ discount.

Refusal to Communicate Out of tactical reasons, at any time in the negotiations one party may (suddenly) entirely refuse to communicate (rejection of communication). This approach often serves to win time. The refusal to communicate is therefore one possibility to cause a delay in negotiations (→ *calculated delay*). This tactic is frequently used in conflict situations, and here especially by negotiators that like to avoid conflicts and want to sit the conflict out.

This strategy is particularly widespread in written correspondence (mail or → *e-mail*), but also during phone calls, e.g. when the assistant/secretary excuses the conversation partner. In this case, the opposing party often attempts to resume communication by sending follow-up e-mails or by making new calls. Particularly in the context of → *permanent business relations*, one side often does not want to approach the next escalation stage too quickly. Hence, in many cases the party first observes a waiting-period before threatening the other party with terminating the negotiations etc., and the threat usually contains a → *deadline*. Moreover, the negotiating partner often finds it very uncomfortable to break off the relationship with the negotiating partner without any direct communication with the opposing party. In this way, the side refusing to communicate can win time. However, this behaviour can cause lasting damage to the parties' relationship and is therefore only to be used if time cannot be gained by mutual agreement.

If the opposing party's negotiator is trying to avoid a conflict situation and therefore refuses to communicate, it can be helpful to point out possible solutions within the framework of establishing contact with the negotiator. Above that, it is highly recommended to not act in a threatening and dominant way.

Renegotiations In Western cultures holding post-negotiations or renegotiations after the conclusion of a contract is oftentimes regarded as a sign of lack of adherence to the contract. Therefore—subject to serious reasons—this is usually frowned upon. In other cultures, (e.g. China, see also Sect. 4.2), where the actual contractual agreement is less important and negotiating and fulfilling a contract are understood as a "living process", the attempt to renegotiate is not perceived as negative.

However, also in Western cultures negotiations do not necessarily end with the conclusion of the contract. This particularly applies to the B2B sector and also includes the contractual terms and conditions already negotiated. The commencement of renegotiations can have various reasons. In continuing obligations and long-term cooperations, circumstances may change and thus trigger the need to adapt the contract. The respective contracts often contain so called → *negotiation clauses*. In order to prevent a premature escalation of disputes, negotiation clauses determine that the parties should first attempt to solve the problem through negotiation. Only then is it possible to appeal e.g. to an arbitration tribunal.

One subcategory of renegotiations are **opportunistic renegotiations** which become possible if the → *negotiation power* has shifted subsequently, as is the case with transaction-specific products or investments that cannot easily be used for other purposes. This can lead to so-called "**hold-up problems**", which refer to the circumstance that the side whose negotiation power increased substantially in a later stage of the negotiation will attempt to shift the negotiation result to their advantage.

The demands for so-called "wedding discounts" towards suppliers are also notorious if a major customer has taken over another (also potential) major customer. Although such conduct is often contrary to antitrust law during ongoing contracts as abuse of market power (prohibition of abuse of a dominant market position), it is nevertheless practised because the supplier risks the business relationship if he/she reports to the antitrust authorities. Even outside wedding discounts, such projects can only be partially avoided by carefully drafting contracts ex ante. If a party tries to get its negotiating partner to make investments with regard to a possible contract, e.g. through → *empty promises*, in order to be able to renegotiate in its own favour afterwards, this is also referred to as an over-commitment tactic.

On the other hand, renegotiations could also be used to increase the → *negotiation pie* and to achieve an even better negotiation result for both parties. At first glance this idea seems very unusual and is not very common in practice. However, an existing agreement takes the pressure off the negotiations. At any rate, it constitutes a safe alternative for the renegotiated contract conclusion. After an agreement has been reached, the parties may be willing to disclose their key interests and preferences. This could in return increase the → *negotiation pie*. The parties could then negotiate the added value and amend the original contract accordingly for a better result.

Respect Respect is an essential framework condition for successful negotiating. If the negotiating partner lacks general respect for the other side, negotiations quickly run the danger of failing. This applies even if the lack of respect felt by the other party is only perceived rather than actually existent.

Even rationally oriented negotiators have difficulties to accept attacks, and lack of respect certainly constitutes such a attack, on the own person. If the opposing party is uncertain regarding their own self-esteem, they will value respect particularly highly. This implies in turn that a convincing expression of respect in these cases can have a positive influence on the climate of the negotiation. Respect and appreciation are closely linked to one another (for this topic area also see under → *core concerns framework*).

Retracking the Deal In negotiations, especially if they are extensive, a particular negotiation point might be very quickly forgotten, which can give rise to problems. It therefore makes sense to go through the whole contract once again before concluding it, in order to pick up on any points which might potentially have been overlooked and improve their formulations. Doing so also affords the opportunity to bring up a topic that was not forgotten but held back purposely (→ *salami tactic*).

Rule of Pen The term rule of pen refers to the advantage enjoyed by the person who, in the context of contract negotiations, sets the compromises reached (→ *interim results*) in written form, and amends the contract draft (→ *single-text negotiation*) in accordance with the agreement reached; or who keeps the minutes (→ *protocols*): The recording clerk has a greater influence on the exact wording than any of the other people present. Small advantages for the own side can be achieved by single words or individual details (also see → *foggy recall*). The recorded results must however generally correspond with what has actually been agreed as otherwise the negotiation trust could be damaged substantially.

Russian Front Based on movies and series, there is the widespread opinion in the U.S. that German soldiers were intimidated during the Second World War with the threat of being posted to the Russian front. This was supposed to induce them to strictly behave according to certain rules. The name of the tactic alludes to this: The opposing party has the choice between an intimidating, and at the very least dissuasive option and one which, although far from good, is at least acceptable. The opposing party will "voluntarily" choose the less intimidating option. This tactic is applied whenever a "voluntary" decision is required from the negotiating partner for a certain option for whatever reason. As likely as not, this negotiation tactic finds application, if at all, in the relationship between superiors and employees rather than in B2B relations.

Salami Tactic The salami tactic is probably one of the best-known negotiation tactics. Shortly before the conclusion of the contract, small claims are repeatedly brought forward by the negotiator "bit by bit". The negotiating partner may accept these demands out of consideration for the contract which is about to be closed. In a broader sense, the salami tactic also comprises cases in which small demands are not only brought forward immediately before the contract is concluded, but throughout the whole negotiation. In these cases, the main idea behind the tactic is the inconspicuousness of the individual demand: By demands being made "bit by bit", the negotiator is potentially moved to grant more concessions than s/he would do if all demands were presented at the same time. On the other hand, this tactic will often lead to a deterioration of the negotiating climate (especially if the demands are concentrated in the period before the contract is concluded).

In the English-speaking world, there are many synonyms for the salami tactic, e.g. **fractioning**, **the nibble**, **nibbling**, the sentence: "**just one more thing**", **add-ons** or the term **quivering quill**. This latter refers to the situation in which one party already has the pen in his/her hand to sign the contract but hesitates; and in this instant, additional demands are made. Sometimes an additional demand is introduced with the words "Did I forget to tell you (…)?", followed e.g. by charges and surcharges, which had not been included in the price until then.

The basic underlying idea of the tactic is that a conclusion of a contract should usually not be brought down by small details, since the parties have already achieved an agreement regarding various substantial points. The negotiating partner is therefore induced to make concessions concerning these small demands. One way to prevent this approach is to consistently make counterclaims (also see → *keep something in reserve*). Another option is to agree with the negotiating partner that all demands must be made by a certain point in time. Agreeing on this procedure makes it much more difficult to add unannounced demands, even if such an "agreement" is normally not legally enforceable. Another way of counterfeiting this tactic is strictly sticking to the so-called principle of "nothing is agreed until anything is agreed". In this way, if one side makes use of the salami tactic, the other side can equally initiate renegotiating points it has already agreed to.

Another tactic related to the salami tactic is the **after agreement demand**, in which (usually minor) additional demands are made after an agreement has already been reached (→ *renegotiation*).

See You in Court Beyond the literal sense, "I will see you in court" can be understood as a threat to involve a higher or public authority, or a court. The escalation of a dispute is at issue. All variations of this threat—i.e. calling a higher authority, publicity, a court—can be effective. This applies in particular to the threat of legal clarification. This is because legal clarification often incurs very high costs (workload within the company, lawyer's fees, court costs, disruption of business relations, reputational damage), which can, even if the litigation is won, only be partially compensated. The threat of litigation is thus often not economically advisable (for either party), since there is always uncertainty concerning the outcome of the legal dispute. Threatening the start of legal proceedings can therefore easily constitute a lose-lose scenario. In the other forms listed here, this problem does not arise to the same extent. As a rule, this threat is formulated with linguistic restraint to prevent an emotional escalation of the conflict. In the event of an open threat, some negotiators tend not to give in, even against rational reasoning.

The issue of legality, which is important for many threats, does not generally arise with regard to threats to take legal measures. It is true that legal disputes can have a substantial negative impact. However, the right to judicially review legal opinion in court is an essential component of the rule of law. This is the reason why not only the legal process but also the threat of taking legal measures cannot depend on the justification of the claims. In B2B relations, there are only very few constellations in which the threat of legal recourse proves to be immoral.

As with any threat, the person making them needs to express clearly whether s/he will actually follow it through. To do this, s/he has to think through the scenario and estimate the potential consequences. If the person issuing the threat is not prepared to bear the consequences, s/he would suffer a loss of credibility and → *negotiating power* by simply threatening to apply sanctions or an action but not carrying them out. If the opposing party gives in to the threat, this could also be very risky as the party may seek revenge. Either the position of the person making the threat is so strong that s/he doesn't have to fear any serious disadvantages when the contract is implemented or in any other instance; or s/he should at least initiate an intensive reconciliation strategy once the threat has been made.

Seven Elements of Negotiation The seven elements of negotiation refer to an approach for the support of successful negotiations, developed by *Bruce Patton.*[104] The seven thematised elements include:

1. Interests,
2. Alternatives,
3. Options,
4. Legitimacy,
5. Commitments,
6. Relationship and
7. Communication.

The primary task is to determine and analyse the interests of both parties. In this regard, the term alternative designates alternatives to the conclusion of a contract (whereas the best alternative is the → *BATNA*). Options however, refer to possible options of how the interests can be realised in the course of a contract. Realising both party interests requires the approval of both sides, while each party can unilaterally decide to pursue an alternative to the contract agreement. The interests of both parties and the resultant demands should by all means be legitimised. This simultaneously contributes to a good rapport between the parties. The element of "communication" emphasises the significance of good communication for the overall negotiation success. On the whole, this approach includes various aspects, which can be found in the general negotiation literature, particularly in the course of the → *Harvard negotiation concept*.

Several Small Concessions People are more pleased with frequent—albeit smaller—victories than with one big victory at once. Referring to defeat and loss, the exact opposite applies. People can accept one big loss or defeat more easily than several small ones. This conclusion is called **hedonic framing.**[105] When applied to contract negotiations the conclusion is, that it is better to make smaller concessions more frequently and to allow the negotiating partner small negotiation successes more often than to grant the opposing party every concession regarding their

[104] *Patton* in: Moffitt and Bordone (Eds.) (2005), 3rd pt., chap. 18.

[105] Cf. Thaler (1999), pp. 183–206.

demands at once. Conversely, several pieces of bad news should be presented to the negotiating partner at once. These findings cannot, however, be directly transferred to the demands in negotiations ("bad news"). Particularly in these instances, it would be more sensible to use the → *salami tactic*. It should also be considered that too much bad news at once can cause the termination of a negotiation, while this could have been prevented had the pieces of bad news been presented separately, each at different times. This effect can also be used in the presentation of an offer. It is better to mention several smaller concessions than presenting the whole sum of advantages granted in one piece. This tactic is also called **smart bundling** (smartly tying packages of demands and concessions).

Sharing Information Sharing information with the other party, can build trust and substantially contribute to enlarging the → *negotiation pie*. In this context, it is particularly important to exchange information about interests in order to find *common interests*, or at least *divergent interests* and reveal *conflicting interests* (cf. → *Harvard negotiation concept*). The sharing of information is thus a decisive factor for the success of negotiations. Sharing information is particularly necessary and advisable in interest-oriented, integrative negotiations. It is not expected—and indeed it would not make sense—that the negotiating partner will be provided with all relevant information. Especially with regard to sensitive information, it should be considered beforehand whether and, if so, how this information should be disclosed to the negotiating partner (→ *information control*). In the case of information disclosure, it should be considered whether the exchange and possible transfer of information should be regulated (e.g. by way of a NDA (non-disclosure agreement)).

In order to exchange relevant information, it is crucial that there is a high degree of negotiation trust between the parties, as otherwise the information exchange dilemma (→ *negotiator's dilemma*) arises. Both parties generally fear that the other side will not disclose equally valuable information and may perhaps use the information gained to achieve unilateral negotiation success. If a particularly large amount of information is shared by one side, the negotiating partner might perceive this as a sign of weakness. The danger of this is particularly high if the negotiators themselves are very restrained in sharing information. There will therefore often be a cautious probing when sharing information and some kind of → *generous tit for tat* will be used.

When selecting information, it must carefully be ensured that the overall picture is not misleading, as otherwise liability for misleading information could arise.

Signalling Whether intentionally or not, both negotiation sides constantly send signals (e.g. by → *body language*). Negotiating partners should therefore endeavour—to the extent possible—to monitor the sent signals and should in advance be aware of the signals they want to send, as this can have a significant impact on the negotiation outcome. If one negotiating party sends out signals that justify trust, there is a greater chance that the opposing side will enter into a trusting negotiation. On the other hand, signals can cause the negotiating partner to negotiate competitively. Particularly in negotiations with unknown partners it is important to be aware of this problem. If in doubt, an uncertain negotiating partner will tend to perceive ambiguous signals as an indication of a competitive negotiation which is mainly why it is especially important to clearly signal confidence in these circumstances.

In emotionally charged situations, the people involved often react spontaneously and imprudently. In these cases, often more than intended is revealed.

Silence Remaining silent is one of the most important tactical measures in → *face-to-face* negotiations. Different forms of remaining silent can be distinguished:

1. Initially, silence can signal consent. A consenting silence is, however, a weaker consent than an explicitly stated assent and gives more scope to undo the given consent. It is therefore advisable for the opposing side to obtain explicit consent by means of a → *Yes/No question.*

Example
"So, we agree on that …?"

2. Further, there is the contemplative silence, particularly when the silent person had not expected his/her partner's question or statement and therefore wants to rethink his/her negotiating position. Here the opposing party can attempt to discover, at least partially, the content of the reflection, or can disturb the reflection by means of pointed questions.
3. Moreover, there is the dismissive silence. As a rule, silence in response to an offer is perceived as rejection. This corresponds to current legislation in most jurisdictions, according to which silence principally implies the legal rejection of an offer (an exception in German las is the letter of confirmation[106]). As complete silence rarely occurs in negotiations it can be perceived as very intense, particularly if it lasts for more than a few seconds. This makes some negotiators so tense and nervous that they are immediately willing to meet their negotiating partner in their demands, in order to start up negotiations again. This is why silence is also used as a tactical means, e.g. in order to achieve anchor displacement (→ *anchoring*) or set a counter-anchor.
4. Finally, silence can also have an interrogative character. Distinguishing between the different forms of silence is not simple. Many negotiators feel uncomfortable about silence which is why they will continue speaking and explain their offer

[106] See on this aspect Jung and Krebs (2016), p. 246 et seq.

further. In this way, silence can help to reveal information that would otherwise not have been disclosed.
5. For tactical purposes, one party may entirely refuse to communicate (further explanations under → *refusal to communicate*) at a certain point of the negotiations. However, this only rarely occurs in → *face-to-face* negotiations.

Context and → *body language* are often the clue as to which form of silence is on hand. As uncomfortable as it may be, it is advisable to first of all—in silence—briefly consider the potential reasons for the negotiating partner's silence. If it is not clear whether it is a question of contemplative or negative silence in response to one's proposed offer, it may be advisable to ask the opposing party about their expectations, since this question covers all the different forms of silence.

Similar-to-Me-Effect In negotiations, and particularly in → *permanent business relations*, the sympathy between the two parties is an essential factor for success as it facilitates cooperation. Studies prove that people are more congenial towards people who are similar to them and are more positively aware of them than of people they don't share any similarities with. People with similarities are favoured, e.g. in recruitment.[107] The similarities can relate to various different aspects, such as age, → *gender*, profession, values, social affiliation or mutual interests. Especially in brief contact conversations, e.g. in the course of *small talk* (→ *chit-chat*), it is thus advisable to find similarities with the conversation partner, to build rapport by way of appeal (→ *find something in common*). Sometimes negotiators are specifically chosen because of their high degree of agreement with the negotiating partner's preferences. Since people lay great emphasis on their own individuality, the concordance of mutual preferences should not be too high either, so that one does not appear as a clone of the other. This behaviour is also called the **similar-to-me-tactic**. With the aim of creating a positive negotiating climate it is not uncommon for one side to be deceitful, e.g. regarding (personal) preferences or hobbies. If this is the case, the question arises as to whether such deception can be classified as lawful (→ *cunning deception*). The authors of this book affirm this evaluation, because a rational decision for or against the actual conclusion of a contract should not be based on inclination alone. Any negotiator basing his/her decision merely on the existence of mutual preferences is not very worthy of protection. Furthermore, the fundamental worthiness of the protection of any negotiator who commonly uses and accepts this tactic has to be challenged.

Single Text Negotiation This is a negotiation technique with considerable tactical implications. If negotiations are only conducted on the basis of a single text, i.e. a specific contract draft, usually presented by one side, the negotiation process is abbreviated, the objectivity of the contract is increased and in the same manner both the level of complexity and the error rate are reduced. It is especially favourable to opt for single text negotiations if the contract is only being negotiated in writing, since it is difficult to deal with several parallel texts in exclusively written

[107] Sears and Rowe (2003), pp. 13–24.

negotiations. Conversely, single text negotiations are less advisable for constellations where the negotiation requires a creative solution, since the written text can easily cause a kind of mental → *path dependency*, which hinders creativity.

If the given text is provided by a neutral third party, the procedure may be more time-consuming due to the interpolation of this third party, but it offers neither side an advantage. If the third party is involved in the negotiations and modifies the proposed text which s/he contributed according to the interim agreement between the parties, this is referred to as a **single text procedure**.

Example
A well-known example for a single text procedure, taken from the political field, is the peace treaty Camp David. This treaty, between Egypt and Israel, was developed by the USA and the warring parties. In Germany, this cost-intensive ideal is applied in notarial contracts, provided that the draft comes from the notary. However, as a rule, the notary does not usually participate in the negotiation steps, which is why this cannot be regarded as a single text procedure. In some cases, contract drafts also originate from a third party, without the respective third party being involved in the negotiations in any kind of way. In this way it becomes possible e.g. to access texts from legal form manuals.

In the case of B2B negotiations as a rule, the draft originates from one of the sides involved in the negotiations. This side may have developed the draft themselves or may use a model contract developed by affiliated companies.

The party which provides the draft generally has significant advantages in the negotiation. This, on the one hand, follows from the fact that the side who provides the text is more greatly aware of the content as well as the effect of the draft (information asymmetry). On the other hand, the negotiating partner holds the burden of justification for any changes s/he wants to enforce. Moreover, the text constitutes a strong anchor (→ *anchoring*), which cannot usually be opposed by a strong counter-anchor (→ *anchoring*).

The side that composed the contract draft will largely enforce the presented individual clauses on a regular basis. This phenomenon can also be explained by the → *status quo bias* which states that decision-makers, when faced with the choice between the starting position (default option) and a new situation, will usually opt for the starting position, even if a change would be advantageous. As far as single text negotiations are concerned, the draft proposal is a kind of default option. One option for setting a counter-anchor is to introduce one's own contract draft. This enables the own party to communicate the own position clearly. If there is no great disparity in → *negotiation power*, the parties may decide to draw up a draft which combines both of the existing drafts. Introducing the own contract draft can thus potentially prevent single text negotiations. If, on the other hand, one party has stronger negotiation power, it will prevent the contribution of another text and insist on the sole negotiation of their draft, i.e. force single text negotiations.

SMART Goal Formulation Technique This is a general technique for developing and formulating the own goals. The term was coined by *George T. Doran*.[108] In this context the acronym SMART originally stood for

S specific,
M measurable,
A assignable,
R realistic and
T time-related.

However, due to the great success of this list of criteria, there are now numerous variations. This tactic can also be applied in negotiations, since it is particularly important to set ambitious targets (→ *ambitious target price setting*) beforehand. In this case, the A stands for attractive. Hence in negotiations, SMART requires a specific and binding formulation of the negotiation goal. Main and secondary goals must be measurable to determine whether they have been achieved or not. In addition, the goal should be attractive, formulated realistically and clearly, stating the necessary steps to achieve the goal against the backdrop of a clear time frame. Such a target formulation technique can help to decrease the error rate. Likewise, the extended acronym **SMARTER**—where the E stands for evaluated and the second R for reviewed—can be implemented to optimise the management process of contract negotiations.

Soft Bargaining The negotiation style of soft bargaining, which simultaneously includes a strategy, relinquishes the use of leverage and deception manoeuvres. It is not confined to the aim of improving one's own profit at all costs, but rather takes → *win-win* options into account. Thus the focus lies on a good negotiation atmosphere and relationship between negotiator and negotiating partner. However, experience shows that this strategic concept only functions efficiently if both sides negotiate in the same way. If the opposing party prefers the hard bargaining negotiation style, the negotiation results are often disadvantageous for the party that chose soft bargaining. Soft bargaining is closely linked to integrative negotiations and the → *win-win strategy*. Here, hybrid bargaining strikes a balance between hard bargaining and soft bargaining.

Someone-I-Want-to-Be-Associated-with-Effect The someone-I-want-to-be-associated-with-effect is akin to the similar to me effect. There is often a specific type of person someone likes to work with. This effect is particularly pronounced between the genders, where there are sometimes strong preferences for specific phenotypes. But apart from this, it is not uncommon that people appear more likeable when they possess a certain quality that one would also like to possess. There is an overlap

[108] Doran (1981), pp. 35–36.

with the similar-to-me-tactic insofar that it is not uncommon for people to be convinced that they too possess the property that they particularly appreciate, albeit to a lesser extent. This effect can also be used tactically if the respective preferences are known.

Split the Difference This classical technique suggests meeting in the middle whenever two negotiating positions have quantifiable differences, i.e. the suggestion is to split the difference. In the absence of other measures, the parties deem as fair, splitting the difference is perceived as an equitable compromise. It is a technique used particularly often in the context of the → *last gap*. However, one should not be tempted to make a numerical offer, since there is the risk that the opposing party will take this number as the starting position and will only meet in the middle on this basis.

Example
Company A offers 60 EUR. B demands 100 EUR. Splitting the difference would lead to 80 EUR. If, however, A offers B 80 EUR as a number, B will only now offer to split the remaining difference, which would result in an agreement of 90 EUR and in the end, the difference would be split in the ratio three quarters to one quarter.

Conversely, the proposal to split the difference could be made at a time when the side making this proposal would actually have to make most concessions. Contrary to the assumption that splitting the difference is fair, it can in fact be more equitable to choose different measures for decision making. The → *Harvard negotiation concept* rejects the split the difference approach and rather recommends the use of neutral assessment criteria instead.

However, the → *burden of justification* generally lies with the person who rejects this method.

Status Quo Bias Given the choice between change and status quo (the so-called default option), decision-makers tend to opt for the latter. This situation is known as the status quo bias (→ *bias*). To a certain extent, this is true even if the new situation proves profitable. This effect is explained by loss-aversion and the → *endowment effect,* among others. Weighing losses high implies that change is only preferred if the loss will be compensated for by a significant gain. In addition, people are reluctant to admit → *mistakes,* preferring instead to commit themselves consistently once a decision has been made and they have an aversion to remorse for a wrong decision. Regret aversion can be considerable, especially if the decision taken represents a deviation from what would have been the usual choice. In these cases, even adopting the worse option can become acceptable in order to avoid a later feeling of remorse.

The status quo bias was proved in the course of several studies.[109] The status quo bias also affects negotiations. If the negotiator succeeds in presenting the desired action as conducive to maintaining the status quo, the negotiating partner can be more easily persuaded to carry out the action or support it. The → *burden of justification* always lies with the party that wishes to deviate from the status quo. The status quo bias particularly influences single-text-negotiations and → *boilerplates* since the contract draft or the clauses under discussion are regarded as the default option. Contracts concluded between the parties in the past have an ever stronger effect. The often conscious recourse to concessionary law can also be explained by the status quo bias.

Strategic Misrepresentation This tactic is strategically based on deliberately making a false promise. The party making the promise knows that s/he will not be able to keep it, e.g. concerning the technical capacity of a product not yet invented; or regarding the completion date. Failure to comply with the promise gives rise to liability in practical all legal systems. Intention is usually not verifiable, since the involved parties are often overenthusiastic (→ *optimism bias*), particularly at the beginning of a project. There are no peculiarities in relation to other breaches of duty. Nonetheless, particularly in the context of large projects and projects with unrealistic expectations made by the client, deliberate false promises are not uncommon. The party making the promise hopes that in the course of the project the other party will realise that the expectation were completely unrealistic and will thus refrain from bringing any claims. Even before the contract is awarded, the principal's representatives often know that the promises and the underlying idea are unrealistic. It has, however, been known even for the responsible persons assigned by the principal to have worked with unrealistic, over-optimistic assumptions in order to have the project approved by their own side. In other words, there is sometimes a kind of "complicity" between the principal's representatives and the supplier's negotiators. In other cases, especially in large public-sector projects, it is not uncommon that subsequent requests made by the client to effect changes that will render schedules and budgets completely unrealistic. That is why nobody questions whether the originally planned time scale and financial frame were ever realistic in the first place.

Particularly in the case of ongoing major projects, there is often no economic alternative available to clients than the present contractor. For this reason alone, the supplier can hope for an amicable settlement. In some cases, the occurrence of strategic misrepresentation is also facilitated by the legal order. This is particularly true for public clients, as in most cases these do not suffer a material damage if a project is finished later than scheduled.

Sunk Cost Bias The sunk cost bias (the distorted view of already incurred, irreversible expenditures) is an important effect of → *behavioural economics*. The

[109] For fundamental research cf. Samuelson and Zeckhauser (1988), pp. 7–59; Kahneman et al. (1991), pp. 193–206.

effect consists of the fact that previous expenditures for a project, which can no longer be reduced or reversed (e.g. by means of a sale), are taken into account in the evaluation of a pending decision—despite the fact that, from a rational point of view, only the potential future advantages and disadvantages of the decision should have to be considered. The background of this distorted view of economic thinking (for these distortions in general see → *bias*) is on the one hand the desire to maintain the value of past investments. "Wastage" should be prevented. On the other hand, it is also important to realise that organisations and, even more so, people who act for companies do not like to acknowledge → *mistakes*. If the project were not to be continued, the previous costs would generally be perceived as having been based on an objectively erroneous decision. Thus there is the problem of *hindsight bias* (→ *bias*). As a result, the willingness to take risks and also generally the willingness to continue projects increases according to the amount of the sunk costs, since the → *reference points* drop further into the context of loss. In addition, there is a **security-effect**: the uncertain risk of potential loss (i.e. continuing the project and a potential compensation of the losses suffered) is preferred over certain loss (i.e. termination of the project leading to final, irreversible loss).

In negotiations, it is important to be aware of this effect and avoid its negative impact on the own side. If the other party argues e.g. for the continuation of a project by employing such statements as "then the previous expenditure will also have been worthwhile", alarm bells should ring. In this situation, the negotiating partner is presumably subject to the effect of the sunk cost bias.

Further Formulations That Indicate the Sunk Cost Bias

"I think we should strive to finish this project, since we have already worked so long on it."

"After we've all invested so much, we really should run the project."

For the negotiating partner, a sunk cost bias can open up opportunities for concluding the contract but can also impede an agreement. In the latter case, one should consider contract constructions that aim to prevent the (open) realisation of the lost costs as a loss for the negotiating partner. The sunk cost bias also influences the time investment (theory) with regard to the consideration of the previous negotiation effort. The sunk-cost phenomenon was also researched in the context of → *BATNA*. The more effort a negotiator invests into determining his/her negotiating power (→ *negotiation power*), or more generally speaking, the more effort s/he puts into negotiations, the higher his/her expectations of concluding a contract from the ongoing negotiations. Only then does the negotiator have the feeling that his/her efforts were "worthwhile".[110] Negotiators should be aware of this effect in order to lead negotiations objectively. It is hardly conceivable that mutual satisfaction will be attained in very complex negotiations if it wasn't realised in advance that this effort would be required. Both sides should therefore aim to develop realistic expectations of the required negotiation efforts.

Nonetheless, the sunk cost bias can also be beneficial for concluding the contract. If one succeeds in engaging the negotiating partner in lengthy, costly negotiations, the partner's willingness to actually conclude the contract is generally increased. This phenomenon is known under the term "wasted work principle". After all, negotiators do not want to have made this effort in vain. After long negotiations, the negotiating partner may therefore be willing to make further compromises to safeguard the conclusion of the contract, even if the result is not fully satisfying.

SWOT Analysis The acronym SWOT stands for **strengths, weaknesses, opportunities and threats analysis**, and refers to an analysis technique that should be conducted before major deals are closed.

SWOT makes it easier to find an appropriate negotiation strategy and, for example, to put together the right negotiation team. In the context of negotiations, the analysis should be carried out both, for the own company, as well as for the potential contract partner (primarily by determining the existing and expected → *BATNA*), differentiating between the current situation, short-term, medium-term and long-term perspectives, as well as taking negotiators (→ *principal-agent-problem*), → *decision-makers* and stakeholders (→ *think beyond the table*) into account. The respective individuals have the potential to open up special opportunities thanks to their strengths; they can, however, also constitute a weak spot. If the analysis suggests, for instance, that an improvement for the own side is to be expected in the short term compared to the current status quo, it follows that the negotiation should either be postponed or extended until this improvement is realised (→ *calculated delay*); otherwise this improvement should become part of the negotiation strategy.

Tactic of Small Quantities The tactic of the small quantities was developed in the sales sector and is particularly used in B2C relations. It is based on the principle that the scarcity of a product encourages customers to buy it.

Example

On booking sites on the internet, statements such as the following can be found:

"Only 3 rooms available"

"Only 2 available seats left on this flight"

[110] Cf. for this Malhotra and Gino (2011), pp. 559–592.

In order to make a product appear more attractive, sellers call attention to its limited availability. At the same time, claiming limited availability is usually directly or indirectly associated with the statement that the product is also very popular with other customers. Customers tend to rate products better if other customers (especially those from a similar social environment) also use the product (**bandwagon effect**). Thus, this tactic is also referred to as **jumping on the bandwagon**.

In the B2C field this tactic is generally considered unfair, if the scarcity of the product is merely faked. In B2B relations, this tactic is seen as a borderline case (→ *cunning deception*).

Example
In 2015, *Zalando* (an online fashion store) received a warning notice from the Centre for Protection against Unfair Competition for using statements such as "only 3 items available", even though a higher quantity was in stock.

Take It or Leave It The tactic of take it or leave it is a pressure tactic and can be applied to individual negotiation points or to the entire offer. It involves one side making an offer without giving any scope for negotiation. This signals to the opposite side that they can either accept the offer as it is or no contract will be concluded. This builds up very high pressure and the risk of the contract failing increases substantially. The tactic is very similar to the → *Boulwarism* strategy. As opposed to the take it or leave it tactic, Boulwarism applies to the whole contract, or at least to very substantial parts of it. From the outset, consideration should be given to how to proceed in the event that the offer is actually rejected. If negotiations are then to continue, an explanation that saves one's own face should be worked out beforehand. This case is rather the portrayal of stubbornness than the actual application of the take it or leave it-tactic. If, opposed to that, the tactic is used in relation to a point that represents a → *deal-breaker*, it will come to termination of the negotiations.

Think Beyond the Table The call to "think beyond the table" is intended to draw attention to the fact that it is important to focus not only on the negotiators sitting at the negotiating table (*at the table*, → *principal-agent-problem)*. This is particularly true for negotiations involving several parties and negotiations in which various **stakeholders** (i.e. representatives of diverse interests) are directly or at least indirectly involved. Indeed, all stakeholders should be identified and their interests taken into account in the ongoing negotiation. These stakeholders include all those within the company who have a direct or indirect influence on the conclusion of the contract, as well as those who will implement the contract; those who benefit from the contract; those who suffer (seemingly or actually) disadvantages from the conclusion of the contract, and, depending on the individual project, external parties such as trade unions, environmentalists, suppliers, governments, communities, activists etc.

These stakeholders can exert a certain pressure for or against the conclusion of the contract or behave neutrally. It can therefore be important to negotiate directly with those who are only indirectly involved, in order to gain their support. The focus thus lies on developing coalitions to help implement a project. Conversely, it is equally important to prevent the establishment of coalitions of stakeholders that unite to block the project.

In such complex situations, it can be helpful to draw a so-called **all-party map**, i.e. a sketch with all stakeholders and their respective interests as well as the relevant relations and potential influence. The map should also include whether and how these stakeholders could be incorporated—or, on the contrary, how their incorporation into the process can be inhibited. This method is also known as **mapping influential players.**

In a broad sense, it should also be investigated whether third parties might be included in the contract to enlarge the → *negotiation pie*.

This Will Hurt You More Than Me The expression "This will hurt you more than it will hurt me" is a commonly used pressure tactic (or strategy if it is used throughout the whole negotiation), in which both sides may (initially) lose. Here a certain behaviour that will harm both sides is threatened. However, the side which announces this behaviour is convinced that the opposing party will absolutely or at least relatively suffer the greater damage caused by the conflict and therefore be forced to yield in the end. This tactic is extremely aggressive, which massively endangers the parties' confidence in the negotiations and thus also the business relation and leads to an escalation of the situation.

Examples

One example for the application of "this will hurt you more than it will hurt me" as a strategy are labour disputes as a means for enforcing the collective bargaining demands of labour unions. Another example is the work stoppage of a subcontractor in relation to the general contractor in a critical phase of the project. As a rule, the subcontractor would then like to renegotiate certain points (→ *renegotiations*), presuming that the general contractor will suffer much greater damage as a result of the work stoppage. The general contractor will thus accept the additional demand (if it is not too high), even though the subcontractor's behaviour is unlawful and consequently s/he will also be liable to pay compensation. Sometimes, the work stoppage at a construction site, due to the dispute regarding the reasons of a delay or non-conformity, is based on this strategy. Furthermore, the EU used this as a strategy during Brexit negotiations with Britain.

Oftentimes, before the threat is implemented, the parties involved calculate their potential damage appropriately and achieve an agreement on the basis of this without a costly conflict. Sometimes, therefore, only announcing damaging behaviour is sufficient to induce the opposing party to make concessions. Frequently, however, the amount of damage to one's own side or that of others, or one's own endurance or that of others, is misjudged. Even if a side succeeds with this tactic (strategy) and gains a short-term advantage, this can have negative consequences in the long-term. Hence, it can for instance occur that the side acting in this way is excluded from the circle of potential suppliers for future deals. In industrial disputes, the consequences can be a severe wave of rationalisation, including the loss of work places or the migration of customers to a neighbouring field and accordingly a necessary reduction of jobs. The use of such a tactic (strategy) therefore always requires a prior analysis of the potential long-term consequences. Moreover, it is precisely here that the question always needs to be asked whether the exerted pressure is lawful, i.e. particularly proportionate.

TINA The acronym TINA stands for "**there is no alternative**". Historically, this term is attributed to Margaret Thatcher, who, in her first period of office often used the wording "there is no alternative" as justification for the radical changes she made. This gave rise to one of her nicknames: the acronym TINA. The approach of claiming that there is no alternative to a certain action or rule can also be observed in contract negotiations. It is an argument which, as such, aims at preventing discussion. The same goal is pursued with the → *undiscussable* tactic. In addition, this technique can be used to weaken the negotiating partner's → *BATNA*, e.g. by stating that there is no existing alternative to a certain technical standard.

For the negotiating partner it is advisable to find out the reasons for TINA. In the political arena, it might be that the true reason is too complex to explain in public appearances. It is, however, also possible—especially in contract negotiations—that the person using TINA cannot think of an argument, or that disclosing the real argument would not be in the interest of the company, for example. It can also be an indicator that the negotiating partner attaches particularly high value to this aspect. There can, after all, be emotional reasons why one side does not want to negotiate an issue. If the reason for the use of TINA can be determined successfully, the negotiating partner has to deal with the reason and thus persuade the opposing side to adopt a more constructive position.

Tit for Tat (TFT) The name "tit for tat" has its historical origin in the phrase "tip for tap" (blow for blow). This strategy begins with cooperation and trust. However, if the negotiating partner does not cooperate, the other side will also switch to non-cooperative behaviour. If the negotiating partner returns to a cooperative negotiation style, the first side also adopts a cooperative negotiation style. Contrary to the → *generous tit for tat strategy*, the first side does not offer a return to a cooperative style of negotiation.

This strategy was developed by *Anatol Rapoport* in the context of a competition and is perceived to be a convincing solution from the point of view of game theory.

Tit for tat has proved reliable under practical conditions, as long as it is applied within the scope of a relative fairness and there are several negotiation rounds.[111] The TFT tactic is an application of a situation-specific strategy. However, there should not necessarily be an automatism between the opposing parties' tactic and the own followed tactic. This would render the behaviour of the own side predictable and ultimately manipulable. Also, the own position may not always appear consistent. Lastly there is the risk of tensions building up in the negotiations. The → *generous tit for tat* strategy was developed particularly in order to prevent escalation which also entails a loss of control. Here, the generous tit for tat strategy makes it possible to take steps of de-escalation.

Traffic Light Systems Traffic light systems, also known as scoring systems, are qualitative assessment systems and thus a negotiation technique used particularly when quantitative systems are too expensive or too time consuming. They are frequently used in the context of legal risk management, because it is difficult to quantify the legal risks associated with a contract. Such systems are especially significant for more complex contract negotiations.

Individual negotiation points are internally classified according to their importance, on a scale of fully disposable to indispensable. Scoring is generally carried out by way of a points system (e.g. from 1 to 5) or using traffic light colours. Another possibility is to use characters such as "+", "0" and "-". Compared to red flags, traffic light systems have the advantage that they not only warn of potential risks, but also give a more differentiated view.

Example
Green = fully disposable; orange/yellow = negotiable, depending on the offered return; red = indispensable.

Depending on the evaluation, it is determined whether the negotiating positions are available at all and what is expected in return. This internal assessment is under no circumstances disclosed to the negotiating partner. The internal assessment should be strictly separated from the assessment communicated to the outside world. If different information and assessments are put together in tabular form, the result is a so-called **decision matrix**.

Transaction Costs During negotiations, negotiators should aim to keep transaction costs to a minimum.[112] Negotiations generate transaction costs, which are traditionally divided into four different categories:

[111] For basic notes cf. Axelrod (1984).

[112] Basic notes on transaction costs cf. Williamson (1985), esp. p. 15 et seq.; Williamson (1989), pp. 135–182.

- Information and research costs (which, among other things, cover the costs incurred while searching for alternatives as part of the determination of the → *BATNA*)
- Negotiation costs (due to the expenditure for the actual negotiation (time and resources) and for the conclusion of the contract (e.g. fees))
- Monitoring costs
- Enforcement costs/costs for renegotiation

Transaction costs can thus be distinguished into ex-ante and ex-post incurred transactions costs, whereby the first mentioned two cost types are incurred before the conclusion of the contract (ex-ante) and the latter mentioned two types of cost occur after the conclusion of the contract (ex-post).

Enforcement costs also include the costs incurred when dealing with disputes within the company itself. From the company's point of view, it is not unproblematic that these internal costs cannot be reimbursed under general damage claim rights.

From an organisational point of view, minimising transaction costs is a general goal. This goal can be achieved if negotiators ensure that future negotiations are already facilitated by the current negotiations. A good relationship with the negotiating partner can contribute to this, and the standardisation of negotiations helps to reduce transaction costs. This area also encompasses precedence cases. If both parties recognise a precedent, future negotiations can be spared unless the determining circumstances change. Agreeing on standards can also help reduce transaction costs. It should also be an objective to keep the negotiations as short as possible. Among other things, setting → *deadlines* can help. Nonetheless, it should be borne in mind that the minimisation of transaction costs is in conflict with the quality of the preparation and conduct of the negotiations, which in turn can also decisively influence the negotiation result. Under these circumstances, negotiators need to weigh up the advantages and disadvantages.

Two Against One This expression is synonymous for a personell predominance within a negotiation team. The larger a negotiation team is, the more (intellectual and specialist) resources are available. However, from the company's point of view, this gain in resources is very costly—due to high personnel and time expenditure (→ *transaction costs*)—and the coordination of the company's own negotiation team is time-consuming, depending on the size of the team. This use of resources can, however, be profitable. In a "two against one" negotiation, the negotiating team has a clear advantage over the single negotiating counterparty, at least where the negotiations deal with relatively complex negotiating issues. The intellectual capacities of both negotiators are in sum higher; they have the opportunity to take turns, make analytical observations and perhaps apply tactics such as → *good guy/bad guy*. In order to avoid such inferiority, it should be clarified beforehand how many negotiators from the opposing party will actually take part in the negotiation. "Two against one" may be viewed as unfair, which is why the negotiation side with more negotiators could look for an excuse to send some of their negotiators away.

For various reasons (costs, no suitable second negotiator, only one person allowed to participate etc.) there may be cases when a negotiator is faced with two or more negotiators from the opposing party. Various measures can help to compensate the negotiating partners' preponderance to a certain extent:

- Preparing well for the negotiation—in particular for the opposing party's negotiator and his/her arguments and demands (i.e. especially preparing for their diverse interests),
- increased use of → *questions* and intensive observation of the opposing party's negotiators,
- increased use of contact with the back office,
- thinking pauses (→ *negotiation pauses*, → *silence*) and
- establishing a good relationship, in particular with one of the opposing party's negotiators (allies).

Two Negotiators Except for very large and very small negotiations, a two-person negotiation team is often the ideal size. As opposed to one-person negotiations, in negotiations where two negotiators are present, there is less likelihood of (content-related, psychological or other) overload. In addition, a negotiation team of two negotiators has the advantage that the one who is currently not negotiating can take on the role of → *analyst*. Furthermore, content-related specialization, e.g. in a technical and economical-juridical part, is also possible and is frequently carried out in practice. In this regard, it is generally beneficial if the negotiating partner in the own team has basic knowledge of the other specialist area, so that s/he can properly follow the negotiation and assess the current negotiation situation.

Further advantages of using two negotiators include:

- Two negotiators can use the → *good guy/bad guy tactic*, whereby in case of doubt, the technician can take the role of the good guy, and the lawyer the role of the bad guy.
- Two negotiators and their varying manner of working together are sufficient to cover and convincingly represent different styles of negotiations and to be to some extent tactically unpredictable (→ *unpredictability*) from the opposing side's point of view.
- Two negotiators are less likely to be taken by surprise or manipulated than a single negotiator.
- The negotiation costs remain relatively manageable.
- The coordination effort between the negotiators remains controllable.
- Particularly where two people negotiate, it is convincing that the → *decision-maker*, as the third person, in charge of deciding, remains in the back-office.
- Two negotiators can check each other (→ *principle of dual control*).
- Two negotiators have a clear advantage in a → *two against one* situation.

Of course, there may also be cases, where two negotiators do not harmonise with each other and thus hamper each other during the negotiations. The challenge for the decision-maker is often to recognise this issue. This can be achieved, for example, by the negotiators reporting back separately.

All in all, the system of two negotiators is so convincing that in large negotiation rounds one should consider working with teams of two negotiators, each assigned to different fields of the negotiation (e.g. two technicians and two commercial-legal negotiators)

Undiscussable The term "undiscussable" refers to points that are so important for the respective side that they are not even willing to discuss them. In English-speaking areas the term **non-negotiable** is also commonly used.

Classifying something as undiscussable can have the purpose of saving pointless (expensive) negotiations. The other side has to decide for themselves whether they can accept this or not. A point designated undiscussable is thus immunised against any argumentation, i.e. virtually taboo. However, it is not always easy to convincingly present a point as being undiscussable. One way to achieve this is the self-gagging method, in which one side manoeuvres itself into a situation beforehand, from which there is no way out without a major loss of face or substantial loss from a material point of view.

Declaring a point as undiscussable can be reasonable if it really is especially valuable for the own side (e.g. a → *deal-breaker*), but the reason for this cannot be given, e.g. because the negotiating partner would thus receive important information that would influence the further development of the negotiation. This is due to the fact that the undiscussable tactic is often simultaneously used to avert the negotiating partner's desire to gather important information on that specific issue. Since the interests behind the blocking of negotiations on this point are thus not disclosed, it can additionally be an element of position-oriented negotiating; or at least the opposing side could get that impression. If something is undiscussable and hence has the effect of a premise, there is even the risk that this point will not be taken into consideration in the process of determining mutual yielding, since this point was not negotiated (yielding is only measured on the basis of actually negotiated points). In such cases, however, it would be fair to compensate the undiscussable point with a particularly broad concession in another point.

The application of the undiscussable tactic increases the risk of a failure of the negotiations and may even negatively affect the negotiation trust, since even requests for information are rejected.

Unpredictability Having an unpredictable negotiator can bring both, advantages and disadvantages for the negotiator's side. It is not desirable that a negotiator is unpredictable regarding the implementation of the agreed contract (insofar as s/he is responsible for this specific task); there is far less willingness to negotiate with this kind of negotiator and the risk of a failure of negotiations increases.

In contrast, a certain unpredictability regarding negotiation tactics can sometimes be regarded as positive. The unpredictability of a → *decision-maker* can result in the opposing side, who is interested in reaching an agreement, yielding more than would otherwise be appropriate, in a kind of security surcharge. Conversely, there is the danger that less trustful relationships will be established if one side acts too unpredictably and volatile.

In general, negotiation behaviour should not be arbitrary and irrational. The suggestion to remain unpredictable is rather to be understood as suggesting that the negotiator should act variably so that s/he does not become too easy to predict and manipulate.

Warning Instead of Threatening Lawyers in particular recommend stating a warning rather than an actual threat towards the negotiating partner. This is based on the assumption, that when a person utters a threat in which s/he attributes the occurrence of promised negative consequences to his/her person, liability and prosecution may follow. It usually also creates the right to challenge the contract and justifies general damage claims. A warning, on the other hand, merely describes the disadvantages which could occur, regardless of any influence of the person giving the warning. In principle, it is legally harmless. In this respect, a warning can also be regarded as **calling attention** to something. In this way, one appeals to the negotiating partner's rational behaviour. This tactic serves to draw the negotiating partner's attention to real circumstances and thus induce a certain behaviour in favour of the own interests.

Frequently, however, a threat that is meant and should be understood as such is linguistically worded as a warning in order to appear less aggressive. However, the legal categorisation is not a question of skilful formulation, but is rather based on the qualitative overall impression that the behaviour makes on a rational recipient. Hence a threat, whether or not it is disguised as a warning, remains an intended threat, with all the associated consequences both legal and otherwise (e.g. on the relational level, by termination of the → *permanent business relation*).

What-If-Questions What if-questions ask the other party to imagine a certain situation (hypothesis) and to state how they would behave in that situation or what consequences this would have. In this case, the hypothesis technique which utilises what if–questions, is applied. This questioning technique pursues various goals. On the one hand, it might be aimed towards the other party drawing their own conclusions. Conclusions drawn by oneself have a higher persuasive power than arguments presented by the opposing party (→ *reactive devaluation*, also see → *incomplete solutions*). Furthermore, the what if-question can develop the vivid image of a probable constellation in the future, the possible settlement of which will be initiated by this question. On the other hand, the what if–questions can also be used in the course of a so-called test balloon to test potential solutions for a problem. Similar to the → *premise questions*, a corresponding questioning technique can be used to inquire whether the negotiating partner considers this scenario desirable. In this way the preferences of the negotiating partner can be determined, thus simplifying the problem solution process. Finally, using this questioning technique can encourage the other party to put themselves in the position of the inquirer, in case a reversal of roles is intended.

Win-Lose Strategy This strategy aims at maximizing the own profit. at the expense of the negotiating partner; or, when it comes to eliminating a loss, to minimise it. This strategy is also known as **competitive strategy**. In the context of this strategy, the size of the overall profit for both parties is only relevant if it also has an actual effect on the interests of the own side. This strategy is thus closely linked to → *hard bargaining* (→ *distributive negotiations*). As a result, chances for both sides, deriving from the expansion of the total profit (*expanding the pie* (→ *negotiation pie*)) tend to be lost, since in this approach the focus is too strongly on distribution. In addition, negotiations following a win-lose strategy are more likely to fail than more cooperative strategies, since confidence in the negotiation, including the trust in the fair performance of the contract, is far lower. Despite these facts, there are still proponents of this strategy.[113] The promoters of the win-lose strategy presume that there are only low chances of creating a → *win-win* situation, whether regarding one-time deals or in the context of → *permanent business relations*. If there is the chance to achieve a win-win situation, one should resolutely strive for the largest possible share of this additional profit. In practice, it is assumed that the win-lose strategy is still very commonly represented. From this perspective, the competing → *win-win* strategy stands accused of not sufficiently representing the interests of the own side and thus achieving worse results. Particularly in → *permanent business relations,* the parties' relationship and trustful cooperation are key factors. However, the win-win-approach is not the only alternative to the win-lose strategy. Other alternatives include e.g. the so-called **hybrid-strategy** and interest-oriented negotiations.

Win-Win Strategy There is no denying that the win-win strategy, also referred to as the cooperation strategy (in connection with → *soft bargaining* and integrative negotiation) is concerned with the distribution of potential profit, and that this distribution must form an essential part of the negotiation. However, one central goal of this approach is to construct a contract that promises the greatest overall return through cooperation (*expanding the pie* (→ *negotiation pie*)). Moreover, it also generates a profit for the opposing side, since only this approach ensures a stable structure, also regarding the subsequent implementation of the contract. Even with superior negotiation power (→ *negotiation power*) it makes sense to concede a small profit to the opposing party, additionally in order to maintain the negotiating partner for future partnerships. In comparison to the win-lose strategy, this approach increases the likelihood of a successful contract conclusion and also establishes a higher degree of trust in the implementation of the contract. In practice, win-win oriented negotiators face the disadvantage that their advantages (a lower failure rate in negotiations, a more trustful implementation of the contract) are often not sufficiently taken into account. Instead, companies tend to focus merely on the content of contracts actually concluded.

In response to the criticism of the win-win approach, the term **mutual gains** is sometimes brought into play. In contrast to the win-win approach, the main focus

[113] Cf. Cohen (1982).

here is to enlarge the → *negotiation pie*, i.e. create added value through negotiations. However, this term makes no reference to the distribution of the negotiation pie. The Consensus Building Institute has developed a negotiation approach that focuses on mutual gains (win-win strategy).

Wince In the course of this tactic, the recipient of the other parties' offer openly expresses his/her astonishment/dismay. This is not only achieved by words but particularly by means of his/her behaviour and → *body language*. His/her physical reaction evidently shows that the offer as it is proposed at this moment in time is clearly unacceptable. The name of this tactic alludes to the fact that the person receiving the offer "winces" in horror. Accordingly, this tactic is also known under the term of **flinch**. In practice, the tactic is implemented by loudly repeating the price offered by the negotiation partner with a negative undertone. The rejection is emphasised by deprecatory gesticulation (e.g. shaking the head, frowning, waving aside). This reaction is usually subsequently followed by → *silence*. The idea behind this action is that such verbally and particularly non-verbally expressed rejection is perceived stronger than purely verbally manifested rejection. In this way the recipient of this hard rejection is more willing to make concessions. During price negotiations wince is frequently used to shift the negotiation partner's anchor (see under (→ *anchoring*) without setting a counter-anchor. This approach does however require that the non-verbal rejection seems credible and does not appear to be rehearsed.

Working Groups Working groups are a technical means of dealing with complex situations in negotiations. There are two forms of working groups (working groups/work teams). One option is that there are working teams on both sides. This can be particularly useful in larger negotiations. It should be noted that as the number of participants grows, coordination effort and costs increase and, as it is the case with too many participants, can even reduce the efficiency of the group.

On the other hand, when negotiating on very comprehensive matters with large negotiation teams, it can make sense to form working groups in which the specialists of both sides look for common solutions. Discussing certain points between specialists minimises the likelihood of → *misunderstandings* and, due to the smaller number of people present, allows the heart of the issue to be reached more quickly. In addition, the parallel negotiation of individual points can result in time savings. Dividing the parties into working groups can also be used to separate certain fundamental questions, which, generally speaking, tend to be very loaded with the positioning of the parties.

Overall, the allocation of certain issues (summary, breakdown) to the working groups is an important means that can influence the negotiation process. Working groups constitute another escalation stage (→ *calling a higher authority*), since the negotiation leaders are not involved in the working groups.

Problems can arise, however, if working groups do not picture the whole negotiations (→ *missing the big picture*). It is possible that the results delivered from several working groups may also culminate in a big picture which one side may find hard to accept. However, disregarding the big picture would substantially shake the confidence in the negotiations. In order to prevent this from happening, the objectives of the working groups of the own side should be clearly determined beforehand and the working groups should be coordinated. To do so, all intermediate results must be delivered to the leader of the overall negotiations.

The problems arising from missing the big picture and the impact of a factual binding effect, based on agreement within a working group, are sometimes specifically used to reap benefits. To do this, a (mostly low ranking) working group is formed, in which one side hopes to enforce their interests. This procedure can prove effective, since the participants of the other side are often unaware of the overriding interests. Using working groups in negotiations is widespread, especially in political negotiations and larger organisations. This is thus one of the areas in which experience from political negotiations can be transferred to economic negotiations.

WWW In the context of negotiations the abbreviation WWW stands for **what worked well**? Negotiating is a continuous learning process, which can be enriched by practical experience and theoretical background knowledge. The WWW-method is a recommendation to encourage people to reflect on their own negotiations and consider, which tactics, techniques or strategies proved successful. This insight can then be used for future negotiations. However, it should be considered that the success or failure of a negotiation tactic, technique or strategy depends on many basic conditions. Accordingly, before applying a tactic again, it is crucial to consider whether it can be adequately transferred to the new negotiation situation.

The question "what worked well?" can also be answered by means of deal sheets. This way, it would not only help the negotiator to learn from his/her success but would also contribute in general to the internal improvement of negotiations.

WWYDD The abbreviation WWYDD stands for "**what would you do differently?**". Similar to the *WWW*-method, the WWYDD enables negotiators to learn from past negotiations. Here, however, the negotiators do not focus on the things that went well but rather evaluate what could have been done better.

The question "what would you do differently?" can also be answered in the context of e.g. deal sheets and in this case would not only help the individual negotiator to learn from his/her → *mistakes*, but would also provide suggestions for the internal improvements of negotiations. In this context however, it is not quite so simple because negotiators might tend to deliberately overestimate their own negotiation result to prevent exposing themselves to criticism from within the company. This problem could be mitigated by safeguarding the anonymity of the assessments.

Yes, But-Answer The yes, but-answer, as the counterpart to the → *But-Yes-answer*, begins with basic consent and subsequently adds concerns or limitations. The yes, but-answer is much more common than the but, yes answer. This may be due to the fact that the respondent's concerns or limitations are emerging bit by bit after the answer has been given. It can also be an expression of his/her positive will. The key message of consent is intended to reach the opposing party directly. This should increase their willingness to respond to subsequently stated concerns. There are, however, cultures and individual negotiators who are generally very reluctant to use a clear "No"; with these negotiators, Yes, but-answers are often to be interpreted as a strict "No". Yes, but-answers are also referred to as **Radio-Eriwan-answers**, referring to a fictitious radio station named after the city Eriwan in America. Inquiries ("is it true, that") made by ostensible listeners were always answered with "in principle, yes", yet in the following sentence ("but") the complete opposite was communicated. In this case the yes, but-answer would have a light-hearted element that might loosen up a negotiation. Besides brightening up a situation, yes, but-answers can serve to fend off a question.

Example
"Is it true that you received a large order from C?"
"In principle, yes. But it wasn't C, it was D. And apart from that, it was actually only a typing error that made the overall sum initially appear so big"

Yes/No questions are questions that can only be answered with "yes" or "no".

Examples
"Is it true that…?" "Am I right in thinking…?" "Does the car have air conditioning?" "Is the house connected to the sewer system?" "Have you obtained authorisation for the roof extension?"

Yes/No Questions So-called yes/no questions are often also referred to as if-questions, since the answer is supposed to clarify if something is true or not. As opposed to → *open questions,* the potential information gain from asking yes/no questions is limited, since respondents have no reason to give a detailed answer. Nonetheless, there is the possibility that the negotiating partner may reveal further information when s/he is asked a → *yes or no question*. The person asking the questions hopes that a revealing answer will be given to the yes/no question. If, on the other hand, a question is asked inexpertly, it is possible for the respondent to give a less than correct "yes" or "no" answer without running the risk of being accused of lying. Moreover, attempts are often made to avoid answering yes/no questions clearly.

Relativisation can be achieved by the → *yes, but answer*, in which the yes is limited in the follow-up. Furthermore, yes/no questions are also liable to result in the respondent giving the answer which, in his/her opinion, the person asking the questions most wants to hear. This risk can be avoided by using or questions and the → *A-not-A-questions*. A yes/no question can also be perceived as coercive, as it impels a definitive answer, although the respondent would prefer to answer softly and without obligation. On the other hand, some important cases demand the conversation partner's absolute commitment for the progress of the negotiation. In these instances, the negotiator should opt for yes/no questions.

ZOPA (Zone of Possible Agreement) The ZOPA—also known as the **bargaining range** or **agreement zone**—describes the area where the respective minimum targets of the parties (→ *deal-breaker*) overlap. Provided the negotiations are rational and interest-orientated, these minimum targets generally comply with the own → *BATNA*. In position-oriented negotiations, however, the minimum target can also be irrational and possibly remain largely unaffected by BATNA. ZOPA was invented as a basic concept by *Howard Raiffa* in 1982.[114]

If there is a ZOPA, in theory there should accordingly be an agreement. If there is no ZOPA, i.e. a **NOPA** (no possible agreement), then from a rational point of view no agreement is possible (cf. further under → *deal-breaker*). A larger ZOPA would allow the negotiation success of both parties to be measured by determining the range of the ZOPA in which the actual agreement was achieved.

To a certain extent, the ZOPA falsifies the actual situation given, since it generally bases on a one-dimensional approach to negotiations. In most cases, only the absolute price is taken into account. Additional conditions such as payment terms, requirements regarding quality, risks and chances are not always easy to represent. In the same manner, the ZOPA does not consider the uncertainties regarding minimum targets, which the parties have to determine before the actual negotiations. As with the BATNA, negotiators have to take the dynamics of changes of the ZOPA into account during negotiations.

The concept of the ZOPA may be significant from a scientific point of view, but it is not, or hardly ever, applied in practice. This is mainly due to the fact that the minimum targets of the negotiating partners are generally not openly disclosed. However, it would be possible to use the ZOPA in negotiation training with specified minimum targets to assess the negotiators' skill in training situations (Fig. 3.12).

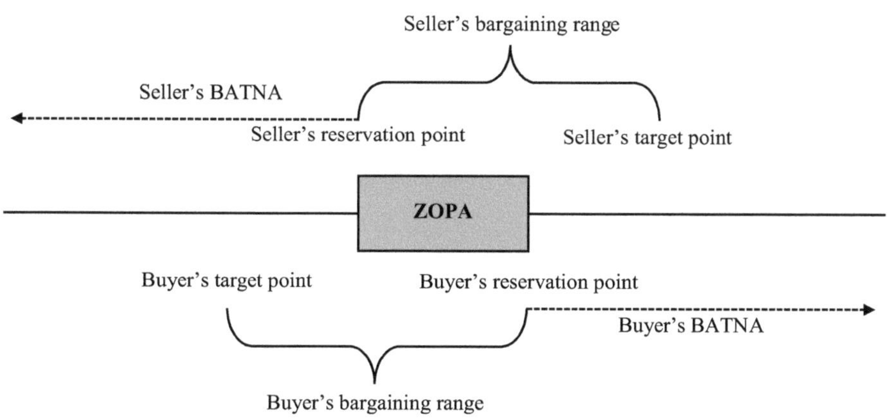

Fig. 3.12 Illustration of the relation between BATNA and ZOPA

[114] Raiffa (1982).

Chapter 4
Cultural Differences in Negotiations: An Overview on the US, China and Germany

4.1 How Germans Negotiate

4.1.1 Preliminary Notes

As with any other nationality, one cannot distinguish "the German negotiator" or the "German negotiation style". Personal mentality (degree of extroversion, ability to manage conflicts, risk aversion, emotionality), circle of friends, experience abroad, gender, age, hierarchy, level of education, professional expertise, branch, region, migration background, ownership structure of the firm (e.g. mother company abroad, large corporation with anonymous shareholders or family corporation), size and internationality of the company, international negotiation experience, corporate strategy, competitive situation regarding the contract object etc. are all factors which influence the negotiator's negotiation type. If, for instance, negotiators lack professional competence, these negotiators negotiate cooperatively less often due to their fear of being disadvantaged. Above that, these negotiators also often act and react emotionally. In Germany, regional differences play hardly any role: the people negotiating are almost never from the same region. Besides, other factors are more formative, such as socialisation in the academic and entrepreneurial environment. In addition, the level of negotiation experience and negotiation training or the concrete composition of the negotiation group can have a significant impact on the negotiation type. Hence it is now commonplace for German corporations to establish international negotiation teams. Nonetheless, there are some statements that generally comply with the behaviour of German negotiators.

S. Jung, P. Krebs, *The Essentials of Contract Negotiation*,
https://doi.org/10.1007/978-3-030-12866-1_4

4.1.2 Negotiation Training

In Germany, training courses for negotiations exist at law faculties and business schools and in business and engineering degree courses, but they are usually not mandatory and only a fraction of the students take part in such a course. This may be due to the fact that, particularly at universities, practically approached knowledge transfer is viewed with fundamental scepticism. Especially in Germany, the different degree specialisations are strictly separated. Interdisciplinary education (simultaneous or consecutive) is relatively rare, and is furthermore hardly honoured in terms of career perspectives. Since contract negotiations combine scientific knowledge from various sciences (social psychology, classical economic theory, game theory, behavioural economics, communication science, law), each German scientist who deals generally with negotiations moves largely within a foreign field of expertise. This situation is avoided as far as possible. Thus, only a few universities offer more comprehensive courses in contract negotiations. Large companies and occasionally also SMEs offer negotiation training for their employees, depending on a needs assessment conducted by the responsible superior manager. Younger lawyers' knowledge in negotiation science can, for instance, originate from mediation training or an LL.M. from an US law school. The fact that German negotiators lack specific negotiation training is often not initially apparent, since the constant improvement of the own abilities, due to progressive experience, is one of the characteristically German ideals. Experienced German negotiators thus negotiate on a professional level, even without negotiation training. In these circumstances, the generally structured and rational approach to tasks can compensate for the lack of specific training, even in the case of inexperienced German negotiators. Yet the effects of a lack of training can be observed in the search for win-win solutions, although these rarely occur; or in the context of the relatively small range of possible strategies and tactics. As, for instance, the effects of → *behavioural economics* are largely unknown, German negotiators often struggle with understanding the importance of background information and utilising this to assume consequences.

4.1.3 Mentalities

Based on the variety of people and environmental influences, ascribing specific mentalities to negotiators from different countries would seem to be hardly imaginable. Firstly, customary descriptions do not relate to the individual negotiator him-/herself, but rather to the average negotiator. Subsequently, this average is compared to the average determined for other countries. Accordingly, this comparison is based on certain tendencies, which do not necessarily comply with individual characteristics.

4.1.4 Orientation on Legal Rules: Safe Harbour Principle

Germans are generally perceived to be "law abiding". Though this may be correct in the sense of a general tendency, it is necessary to take a differentiated point of view. Apart from objective parameters (such as the companies' size, significance of legal risks or whether the transaction is a one-time-deal), the law's importance for the negotiation particularly depends on the level of lawyer involvement. Primarily, business negotiations between SMEs and larger, family-owned SMEs should preferably be conducted without the direct involvement of lawyers.

German SMEs do not usually have a specific legal department but rather take legal decisions in consultation with law firms as permanent external consultants.

Many SMEs try to adhere relatively strictly to beneficial or at least safe clauses, drafted previously and determined by decision-makers within the company, who often consult external lawyers. Other SMEs, however, do not engage in drafting a legally effective contractual relationship, because they are confident that legal disputes rarely arise anyway. Instead, they place emphasis on clauses that benefit their own side. In this way, the question of legal effectiveness is upstaged—even though, worldwide, Germany has one of the strictest sets of rules on content control regarding B2B → *boilerplates*. Occasionally, there are companies that even want to utilise this sharp set of rules on the control of general terms and conditions (*boilerplate-control*) for their own benefit. As a result, these companies readily agree even with critical points because they entirely trust the intensive support of the legal content control as it orders the ineffectiveness of particularly detrimental clauses (so-called "boilerplate-based negotiation tactic"[1]). This protective measure could be abolished if the respective clause were negotiated individually. However, this tactic is only realisable where German law applies. Large companies in particular practice intensive consultation with the legal department. Consequently, these companies often present themselves as less flexible and insist on the use of their standard clauses—even in cases where the alternative desired by the opposing party holds no substantial disadvantages. In total, compared to other countries, the significance of law for negotiations is relatively high in Germany. This is due to the fact that Germans strive for a safe, highly predictable situation for the processing of the contract. For this matter, a legally protected situation appears invaluable. This conforms with the fact that Germans attach great importance to the principle of contract compliance (*pacta sunt servanda*), although it does not imply full compliance of the contracts at all times. In this regard, Germans' high legal compliance as perceived externally, appear to be exaggerated. Yet, renegotiations after the final conclusion of the contract might not be uncommon but are generally not accepted by the side that is unwillingly faced with the renegotiation. However, this does not apply to situations where a fundamental change of circumstances took place after the conclusion of contract. Regarding negotiated contract clauses, German law is strongly influenced by the search for individually suitable solutions (principle of good faith; fair and

[1] See Jung and Krebs (2016), p. 40.

interest-considered interpretation; sometimes even against the exact wording of the contract; gap-filling in accordance with the parties' ideas (supplementary contract interpretation)). The application of this principle allows a complete regulation of each individual case to be waived, as well as enabling a more generous hand with formulations, insofar as the content-related elements are sufficiently clear. This leeway, granted for negotiations, often remains unused however; perhaps since this would involve deliberate risk-taking. Thus, this course of action is especially uncommon among lawyers. In summary, when compared to their international counterparts, Germans are often considered to be risk averse—even though in this context, the world-famous "German Angst" is probably not significant. Still, compared to American companies, German companies generally tend to draft less comprehensive agreements.

As long as lawyers take a key role in contract negotiations (either as the negotiating person or in the → *back office*), it is very common to choose the legally safest way. German lawyers usually follow the safe harbour principle and are not orientated towards pursuing a legal risk management, which evaluates economic risks and chances as well as comprising major risks outside the field of criminal law. Likewise, economically-oriented companies often do not dare to override legal concerns that have been set out in writing, since German liability law is perceived to be very strict. The principle of legality prohibits breaches of law, even if they have been conducted in the interests of the company. Despite the significance of this law for German companies, bringing legal disputes before courts or arbitral tribunals is not a desired option. Settling disputes by means of this procedure is perceived as elaborate, risky and damaging to business. Accordingly, these legal means are understood to be the ultima ratio. Hence in dispute negotiations, legal arguments are only used in order to reach a reasonable agreement—at least by non-lawyers. It is thus very seldom that Germans evaluate the option of an actual legal dispute to be a real → *BATNA*. Company-intern compliance rules, which have gained ground enormously in recent years, are, in a broader sense, another legal element that influences the German negotiator. These rules aim not only to prevent corruption in the form of expenditure for negotiation partners (presents, invitations, joint dinners) but also comprise regulations for German negotiators, supervising their acceptance of presents and invitations from the other party. Compliance rules are generally very strict, particularly within large companies or in SMEs delivering to large companies. The scope to grant exceptions is very small, frequently necessitating a laborious procedure. In this context, German negotiators might conceivably find themselves in an embarrassing situation if handed presents or invited to dinners when the costs incurred exceed company limits. In these cases, German negotiators face the dilemma of either violating company-intern rules or upsetting the opposing party.

4.1.5 Basic Characteristics and Approaches

Despite considerable individual differences among negotiators, certain typical characteristics and strategies can be assigned to negotiators from different countries. This assignation is, in essence, valid—based on the fact that many individuals are involved both at the negotiation table as well as in the → *back office*. Negotiation styles hence do not only depend on the specific characteristics of the single negotiators involved but are characterised by the common behaviour and expectations of the surrounding society. Even single companies very rarely deviate from common behaviour, since divergent behaviour would encompass the consequence of creating social distance and communication risks. Furthermore, the statements made address common behaviour and common basic ideas, and by no means claim to be universally applicable.

In Germany, logical argumentation plays a very significant role for negotiations since the belief is prevalent that logical argumentation cannot simply be disengaged. German negotiators focus on a very intensive justification of the position they presented initially, making a point of not abandoning it in the course of the negotiation process. On an international scale, Germans come across as being comparatively reserved and introverted. They strive for a friendly, yet rarely for an overly friendly negotiating climate. Germans in particular feel the demonstration of → *emotions* during negotiations to be rather unprofessional, irrespective of whether the emotion aroused is positive or negative. Hence, only a few German negotiators deliberately utilise emotionality. Since many German negotiators have no experience with emotional outbursts from the other side, they might even give in when facing an emotional outburst of the other side. Thus, if the other party has a very emotional negotiator, he or she is hardly likely to be highly respected. As body language reveals existing emotions, most German negotiators do not exhibit vivid body language. If negotiations are held between male negotiators, the accepted level of aggression is higher than in mixed negotiation teams. However, the negotiations themselves are conducted in a relatively distanced and formal manner. Throwing in jokes during the negotiation is not standard behaviour for German negotiators, and this applies all the more for the use of irony. Generally speaking, German negotiators are found to be serious, focused, careful listeners and patient (even though they aim for effective negotiations). Some authors even see German negotiators in the internationally leading position for their listening qualities and endurance. What's more, German negotiators are interested in background information, and also find it helps to repeat information when clarifying either a situation or themselves, or to highlight arguments. Frequently, they insist on documents that reflect the already achieved results. Yet there is a study, according to which, in international comparison, German negotiators ask very few → *questions* (see topic list "questioning techniques").[2] As opposed to company-intern meetings, negotiations with third parties are not seen as a stage for self-presentation. Success evaluation is result-ori-

[2] Cf. Hernandez Requejo and Graham (2008), p. 76 et seq.

ented. To an impartial observer, Germans are remarkably fact-oriented and number-oriented: even regarding → *small talk* about the weather, Germans would not usually simply state that it is cold, but rather that it is, for example, −16 °C. From an international point of view, German negotiators are considered to be paper-oriented, since they often prepare written material on various questions. During multi-day negotiations, written follow-up processing also takes place to prepare for the following negotiation day. From an US-American perspective, Germans pay great attention to details in negotiations, and frequently consult with the responsible authorities in the head office. Due to this, Americans perceive Germans to be bureaucratic and slow negotiators. German negotiators often have a very complicated relation to their German identity. For one thing, academics have been brought up not to develop an overly positive relationship to Germany, its history and symbols, or to publicly display any attachment to the country. Hence, such patriotic gestures as, for example, flying the German flag or singing the German national anthem do not generally evoke positive emotions. Positive references to German history made by the foreign negotiators themselves—even if they do not relate to the Nazi or to the imperial era—often cause embarrassing silence, or more often negotiators are very insecure about how they should react. Many Germans are, however, closely related to their region, particularly if they were raised there. Consequently, genuine interest in the region in question is very often received positively by German negotiators. At all events, higher-ranking negotiators generally also favour high culture in Germany (concerts, museums, memorials). Companies that plan evening or weekend events with their guests are usually not interested in conducting informal negotiations during these trips. It may perhaps thus transpire that, in the course of negotiations concerning quality deficiencies disclosed by a Chinese supplier, German negotiators try to force a confession of unattained quality, even though they can see that such an open confession would evidently be in opposition to the negotiation partners' mentality.

The occasional tendency to "instruct" the negotiation partner can in some (particularly negative) cases lead the German negotiator to explain to the opposing party their own interests, or to suggest to the other side how they should organise themselves. In most cases, Germans have every confidence in products which are "Made in Germany"—German technology in particular—as well as in German business practices and legal thought processes. This is so highly developed, even to the extent that specifically German practice is considered to be superior to all other practices, and deviating approaches are rejected intrinsically (i.e. Germans are uneasy with people who do not work in the same manner as they do). This feeling of superiority ("am deutschen Wesen soll die Welt genesen"/"the world should take its example from the German nature") along with a common tendency towards a "know it all" attitude and the way other countries view the very direct way that Germans express their disapproval ("Nein") can provoke critical negotiation situations.

This particularly direct manner of emphasizing disapproval (the "tendency to be blunt" and to "disagree openly"), is a characteristic—and for the overall negotiation success a not harmless—trait of German negotiators. It is therefore unsurprising that the sentence "that is not possible" in telephone negotiations undoubtedly reveals that you are talking to a German lawyer. To put it simply, truth overrides tact. Since

German negotiators are used to this very direct way of communicating disapproval, they must in time improve their ability to assess their negotiation partner's various expressions of approval/disapproval correctly.

Yet, the direct manner offers the advantage "knocking on the bush" and so-called "shadow games" are practised relatively rarely. Even if this does not apply in general (there are exceptions in particular for international groups), academic titles—especially doctor titles (equivalent to PhD)—still play a comparably significant role. In Germany, they are included as part of one's legal name listed in official identity documents. In contrast, using a person's first name is quite common in some US-American influenced companies. One sure sign of American influence within the company is communication in English. Insofar as it is internationally acknowledged/common, German negotiators quickly switch to using first names—even if they are envoys from companies where this practice is not common. In the meantime, so-called function titles, such as authorised signatory (also expresses far-reaching power of representation), department head, division manager, director, general representative, managing director/member of the executive board are emphasised very rarely. Insofar as German companies are not US-American in character, the titles awarded are comparatively reserved in terms of language. Combined with the fact that negotiations are often lead by persons with a relatively low rank, this circumstance may cause irritation among the other party's negotiators, particularly if the negotiation peak in these countries is usually staffed with high-level representatives.

In some cases, German companies therefore tend to use other titles, indicating a higher level of authority for external business transactions compared to company-intern matters. Moreover, Germans tend to strictly differentiate between private and business matters. Private invitations—for example to the lead negotiator's home house—are thus seldom, and private matters are only discussed if the negotiation partners are acquainted with one another. Genuine sales representatives, but also employees of management consultancies, for example, in this regard tend to be more offensive, even if these topics are usually limited to breaks in negotiations. Post-1945, Germany developed into a consensus-society, i.e. all essential decisions are consented to. Together with the preference for rationally-legitimised decisions, this can e.g. lead to a situation whereby the negotiation partner, who has perhaps already made concessions in one issue, is supposed to be convinced that a decision is the only rationally-grounded decision. Among the so-called secondary virtues, characteristic for Germans, are maintenance of order and performance of duties. The latter often ensures that orders, issued by the responsible authorities, are observed, even if they are not favourable from the affected company's point of view. One very common conformist attitude inhibits agreeing on solutions not practised previously. Punctuality is also among the highest-ranked virtues in Germany. For instance, this can be observed when participants arrive slightly late for the negotiation and usually excuse themselves for being late. In this regard, deliberate delays are sometimes also used for power-posing (→ *imperial gestures*).

Prior measures taken to ensure methodical planning (also in combination with a sense of order) is a method which appeals to Germans. In negotiations, this is often displayed in the course of preparing the agenda, for example, and dividing the negotiation subjects into single negotiation phases. In this regard, German negotiators can be classed as being linearly active. This is reflected by German negotiators focusing on discussing only one negotiation subject at a time in accordance with the agenda, thus working through all negotiation subjects consecutively, in a planned order ("tackling each problem one at a time in a linear fashion").

In addition, the negotiation is also influenced by the organisation of the company. Large companies that originated in Germany are seen to be very ponderous, as they have a large set of standardised guidelines. In most cases, following these guidelines is mandatory and the approval of exceptions might be subject to a complex procedure. Usually these companies have clear guidelines regarding communication and the handling of instructions in correspondence with the basis of a hierarchical organisation. Oftentimes, the decision-making process has to include various divisions. Foreign negotiators sense a high rivalry between the departments of German companies. This could mean the responsible head of a division being permanently offended by the fact that negotiations were (seemingly) lead against the interests of one of the affected divisions. Even though SMEs also work within hierarchical structures, the company's director maintains direct power regarding the respective decision. However, this is a privilege reserved only for decisions above a certain size. The afore-mentioned rivalry is less pronounced in SMEs. In regard to essential negotiations, it is not uncommon that the company's director will participate in the final negotiation. Hence large companies utilise the attendance of a branch manager to express the relevance of the negotiations. Compared to the reference areas of western Europe and North America, gender equality in Germany regarding women's positions within company management is not extensively developed. One may only carefully assume that this circumstance facilitates a lower dissemination of an cooperative negotiation style.

When distinguishing between dealmakers and realmakers, German negotiators tend to be realmakers. In other words, when confronted with complicated situations, German negotiators approve intricate solutions that appropriately consider the complex circumstances. These solutions are aimed towards an almost perfect contract in view of technical, economic and legal elements, oftentimes leaving no option for entirely unregulated points.

4.1.6 Negotiation Preparation

It is expected of German negotiators that they are familiar with their own party's facts and figures in their entirety, as well as with those of the opposing party. This not only demands intensive preparatory measures; it also generally applies to previous business deals between the parties as well as to the current competitive environment regarding the negotiation subject. The strived-for ideal is that the German negotiator has a general understanding of the opposing party's economic situation and economic positioning as well as their customer and supplier conditions.

Apart from being familiar with individual data, an overall analytical understanding of the project under negotiation is desirable. This encompasses a general understanding of strengths and weaknesses. In more complex situations, i.e. whenever the negotiation subject is linked to several subject matters (e.g. in the course of diplomatic negotiations), the German understanding ideally demands an "overall concept" to be used as the guiding principle for all sub-projects.

The aim of thorough preparation is not just to discover party interests but also to develop a comprehensive analytical and rational argumentation and also to prepare for counter-arguments. According to the German point of view, ideal negotiations are defined by the use of analytical and rational argumentation to realise these own interests to the greatest possible extent. German negotiators thus demonstrate a high willingness to engage in the content related discussions.

Viewing the negotiation from a technical angle, the → *agenda*, which declares a clear order of discussable points and content drafts, is virtually indispensable. This preparatory measure also includes a timetable. The parties often hold intensive pre-negotiations, specifically to deal with the agenda and timetable. However, a "know-it-all"-attitude can be imputed, should knowledge elicited from this intensive preparation—which discloses facts and figures—be disseminated offensively, thus provoking negative psychological consequences. On the other hand, if these facts and figures are actually essential and the other party has simply neglected to prepare in the same manner, being prepared can make the other party feel inferior. This in return may facilitate a fundamentally negative attitude towards the negotiation.

In contrast, even if it means exposing the other party's deficiencies, German negotiators are often convinced that exerting pressure by citing facts is an appropriate means to incite the other party to (partially) make concessions.

Holding company-intern preliminary meetings is also very common. These meetings serve to determine so called "red lines", negotiation goals and options, complete proposals for single negotiation points and the individual roles of each negotiator. Company-intern hierarchy is often expressed by the fact that the highest-ranking negotiator opens the negotiation and the specialists subsequently negotiate within their respective expert fields. Yet frequently, lower-ranking participants in the negotiation are not given the chance to speak at all. This is often the case when negotiations take place between lawyers. Typically, a chief negotiator will not uncover any special competence among lower-ranking members of the negotiation delegation and the group proceeds strictly according to hierarchical structure.

Unless warranted by previous negotiation experiences that have contributed to a negative undertone for present negotiations, preparing psychological and emotional subjects is not usually widespread. Similarly, preparing tactics is also relatively uncommon. From a formal point of view, time is often the reason. However, it can also be explained by the little significance that is attached to these preliminary meetings. This is partially due to the fact that German negotiators (often) lack (tactical) training in the field of contract negotiations. What's more, rational-argumentative based agreements that consider both parties' interests make very little use of tactics. Nonetheless, preparing tactics is decidedly a part of negotiation preparations. This is at least true for negotiators who have already been confronted with certain tactics by the other party: defensive measures and counter-tactics are called for. As situational behaviour qualifies as being tactical, experienced German negotiators often have quite a large repertoire of tactics at their disposal, albeit unwittingly. Thus in Germany, → *silence* is rarely used as an intentional tactic. Yet when questioned, one professional negotiator reported that s/he has acquired the skill to remain silent for longer than his/her Chinese negotiation partners. This, however, is not the norm: German negotiators often cannot maintain a poker face, or do not alter their → *body language* in order to disguise their true emotions. Despite emotionality being generally more reserved among Germans, feelings are expressed openly which makes it easier to identify differences of opinion between individual negotiators. According to one study,[3] German negotiators have the highest self-disclosure rate among all the nations evaluated. As such, German negotiators tend to disclose a considerable amount of information about themselves, whether consciously or not.

4.1.7 Mock Negotiations

Mock negotiations are often conducted as preparation for the negotiation proper, but in Germany this practice is rather uncommon, even for high-profile business negotiations. If at all, big negotiations are theoretically thought through. It is likewise very rare to create notes on the other party's negotiators as a follow-up to previous negotiations. Nonetheless, past negotiations—especially if they were high profile—are analysed and their results subsumed in upcoming negotiations. Due to the lack of knowledge management in this field, it is generally the negotiator him-/herself who is usually in charge of remembering past negotiation experiences.

4.1.8 Location, Time and Composition of the Negotiation Team

German negotiators prefer offices as negotiation locations. This umbrella term encompasses conference rooms at airports and (occasionally) hotels, too. In companies, negotiations are generally held during office hours, which is why they rarely take place on Friday afternoons. This is closely related to the increasing importance of the work life balance and the fixed working hours of most employees; a circumstance which is also sometimes exploited in order to create time pressure (→ *deadline*) for a final agreement. In the context of international negotiations however, and particularly those held abroad, this time constraint is comparatively irrelevant. In these instances, German negotiators have no option but to adapt to the situative requirements. Generally speaking, German negotiators, who negotiate abroad to be more flexible and take local customs into account.

[3] Cf. Hernandez Requejo and Graham (2008), p. 76 et seq.

Unless the negotiation is very small, negotiation teams are ideally comprised of two members (→ *two negotiators*): for example one expert for technical questions and one for commercial-legal matters. However, negotiations on industry plants, company acquisitions and similarly important, complex negotiation subjects customarily require larger negotiation teams. Here, the technical, commercial and legal sides are represented separately. Even in very big negotiations, negotiation teams from Germany are routinely smaller than those from comparable countries, e.g. China or USA. In medium-sized negotiations, noticeable differences in team compositions can cause severe issues which in turn can quickly lead to deadlock situations. It is accordingly in the interests of both parties to strive for balanced negotiation teams. Due to the participation of a lawyer being relatively uncommon in certain sectors or negotiation situation, their participation is often perceived as an imbalance. Unless the opposing party's interests oblige a particular composition of the negotiating team, in Germany negotiators tend to be selected from the lower echelons within the company—even in very important negotiations. In addition, German companies seldom employ negotiation → *analysts* or other professional negotiation consultants.

4.1.9 Small Talk

German companies deem small talk (→ *chit chat*) to be of little significance for the overall negotiation process. Neglecting small talk means that German businesses often disregard its potential for creating a positive negotiation atmosphere. They preclude understanding the group dynamics of the other side, and forego analysing the emotionally normal behaviour which can be useful for evaluating emotions during the negotiation itself. Experience gained from students and professional negotiators confirms this assumed disinterest or lack of knowledge. It would seem that Germans tend to believe that the risks incurred by small talk (i.e. offering insights to the other party) and the costs occurred far outweigh the potential advantages (i.e. understanding of the other party and trust building).

This said, small talk harbours practically no "taboo topics" for German negotiators; and yet only a handful of topics are deemed appropriate. This is to prevent the risk of creating an uncomfortable atmosphere whilst at the same time being able to use these topics as the basis for the following main negotiation. For instance, although a very common topic, small talk about the weather is unpopular as it proves difficult to link to other conversations. Unsurprisingly, private matters are very rarely discussed (see above). Topics such as the journey, traveling and sports (particularly soccer) are prevalent. If the host of the negotiation openly communicates his sympathy for a specific hobby or interest, e.g. illustrations or models displayed in the office, this may be used to form the basis for small talk. Business dinners might be organised as part of the actual negotiation, although their attendance is subject to observing the compliance rules as mentioned earlier. As a rule, when negotiating with German corporations, an invitation to the company canteen is a common practice. Pursuant to the → *similar to me-effect*, German negotiators prefer negotiation partners with similar negotiation behaviour and values.

4.2 How Chinese Negotiate

4.2.1 Preliminary Notes

In the chapter on German negotiators, we stated that it is not possible to distinguish a general type of German negotiator. Likewise, it is also not possible to distinguish a general type of "Chinese negotiator" or "Chinese negotiation style". In fact, there are huge regional differences within China—far greater than those found in Germany for example. Hence, negotiators from Hong Kong are closer to the western mentality than Chinese negotiators from the mainland, due to Hong Kong's historical experience with being an English colony and their recurrent special status. Then there are single ethnic minorities, e.g. the Uyghurs, with specific characteristics in their mentality (direct and emotive communication) which can have an effect at negotiation level. Likewise, there are relatively big differences between large, modern cities and more rural provinces. There are also significant differences between state-owned companies and, in particular, internationally operating private companies. The negotiators of the latter companies are regularly fluent in English and usually also have experience with international negotiations. Both are much less common for employees of state-owned enterprises. Moreover, it should be borne in mind that the People's Republic of China has passed through one of the most outstanding, dynamic change process of the last centuries, even by global standards. From being a self-contained, communistic, economically weak developing country before economic reforms began in 1978, the PRC has developed China at great speed to become the worldwide No. 1 export nation, and even has the prospect of becoming the biggest economy in the world. The PRC is most definitely on the way to dominate strategic future markets both economically and, in parts, technologically. By the same token, the PRC is also developing into a world power politics-wise.

These developments have taken place within the framework of a capitalistic economy in which not only the communist party but also the state have been granted strong influence regarding strategical economic questions—and even more comprehensively regarding political matters. From the Chinese point of view, and in light of its status as a historical, cultural and political superpower, China has currently regained its standing, to which it sees itself entitled. Many negotiators have now gained experience abroad which was not the case until just a few years ago. Although the practice of including government agencies in the negotiation process has decreased significantly in recent years, governmental involvement is still higher, compared to the western negotiation culture. In negotiations with other companies, Western companies can reap benefits from the fact that they have developed good relations both with the Chinese authorities and their own Western government. This—seen from a Chinese perspective at least—is beneficial for overcoming bureaucratic obstacles.

These rapid developments inevitably do not apply to all areas and relate more to younger people than to the older generation. Yet despite this, they facilitate a certain heterogeneity. Opposed to this, traditional Confucianism and the communist party's guidelines as well as the general orientation towards collective wealth ensure a comparably homogenous socialisation.

Following the roots of the long-established principle of Yin-Yang, traditional and communistic guidelines also match dialectically. With regard to contract negotiations, they also promote the pursuit of outer harmony. Moreover, this approach also complies with the ambiguity tolerance. i.e. the positive fundamental philosophy towards ambiguous communication.

4.2.2 Negotiation Training

In the meantime, the leading Chinese universities offer specific courses on contract negotiations. Besides the educational programs that follow the example of US-American courses, there are also offers that are more closely aligned with their own traditions and preferences. There is great demand for these courses. Already by 2008, the Chinese negotiation teacher *Liu Birong* (author of approx. 25 books on negotiation) boasted of having taught over 10,000 people the secrets of negotiation.[4] From a traditional point of view and right up to this day, mastering strategies and tactics is very important. Accordingly, President *Xi Jinping*'s televised new year's speech for 2018 showed a wall of books in the background including, for example, the ca. 2500 year old "The Art of War" by *Sun Tzu* as well as "On War", written by *Carl von Clausewitz* in 1832. In Chinese culture, the use of traditional strategies as well as the development of new strategies and tactics would appear to be more highly esteemed than in Western negotiation culture (see examples under tactics).

4.2.3 Mentality

As stated above, not all negotiators are the same. Various factors can influence the individual negotiator's mentality and, more particularly, their actual behaviour. However, it can generally be stated that Chinese negotiators can be characterised as being collectivist and, with regard to personal contact, more oriented towards tradition. Hence, the actions of Chinese negotiators are on the whole rule-based. This point, alongside the Chinese language as a characterising element, promotes a comparably homogenous mentality amongst negotiators and a fortiori in relation to their

[4] Cf. Mehring (2017), p. 39.

conduct. Thus, the understanding of negotiations as complex strategy games, which can be won not with mere recipes, but with situation-appropriate strategies and tactics, is also relatively widespread.

4.2.4 Orientation Towards Legal Requirements

In the course of negotiations, the level of orientation towards legal requirements still remains limited. Up until a few years ago, the Chinese legal system exhibited substantial defects—even in fields not relating to the interest of the communist party or the state. Substantial law did not comply with the needs of a modern economy; procedural law and enforcement proceedings were hardly effective; judges did not receive comprehensive education. They were both underpaid and vulnerable to corruption. In addition, they perceived themselves to be dependent on local officials.

The People's Republic of China is, however, putting major effort into reducing the deficits of their legal order. Yet—with the notable exception of the legal regulation of corruption—these developments do not seem to have decisively impacted the negotiator's attitude towards law. From a Western perspective, there is a peculiar absence of fair procedures regarding legal proceedings with any of the numerous state-controlled or strategically important companies.

Chinese negotiators do not judge Chinese law to be a decisive safeguard against any breach of duties by the opposing party, which would create enough trust to allow them to take economic risks. In this regard, many negotiators lack a positive attitude towards law. This assumption was supported in the course of a study, conducted internationally by the authors and stated that the majority of the surveyed Chinese did not agree that a deliberate deception on the legal situation should be sanctioned legally. Notwithstanding, there is quite a significant tendency for Chinese negotiators to actually use the law for their own benefit. These days, as opposed to the past, negotiations include lawyers more often. What's more, the increasing importance of the law is reflected, for example, in the contract clauses, in which Chinese companies certainly invest time and specialised manpower during big projects. Further indications of the greater importance being attached to the law are the Agreement on Chinese law, the Agreement on the authoritativeness of the Chinese language version of the contract, and the Agreement on a Chinese arbitration institution (CIETAC) as the responsible authority in case of dispute.

4.2.5 Trust Building and Contract Negotiations

Contractual relationships generally necessitate having trust in the other party. This especially applies to long-term or complex relations (→ *permanent business relation*) and those requiring a high level of cooperation. Regarding their substantial content and the according enforcement mechanisms, legal orders can be effective, inexpensive deterrents to infringers; so much so, in fact, that they significantly support both parties' trust in the negotiation. In case any legal orders—such as the Chinese—do not provide this trust (at least, not yet), it is essential to build trust through one's behaviour during the negotiations. Hence, for quite some time now, non-legal trust-building has played a significant role in China.

Guanxi, the relationship between the companies involved and key people within these companies, is built on the basis of trust. Combined with legal measures, this aims at ensuring long-term success. Although the significance of relationships is deeply rooted in the teachings of Confucianism, it also bears relation to modern economic needs. The Confucianist ideal creates ethical bindings between negotiators of equal rank as well as mutual obligations within hierarchical relationships. The main goal is a harmonious togetherness.

Guanxi is facilitated by many people and involved companies who build this network of trust on the groundwork of long-term relationships. Even in countries with efficient legal orders, stable permanent relationships exist without any need of legal involvement. This is due to the parties being hardly ever, or only in extreme cases, willing to risk long-term relationships for solitary points of dispute, irrespective of their magnitude. In addition, normally in a long-term relationship there is also some personal trust between the managers on both sides.

Turning to legal proceedings in case of conflict in permanent relationships is the last resort, even in countries with an efficient legal order. The functioning of these relationships without any legal involvement certainly explains why Chinese companies tend to strive for permanent relationships. If the Chinese negotiation partner only expects a short-term relationship, much lesser investments into the quality of the relationship are made and the offers are usually assessed as less attractive. Ideal Guanxi, comprising several companies and numerous involved people within those companies, would provide a particularly stable basis, since the consequences of serious mistakes could evoke the weakening or even overall loss of this whole relationship network. At the other end of the spectrum, it is possible to observe the overemphasis of Guanxi in China to the point of unfairly giving advantage to companies beyond any economical reasoning and showing a tendency towards nepotism.

Subsequently, a non-Chinese company, desiring to build a business relationship through negotiations, has significantly better chances if it already has a stable permanent relationship with a different Chinese company within the Guanxi of the potentially new Chinese negotiation partner. Employing one of the often-recommended mediators (*Zhongjian Ren*) can, however, be classified as a borderline case of corruption, particularly where relationships with the government are concerned. Nonetheless, a well-connected mediator does have a large Guanxi as well as appropriate social status.

In this way, using a mediator facilitates the Chinese company's trust in the Western company. The mediator thus "lends" a part of the general trust in his person. If the aim is a trustful relationship between two people, it is recommendable to build trust with various people on each side.

This approach prevents being dependent on a single interpersonal trust relationship. The emphasis placed on building trust in China also explains why negotiations with the Chinese include a lengthy period of the negotiators becoming acquainted with those sent by the non-Chinese company. If the aim were merely to gather information, a significantly shorter period of becoming acquainted would be sufficient. The generous hospitality of Chinese companies encounters a strict compliance culture with negotiators from some Western countries (e.g. Germany), where the acceptance of valuable gifts or services is prohibited strictly. If a gift or invitation is rejected, the Chinese host is at risk of losing face, which is why special sensitivity is required. In return, Chinese negotiators are largely very appreciative of the hospitality displayed by Western negotiators towards their Chinese counterparts.

Regarding the exact content of the contract, Chinese companies do not perceive the contract to be fully fixed but rather flexible, depending on the further development of the negotiation. Renegotiations after the conclusion of a contract are thus more significant and it is the planner's task to consider this circumstance at all times. The contract should thus accordingly ensure a balanced power position over the course of the contract period. Therefore, Western companies tend to pay more frequent quality assurance visits to Chinese suppliers and take further measures to monitor their success on an ongoing basis. This relativisation of the agreement over the actual content of the contract (no clear *pacta sunt servanda*) could be encouraged by difficulties to legally enforce the contract. In addition, this circumstance is accompanied by the disbelief of perfectly static solutions. Though Guanxi prevents severe breaches of the expected performance, is not powerful enough to prevent fights for the additional gain of small benefits after the contract has been completed.

Despite the Chinese business interest in permanent relationships, one-time deals do sometimes occur. Since these cases are one-off transactions and the volume of the deal is usually not very high, investing in the relationship is deemed not worthwhile. Neither do these relationships provide the same degree of security for one-time deals as, in these situations, the Guanxi-approach is less relevant for choosing a business partner. The use of "mediators" is not particularly common in these cases, either. Yet, even in these situations trust plays a much more significant part than in other negotiation cultures.

4.2.6 Basic Characteristics and Approaches

Chinese negotiators are very patriotic. They are convinced of the importance and size of their country and proud of its rapid ascent. Linked to these factors is a self-confidence, sometimes extending as far as a feeling of superiority towards other cultures. A high level of self-confidence generally prevails in the context of negotiations, too, which serves to strengthen the resolve of Chinese negotiators against the demands of a non-Chinese negotiation partner. Negotiators from the PRC are often strongly influenced in their behaviour by the prevalent rules and traditions, which particularly include honouring the other party. Special honour is accorded to older people. Inasmuch, Chinese people speak of the so-called Shehui Dengji (social hierarchy/social status). According to a study by *Geert Hofsteede*,[5] the social distance between superiors and subordinates ranks among the highest worldwide. From the Chinese point of view, respecting the social hierarchy starts with the choice of negotiators. However, the hierarchical organisation is essential during the negotiation, too. Since the Chinese also attach great importance to punctuality, it can often be advantageous to arrive slightly earlier than one's appointment. In China, ceremonies are highly valued, which is why foreign negotiators are expected to behave appropriately in those suituations.

In addition, the Chinese place great importance on keeping face for both sides. The concept of face saving is very prominent in China. The key term Mianzi stands for both "face" and "social capital". Social capital can be lost by indulging in behaviour that does not conform to the rules, e.g. displaying excessive self-centredness; disrespecting the hierarchy; loud or aggressive behaviour. Chinese negotiators very rarely express → *emotions* and, if they do, these might not be entirely sincere. Their → *body language* is characterised by self-discipline, thus indicating very little to the opposing party. Since Western negotiators are perceived to be very insensitive towards gradual behaviour patterns, Chinese negotiators sometimes tend to speak more openly with Western negotiators than they would in exclusively Chinese negotiations.

Demanding to formally concede an earlier breach of obligations by one side is marginally acceptable to the Chinese, which is why this concession is rarely given—even in cases with an obvious breach of duties. If this concession is needed due to legal requirements, e.g. for settling a damage claim through the insurance company, it is advisable to employ a neutral third party to allow the concession to be granted with minimal loss of face.

For Chinese negotiators, listening (tinghua) is much more important than in Western negotiation cultures (see corresponding topic list). Yet, the number of actively conversation-oriented Chinese negotiators seems to increase. Chinese negotiators are known to be very patient. However, this does not mean that Chinese negotiators relinquish the opportunity to use fake time pressure (→ *false deadline*). Chinese negotiators want to win (*kiasuness*), provided that the competition is the reference point. On the other hand, the important influence of Confucianism supports the emphasis on maintaining face and harmony. As a result, this generally leads to a → *win-lose approach*, although, in comparison to e.g. the US, the win is not expressed clearly either during the negotiation or in the contract text. A content-related competitive negotiation is deemed appropriate if the parties are striving for a cooperative relationship, e.g. a joint venture. In this regard, Chinese negotiators specifically distinguish the negotiation process from the future party relationship.

Despite the prevailing turbo-capitalism, the PRC is deeply influenced by collective thinking. Thus, negotiators always say "we" instead of "I". If foreigners consequently disregard this rule, it is felt to be negative. Compared to negotiators from other countries, despite definitely viewing the deal individually, the emphasis of

[5] Cf. www.hofstede-insights.com.

Chinese negotiators lies on viewing the long-term perspectives. This includes considering the overall context of relationships with other companies; i.e. orientation towards the overall picture. Chinese negotiators are said to not negotiate in a linear manner, i.e. one point after another and can thus be described as polychron. One element of this, i.e. various parallel communication processes with different people, are not at issue for Western companies. However, it can be observed that several negotiation points are discussed simultaneously. Accordingly, a negotiation point is not discussed under the condition that a different point has been finalised. This "holistic" way of negotiating is not as aimless as it might seem: It allows, Chinese negotiators to follow the concept of negotiating a general framework of conforming points and then continue with the negotiation of problematic points. Even if several single points are discussed in parallel, the recapitulation of those points is based on conceptional thoughts. Hence, the big picture (→ *missing the big picture*) is always on the Chinese negotiator's mind. In contrast to the majority of the Western negotiating cultures, in China, proposals are often first justified and then put forward in concrete terms. Reactions to the reasons given can be used in this way to modify the proposal in a way that is not recognisable to the other side. Framework agreements, which should be applied in the long-term, are valued as being strategically important. The suggestions often include rules and rule mechanisms which are beneficial to the other party in the short-term but which profit the own party in the long-term.

Traditionally in the whole of Asia, China is famous for its traders. Thus, it is usually common to leave room for negotiation in the course of the first offer. The active negotiator is the preferred negotiation character and is notorious for making an ambitious first offer. This also accords with the high importance of reciprocity as the prevalent principle of justice in China. Regarding other content-related questions and additional conditions the Chinese do, however, wait for the other party's initiative in the hope that at least some proposals are acceptable without further negotiation and e.g. without granting any demands in return. Chinese negotiators ask considerably more questions than negotiators from other cultures. Due to the emphasis placed on building trust, many questions relate to personal details. In addition to the culture of asking questions, comparing as well as presenting available parallel offers from other suppliers to the other side in China play a significantly more important role than in other negotiation cultures. Not only is there an attempt to use the → *framing effect* here, but likewise a well-founded rejection of the several proposals is more difficult. Regularly, the reasoning also reveals more information about the other side.

Despite their strong orientation towards hierarchical order, Chinese negotiators do not refrain from tactical deception concerning their authority to make decisions. Thus, it is quite possible that the highest-ranking person is formally the chief negotiator, but the actual → *decision-maker* (often called teamleader) making the final decision is another member of the negotiation team. As it might be difficult for the opposing party to discover who it the actual decision-maker, this tactic can prove advantageous. If, however, the "secret" decision-maker were ranked significantly higher than the (ostensible) chief negotiator, detection is likely in situations if, for example, Chinese negotiators react to a joke in line with the higher-ranking decision maker, thus giving him away. The authors of this book were able to see for themselves how a Chinese purported chief-negotiator held a conversation out of sight of the delegation, even though in the actual negotiation the gestures, body language and question and answer types implied that he was the final decision-maker. Based on the fact that, in China, many decisions are finalised at the highest company level, it will occur quite often that the final decision-maker is not present at the negotiation, despite there being a delegation of high ranking negotiators present.

Only very rarely do Chinese negotiators utter a direct "no". Essentially, the many forms of "maybe", or soft disapproval, can be a major problem for their western counterparts. In this regard, not even signing the contract means clear agreement with all the negotiated clauses of the contract. Indeed, the other party may well intend to adapt certain clauses during the implementation phase of the contract. Yet, even in China there are cases where disapproval is expressed openly. If negotiators on the Chinese side remain silent and lower their heads, i.e. look down, this points to direct disapproval. In the Chinese negotiation culture, → *silence* and the use of → *negotiation pauses* is highly developed.[6] Even without the aim of tactically creating silence, Chinese negotiators hesitate for a longer period of time before giving their answer. Oftentimes a direct response is given eight seconds or longer after the question has been asked. This delay before answering buys deliberation time (→ *considered response*).

This reasoning also explains why Chinese negotiators always wait for the interpreter to translate, even if the other party's language is sufficiently understood. Intentional silence is often used tactically, since it is presumed that people often cannot stand a longer period of silence. Particularly due to the discomfort caused by silence, but also because it becomes increasingly difficult to break a silence without losing face, Chinese negotiators are skilled in breaking silence. As a rule, the first words to break the silence do not pertain to the negotiation subject but rather offer the guests a cup of tea, for example; or when attending the negotiation as a guest, asking for a drink.

Chinese negotiators are considered to have well-developed communication behaviour, the focus of which lies on indirect statements. As stated above, their ability for ambiguity as well as their tolerance for ambiguity are even more developed. Vague or ambiguous statements are thus used deliberately and are not perceived to be negative. Furthermore, if the other party also makes unclear statements, Chinese negotiators tend not to find this irritating. Pressure is applied indirectly and deceit is also oblique. Chinese negotiators only apply more explicit measures if they feel that their Western negotiation partner is not sufficiently sensitive to their indirect communication signals. If the negotiations require interpreters, this often makes communication considerably more difficult. A dependency on only one interpreter can equip the interpreter with a life of this own, either regarding deliberations on changes in the context of the translation, or by way of independent negotiation contributions.

---

[6]Cf. Mehring (2017), p. 221 et seqq.

In China, the art of negotiation is often compared with the art of war.[7] Therefore the "Thirty-Six Strategems" and Sun Tsu "The Art of War" are very popular literature among Chinese negotiators. This facilitates also a → *win-lose* perspective, even though Chinese negotiation literature also covers the *win-win* aspect of negotiations. This approach is moreover linked to the attempt to utilise the 36 stratagems and other classical recommendations, and to develop effective tactics for the own side. For example, the famous stratagem No. 6 "make noise in the east and attack from the west" is used in negotiations by deceiving about priorities and switching the own concessions in seemingly important questions with concessions of the other party in the questions that are actually essential for pursuing the own interests (→ *padding*).[8]

4.2.7 Negotiation Preparation

In China, major importance seems to be attributed to the comprehensive preparation of negotiations. However, the accessible literature does not offer any detailed information on this specific negotiation phase, although it emphasises the prior analysis of interests, the negotiation aim and possible tactics.[9] Practitioners routinely report that Chinese negotiators are very well prepared. In this regard, Chinese negotiators do not solely gather the information relevant for the actual business deal (→ *information procurement*). According to the overall approach they also inform themselves about the other party's market position, market behaviour and relationship network. Information is essential in the Chinese negotiation culture. This also explains why Chinese negotiators ask so many → *questions*. The value of information is so high that, the use of illegal information procurement methods by Chinese negotiators was at times reported in Western media.

Pre-negotiations concerning the venue, time and the → *agenda* are very common in bigger projects. The first contact before the actual negotiation preparation often takes place using a mediator with a powerful relationship network and high social rank. In some instances, international enterprises have employed the grandchildren of the originally leading cadres of the Chinese communist party as mediators.

4.2.8 Venue, Time and Composition of the Negotiation Delegation

Negotiations with Chinese companies predominantly take place in China. This applies regardless of the fact that many Chinese negotiators are interested in negotiating contracts abroad, not only to get to know the country better, but also the

[7] Cf. Mehring (2017) with further references (translated and commented edition of the book (with the same title) by *Liu Birong*, one of China's leading negotiation experts).

[8] Cf. Mehring (2017), p. 287 footnote 416.

[9] Cf. Mehring (2017).

technologies employed by their negotiation partner. Interest in a return visit is often reciprocated at a later stage. Negotiations usually take place in a conference room of the Chinese company. Other conference rooms near the company are also a suitable location.

Traditionally, Chinese negotiators prefer to set a negotiation date with a long temporal forerun. Having said that, appointments for negotiations with e.g. entrepreneurs are commonly made at short notice. In addition, Chinese negotiations are very lengthy. This is mainly due to the long acquaintance phase as well as proceeding carefully throughout the actual negotiation. In contrast, Chinese negotiators are also familiar with the different practice of short, effective negotiations, as prevalent in the USA or Germany. They do not, however, appreciate this manner of negotiating. Since Chinese negotiators sometimes attempt to use time pressure (→ *deadline*) shortly before their date of return, it is common that foreign negotiators visiting Chinese companies are flexible regarding their return journey or opt for a sequenced negotiation process with different stages and will under no circumstances reveal their return date. For normal length negotiations, periods from Tuesday to Thursday are ideal.[10] Due to the significance of hierarchy and age, the ideal negotiation delegation mirrors the opposing party regarding their choice of chief delegator, taking their hierarchical structure and age into account too. Hierarchical differences among foreign negotiators are generally compensated by the creation of special titles especially to be used in the negotiation with Chinese business people. Age differences can generally be overcome by choice of clothing and attitude. In the past, Chinese negotiation delegations generally included a large number of negotiators. These days, although Chinese delegations are still bigger than Western negotiation delegations, the difference between the two seems to be diminishing. Rank, age, and decision authority matter to Chinese negotiators and are the recommended alignment points for their Western negotiation partners. Chinese negotiation books differentiate between teamleaders and main negotiators.[11] In order to build trustful personal relationships, personal constancy among the respective negotiators is essential.

4.2.9 Acquaintance Phase/Small Talk

Based on the reasons aforementioned (i.e. no trust in legal security, significance of Guanxi for trust in the business partner), Chinese negotiators do not tend to practice short → *small talk*, but prefer a longer period of becoming acquainted. This phase usually includes not only joint dinners but also sightseeing tours etc. At this stage, the parties do not discuss the actual agreement. Observations focus on the other party's group structure and the social behaviour of individual negotiators. The main

[10] Cf. Mehring (2017), p. 285.

[11] Zhang et al. (2018), p. 115 et seq.

aim is to build trust between the negotiators of both sides, especially at the leading level.

4.2.10 Tactics in Contract Negotiations

As previously stated, strategies and tactics are highly valued. This promotes the application as well as the development of new tactics. Since there are numerous specifically Chinese tactics, the following section only mentions selected tactics. In this regard, tactics using deception (see topic list "deception"), which are anchored within the "Thirty-Six strategems" or "The Art of War" by Sun-Tzu, play a significant role. According to these traditional strategems, tactics, as well as the Confucian tradition, indirect deceit is far more common than making explicitly untrue statements. Among others, these deception tactics include bluffing about the value of negotiation points (→ *padding*) as well as the degree of concessions possible on the Chinese side.

Pressure tactics (see topic list "pressure and threats") primarily focus on the competition situation. In some cases, for example, it is common to invite several Western companies which compete with one another for parallel negotiations. This creates an auction-like pressure according to the idea of → *negotiauctions*. In other cases, pressure is exerted on single negotiators once their individual weak spots have been identified.

That is the reason why the open threat to terminate the negotiation is rare. Furthermore, pressure and deceit can be combined. Oftentimes deceit only refers to the aim of pressure (see stratagem 6). False statements concerning content are far more seldom, even though this approach is governed by a specific stratagem (stratagem No. 7). This could conceivably be linked to the fact that the threat of the deceit being disclosed is significantly higher and would inevitably lead to a loss of face. Many tactics are based on the great importance of face saving. Hence, there are specific shaming tactics, whereby Western negotiators are accused of threatening the relationship with their behaviour. Past disputes are mentioned in the hope that this will give the other party a bad conscience. The aim is to achieve concessions in essential points. Chinese negotiators greatly appreciate Western negotiators helping to save the Chinese negotiator's face, e.g. by foregoing a discussion of false statements and rather setting these facts right under four eyes. The importance of Guanxi and the according personal relationship promotes the use of manipulation tactics, aimed at exploiting the opposing negotiator's personal relationship towards the business deal. Chinese negotiators are often very skilled at defeating tactics. Hence, they do not only explore the seriousness of a set → *deadline* but also exhaust the period of this deadline. This procedure aims not only to make the most of the time limit but also to expose the negotiating partner to negotiation stress (insecurity concerning the need to terminate the negotiation if the deadline is exceeded). Sometimes the Chinese side uses bilingual signs for the negotiation. Sometimes the wrong Chinese name sign is deliberately given to a Western negotiator. This is a ploy aimed at discovering whether or not the Western negotiator understands Chinese. In some cases, agreements are purposely paraphrased slightly incorrectly (→ *foggy recall*). This is either an attempt to subtly change part of the agreement, or the objective may be to delay the negotiations. If the Western negotiator tries to imitate his Chinese negotiation partner by trying to avoid a clear no, the Chinese side sometimes tries to interpret this behaviour as approval, in accordance with the Western approach. Above that, it was also observed that Chinese negotiators deliberately negotiated the price in such a hard manner, that the European side wanted a break off of the negotiations. The Chinese side subsequently swaps the chief negotiator and, with the knowledge of the European side's → *deal-breaker*, goes on to negotiate a result very close to the acceptable minimal demand made by the European company. This tactic enjoys a certain popularity because it gives the Chinese side the impression that making the demanded concessions has actually been utilised as a last resort. Antidotes are premature sham break offs of the negotiations in order to force the Chinese side to give in prematurely and not to reveal the own side's real limit.

4.2.11 Implementation of Negotiation Results and Further Negotiation

As already stated, Chinese negotiators perceive the agreement on a contract as an important interim result but not as the absolute conclusion of negotiations. According to this attitude, the implementation phase leaves scope for further concretising or renegotiating and slightly specific points. In particular, points which are presumed to be non-essential for the Western company are often the subject of intensive renegotiations, despite an agreed upon contract. In this regard, the different language versions (e.g. English and Chinese) can also prove problematic. From a Western point of view, the implementation phase is very expensive and lengthy, since it requires equally elaborate measures and processes. Yet, there are also Chinese companies that feel more obliged to conform to the clauses initially agreed upon, particularly if this can create a competitive advantage over other Chinese companies. The Chinese consider oral agreements to be even less binding and are not viewed as being sufficient, regardless of their legal validity.

4.3 How US-Americans Negotiate

4.3.1 Preliminary Note

As already stated regarding German negotiators, there is no such thing as the "US-American negotiator". It can rather be said that there are various influencing factors that shape the negotiation style. From the outset, the USA has always been country of immigration. In the course of history, this immigration has been from various regions across the globe. In principle, the sheer size of the country coupled with its background of immigration would seem to point to a high level of regional heterogeneity between negotiators. Yet, due to the high assimilation power of the country, the negotiation style among American negotiators is comparably homogenous.

If negotiators from California are said to be more open for innovative ideas than their colleagues from the East coast,[12] this may be due to the specific companies settled in California, which are—as part of the Digital Economy—more dependent on developing innovative solutions. The reason would thus lie less in regional specificities but rather in the respective company and its culture. Hence, even though some differences might be observed e.g. between negotiators from New York and the Midwest, the negotiation style can primarily be explained by generally factors of influence, such as personal mentality, experience abroad, gender, age, hierarchy, branch, professional expertise, negotiation skills, the company's negotiation strategy, role (buyer, seller), the negotiation's character as a one-time deal or being part of a permanent business relationship.

In addition, some factors are particularly important in the USA. For instance, in comparison to other countries, a bigger difference can be seen between negotiators who, like the current US President Donald Trump, prefer hard-ball negotiations, and those that strive for a cooperative negotiation following the → *Harvard negotiation concept* (see further below). Furthermore, in the USA the difference between a "business-like negotiator" and a "legalistic negotiator" is more emphasised (for this see further below).

4.3.2 Negotiation Training

The USA is the land that first discovered the significance of negotiations. From the early 1960s, game theory and social psychology discovered negotiations as a scientific field in the USA. In the middle of the 1970s, very successful negotiation books were already being published and corresponding coaching was offered as a guide for business-related negotiations.

In 1979, the lawyer *Roger Fisher* established the Harvard Negotiation Project at the Harvard Law School, which in 1983 became the institutionalised "Program on Negotiation" (PON). This program combines negotiation science and training. This became the basis for teaching contract negotiations not only to thousands of students of Harvard Law School and Harvard Business School, but to tens of thousands of practitioners in the course of PON. Many of the books published on contract negotiations, even those published by famous scientific authors, are geared towards a broad audience. The most lasting effect is ascribed to the book "Getting to Yes – Negotiating an Agreement Without Giving In", 1st ed. 1981 by *Fisher/Ury*. In the

[12] Cf. Hernandez Requejo and Graham (2008), p. 238 et seq.

meantime, this book has been published in many languages and various editions. Worldwide it is associated with the name → *Harvard negotiation concept*. A great number of the underlying basic ideas of this concept—such as the interest-oriented negotiation or measuring the own and opposing side's negotiation power by means of the → *BATNA*—have become a global benchmark for professional negotiators.

Nowadays, negotiation courses are offered all over the USA at law schools and business schools, as well as at engineering schools and for business psychologists. The → *win-win approach* (*expanding the pie*; → *negotiation pie*) which is promoted within the Harvard Program is, however, less relevant within the US-American practice, than could be expected with view to the Harvard negotiation concept.

The openness for interdisciplinary cooperation as well as practice orientation is a special strength of the US-American university system and is particularly beneficial for negotiation practice. In this regard, lawyers, psychologists and business economists as well as classical economists cooperate intensively. The practical consulting actions of many negotiation scientists, the cooperation between scientists and practitioners and the feedback of course participants with practical experience ensure an intensive exchange between theory and practical experience.

Even outside the university sphere, the USA depicts a rich variety of offers for coaching and consultancy. The amount of literature on contract negotiations written in laymen's terms, which invites the reader to private study, is hardly quantifiable and in total attains a print run of millions. Generally, each book focuses on a specific issue or deals with a negotiation approach, which the author propagandises as resounding. The average education level in contract negotiations is estimated to be higher than in all other comparable trading nations. Yet, many US-American negotiators primarily take the gained knowledge to be a recipe that just needs to be applied. Despite the volume of negotiation training on offer, more in-depth understanding of negotiations as a strategy game requiring complex, individually adapted thoughts is less common.

4.3.3 Mentalities

Just like there is no typical contract negotiator as such for each nation (see above), there are also significant differences of mentality among US-American negotiators. Having said that, the law of averages allows similarities in values to be identified, which, from a relative point of view, are a common basis in comparison to negotiators from other countries. Thus, certain basic cultural values are common to US-citizens, regardless of their original country of origin, religion or social status. These basic values coin their mentality. The following notes illustrate these aspects in detail.

4.3.4 Orientation Towards Legal Requirements

The US-American version of common law is, as the common law in general is, strongly based on formalities. Thus, the exact wording of the contract (*plain meaning rule*) is more significant than the economically desired outcome or a fair balance of demands. This also complies with the fact that US Americans emphasise the importance of self-responsibility for the contractual parties. Moreover, US law is case-based and does thus not favour general rules. Likewise, legal rules vary significantly from state to state. Contract-based solutions are therefore the only means to prevent legal divergence.

This approach promotes the inclusion of lawyers in the contract negotiation and also explains the tendency towards very lengthy and detailed contracts that cover every possible case. In general, these contracts are also formulated in such a manner that circumstances outside the written contract are not regarded.

With regard to legal certainty, the parties regularly do not want common law to apply, which is the case where contractual gaps occur. The US-American proceeding law ensures that it is not economically sensible to initiate court proceedings for small sums. Opposed to that, the system of serious penalties with legal means such as class actions, punitive damages and very high and hardly juridically reviewable sanctions by government agencies (e.g. the Securities and Exchange Commission (SEC) or the DOJ (Department of Justice)) ensure that companies are aware of the fact that more voluminous transactions cannot be made without legal consultation. US lawyers do not enjoy great popularity, firstly due to the high sanctions which entail accordingly high costs for US lawyers, but also because of the utilised jury system. This system allows laymen, who are emotionally influenceable, to make decisions, thus allowing a good lawyer the opportunity to achieve results against the objective law. The US have an extremely high number of lawyers, not only in absolute numbers, but also with regard to their ratio per number of inhabitants (the highest per capita rate globally, at least as far as the bigger states are concerned).

US-Americans lawyers tend to think more economically-oriented than for instance German lawyers. This is due to their stronger interdisciplinary-based education, e.g. in the field of law and economics, but also linked to their high degree of willingness to become acquainted with other fields, and to use this knowledge for their further actions. Likewise, their generally positive attitude towards taking risks with respective chances (for this see further below) makes it easier for US-lawyers to take a stance that is more strongly economically-based. Thus, viewing law as an integral part of risk management is not uncommon.

Nonetheless, in the US, a lawyer will employ a different approach to negotiations than an economist. This has led to businesslike negotiators being differentiated from legalistic negotiators in the US-American sphere. Businesslike negotiators are generally very optimistic about the successful completion of negotiations. Hence, they prefer broad strokes and do not insist on a perfectly detailed solution. On the other hand, legalistic negotiators, similar to German negotiators, place great emphasis on dates and facts, often informing themselves of potentially important details beforehand. This type of negotiator is even less likely to apply emotional negotiation methods than business negotiators. The negotiation focus of legalistic negotiators is rather on finalising details and fixating specific legal facts. In essence, this differentiation can be compared to distinguishing dealmakers (completion-oriented negotiators) from real makers (oriented towards a perfectly constructed contract), the mere difference being that the latter differentiation relates more to a personal mentality than being common to a certain group of people.

In rare cases, one can also observe a so-called “moralistic negotiator”. Their behaviour is led by idealism and they often appeal to ideals and emotions whilst being generally sceptical of the opposing side’s moral integrity. This type of negotiator is rarely found in unmitigated B2B-negotiations. This is true despite the fact that even ethical principles in the US are usually conveyed more openly and intensively than for instance in Western Europe. In the US, it is more common than in Europe that companies are based on an organisation with an idealistic purpose.

Even though lawyers in the US are directly involved in a high number of negotiations, there are also negotiations from which lawyers are deliberately excluded. In this context, the primary aim of responsible managers is to achieve an agreement in essential economic points. The second step is to task the responsible lawyer with drafting a signable contract based on these interim results. This basic agreement (deal) is usually sealed with a handshake and often also fixated in writing. This is often done by means of so-called term sheets, where bullet points, i.e. not fully formulated clauses, summarise the current status of the negotiation. Another option is to issue a letter of intent (LOI), which is generally assigned a higher morally binding effect (even though it does not comprise a legally binding effect). Based on the basic agreement, it is generally assumed that the lawyers complete their stipulated tasks swiftly and without the occurrence of any great conflicts.

Insofar, the lawyers involved on both sides are under a great deal of pressure from their principals to achieve an agreement. In classic negotiation structure under the direct involvement of lawyers, differences in the demand clauses are often more conflictual.

4.3.5 Basic Characteristics and Approaches

From the beginning of the twentieth century onwards, the US have been the global economic super power No. 1. In fact, following the dissolution of the Soviet Union and the according union of states in Eastern Europe, the US have been the only political, economic and military super power until the rise of the PRC. This has an enormous influence on the confidence of companies and the agents acting for them and is reflected by the use of the phrase “God’s own country” when referring to the USA.

Since worldwide English is the prioritised negotiation language No. 1, the confidence of US-American negotiators is superior to that of non-native speakers. The opposing party will generally include experienced international negotiators who are fluent in English, yet they are no match for US negotiators who start to express themselves loudly, quickly and in their local dialect.

In addition, US negotiators are known for their very direct and open communication style. Globally, only German negotiators are felt to be more direct. Demands are made and proposals are rejected very clearly and in a determined manner (more on communication under point 4.3.8. in the context of negotiating with Americans).

In the US, reserved and indirect communication is primarily perceived as a sign of weakness, hence US-American negotiators often run the risk of prima facie judging negotiators from stronger context-oriented cultures to be weak opponents. Further details, such as a weak handshake and other cultural differences, may evoke a wrong impression of the other party's negotiating strength. For both sides, this feeling of imparity is often confirmed or even heightened by the behaviour of US-American negotiators at the negotiation itself when they demand space ("*Give me space!*").

The greater the apparent differences in the mentality of the negotiation partner are compared to the US-negotiators, the more likely the behaviour of US-American negotiators is to be evaluated negatively. The other party's negotiators often feel this behaviour signals a lack of respect for their own culture, even going so far as to consider it "imperialistic". In these cases, the term "superpower negotiator"[13] is used. In this respect, the US-negotiator's halting readiness to seek compromises coupled with the frequent use of → *deadlines* and → *take it or leave it* offers may serve to support this assumption. Negotiators from context-oriented cultures often see US-American negotiators as arrogant and—due to their openness—also as rough.

The high self-esteem of US-American negotiators leads them more strongly to adhere to their national perspective for assessing negotiations, emotions and tactics than is the case for other nations. On average, the sensitivity of US-American negotiators towards other negotiation cultures or towards the individual behaviour of foreign negotiators is not very pronounced. Nonetheless, there is an extensive amount of relevant US-literature on intercultural issues, and there are also experienced negotiators who can look back on many years of experience with other negotiation cultures. It is therefore obvious that there are US-American negotiators who are well acquainted with the specific negotiation culture of other countries and who adapt their behaviour accordingly.

Formal power and status games are less significant in the USA as compared to other cultures. Formal education is also less important in comparison to the significance of practically proven skills. Hierarchy in the US-negotiation culture is also not only less important than in other cultures but it is also structured more openly. Using forenames to address someone signifies a more relaxed attitude regarding the adherence to formal rules when dealing with higher-ranked superiors. Thus in the USA, a social event loosely connected to the negotiation can be used to address a problem to the much higher-ranking CEO of the other party without prior warning. This behaviour would cause heads to be shaken in Germany while in China an

[13] Solomon and Quinney (2010), p. 38 et seqq.

abrupt termination of the negotiation could be imminent due to the lack of respect shown. The actual power of a US negotiator and his/her social behaviour are thus determined by the specific situation and less by formal rank.

The implication for competitive negotiations is that a negotiator would do well to acquire a reputation as being a tough negotiator before entering into negotiations with a US-American company. US-American negotiators are often fully authorised to conclude the agreement, hence, their actions depend less on approval than is the case for other negotiation cultures.

The guiding principle for US-American negotiators is to hold short, intensive negotiations. Missing the chance to conclude a contract is perceived to be much more drastic than agreeing on an imperfect contract. This means that so-called "cold calling" is by no means uncommon. Insofar as no specific approval was regulated beforehand, US-American negotiators usually feel authorised to conclude the contract without any further consultation with their head office (hence they have "full authority"). In comparison with other negotiation styles, this means that the American negotiation style saves time. Similarly, → *small talk* (see further under point 4.3.8.) is usually also limited time-wise because the focus of US negotiations is most definitely on the actual negotiation object. With this in mind, negotiations typically consist of a linear sequence of phases (pre-negotiations, opening, main part—the individual points, which again follow a linear structure—and the completion of negotiations with the end result). The Germans and the Swiss lead the field in linear negotiations, closely followed by US Americans. Timetables are often incorporated into negotiations due to their highly binding effect on negotiation procedure.

Accordingly, there is often a substantive → *agenda*, which, as such, is less strict than those used e.g. by German negotiators. Issues are generally negotiated in sequence, i.e. one after the other, if there are no good reasons to do otherwise. In complex negotiations the parties often desire so-called *package deals* (→ *ostensible connexity*) which propose solutions linked to non-contentually related issues. The time factor is also important to US-negotiators due to their acute awareness of the dynamics of the negotiation situation and negotiation power (→ *BATNA*). If the agreement is not finalised quickly, the interim results may become invalid due to the situation changing. Interim results are not usually legally binding and so the interim results are limited both content- and time-wise.

Usually communication between US-negotiators is open and direct (tell it like it is cf. further above) as well as being generally very polite. However, due to the direct tone, negotiators from context-oriented negotiation cultures do not always notice these characteristics as they are often hidden behind a perceived lack of respect towards hierarchies and pressure exerted on negotiation partners. An informal atmosphere is preferable as it is conducive to the main focus of the negotiation, which is on oral (but not written!) communication. The own interests and intentions are not usually fully disclosed to the other side. Although US-Americans are often said to follow the "cards on the table"-approach, closer inspection shows that they point in many different directions, yet—unlike playing poker—not all the cards (i.e. in the context of negotiations, not all interests and positions) are revealed. Proposals are first made than justified. Thus, the focus lies on inductive, pragmatically-based arguments. Their appreciation of rational arguments is, however, not so far-reaching as that US-American negotiators assume that those arguments indicate the rational and achievable negotiation result.

The content and result of the negotiations are more important than a (sharp) rhetoric and argumentation. However, the ability to speak clearly and participate actively in communication is very important. Negotiations are usually focused on rationality and lead without emphasising → *emotions*. Content-wise, the approval or rejection of proposals can reach a seemingly emotional level if intensified or personalised, but even in these instances there is no loss of emotional control. Many of the seemingly emotional formulations are rather deliberate exaggerations. Since US-negotiators often have little experience with real emotional outbursts, they could be taken aback or confused by faked (or real) emotional outbursts.

US-negotiators generally only speak English and do not always know much of the other party's culture. Hence, intercultural competences could still be worked on in many cases. Sometimes they are also perceived to be "naïve". Early on in negotiations they sometimes appear to miss problems and convey the impression of fully trusting their negotiation partner.[14] However, it would be absolutely wrong to surmise economic naivety from deficits in cultural competence. Despite any impression they may convey to their counterpart, US-Americans are aware of potential risks and US-negotiators do not exhibit any deficits regarding the economic subject of the negotiation. On the contrary, focusing on the essentials of the negotiation might help US-negotiators to maintain the overview of the bigger picture (→ *missing the bigger picture*) more easily than negotiators from other cultures. In addition, US-American negotiators usually use translators even if they speak the respective language. This serves the purpose of gaining time to consider their options if nothing else.

The use of metaphors is very popular, particularly to describe progress made up to that point. Using both, slogans and catch phrases, is also very relevant in US-American negotiation practice. Due to the popularity of original formulations, new terms are often coined without communicating what the term actually means. For the opposing side, this implies that US-American negotiators can be won over much more easily by the use of original formulations. Humour is also generally perceived to be very positive. US-American negotiators persist in employing humour even if the other party does not respond to it, due to either not understanding the joke or evaluating it as inappropriate. Excellent American negotiators often stand out due to their ability to make fun at their own expense, which can lighten the atmosphere in critical situations. Even though American negotiation science highlights the importance of → *questions* in negotiations, their own active speaking parts generally dominate (on the relation between listening and speaking see → *70-30-rule*).

It is not uncommon for Americans to address negotiation topics during joint dinners or social events or even to discuss the negotiation subject exclusively for several hours at a cocktail party. The content and not the context is essential. The

[14] Cf. Lewis (2006), p. 181.

primary goal is to achieve a good deal—not necessarily to build a trustful, permanent relationship. American negotiators thus focus on the present and accordingly pay considerably less attention to the past. Indeed, they primarily focus on the near future, which does not, however, in any way preclude the consideration of strategic aspects during the negotiation on a specific negotiation object. The long-term view on relationships is just not a general goal of negotiations as such (for the situation in China see points 4.2.5. and 4.2.6.). A good deal is measured by economic-rational aspects, and particularly by the ROI (return on investment). The less common view on the strategic future concludes that Americans do not like to conclude smaller trial transactions, which, as such, are not profitable. In consultations however, US-Americans are made aware of how customary these transactions are e.g. in Germany and the great potential of possible follow-up transactions.

Compared to the characteristics of German or Chinese negotiations, figures and dates are only important for the core of the negotiation where precise knowledge of the facts and written documents is expected. For long-term contracts, US-Americans place emphasis on monitoring in this core area. Focusing on the core of the negotiation is seen as a special skill which not only decreases the complexity but also shortens the negotiation time and reduces transaction costs.

By focusing on the core area of the negotiations, US-American negotiators simplify complex issues and problems to be solved. In this regard, they often tend to exaggerate chances and play risks down. Regarding important performance dates, there is a tendency towards a very generous representation for their own purposes. This may partially be due to the drive and optimism which many US-American negotiators exhibit in negotiations. Another reason may be the legal order, since Common law sees contractually fixed promises as essential and does not use statements made pre-contract to interpret the actual content of the contract. In B2B-contracts, which comprehensively and finally determine the party's rights and obligations, there is practically no chance to enforce demands based on statements made during the negotiation, since the contracting parties are aware that only the facts included in the final contract count. The value of the justifications made by US-American negotiators can thus only be assessed with view to the actual contract content. For negotiations with cultures that value the truth of statements during the negotiation phase, American negotiation textbooks suggest limiting the negotiations to attainable performance promises.

Linear compromises, whereby both sides approach each other regarding a topic, are not very popular with American negotiators since this type of compromise requires submission. Making this kind of concession is understood to be a weakness to avoid. Nonetheless, finding a synthesis after both parties have presented their theses and antitheses requires a great sense of creativity and, as such, it is highly regarded by US-Americans. If enabled to find this kind of synthesis, US-American negotiators do not perceive the attained compromise to be an expression of their own weakness. Another exception regarding this point applies to the price, since the first offer is deliberately set far away from the ambitious goal which is actually desired (→ *ambitious target price setting*). Instead of granting linear compromises, the focus lies on give and take with regard to different questions (→ *non-linear compromises*). If at all, concessions are generally made late in the negotiation process. Before this point, a US-American negotiator will try to assess if the desired goal can be achieved without giving in. When negotiating with US-Americans, the suggestion is thus to accordingly remain very patient.

Regarding constructions and formulations, US-American negotiators are often very pragmatic. If they are satisfied with the economic result, they often accept changes of formulations or constructions within the contract. According to the basic positive attitude displayed by American society towards taking risks, given the corresponding chances and the basic optimism "to make it work", US-American negotiators are willing to take relatively high risks. This facilitates setting ambitious goals (→ *ambitious target price setting*) and making even more ambitious first offers (→ *first offer*). In order to reach an agreement, various techniques are applied. Apart from offers, arguments and the attempt to convince by means of logical conclusions, aggressive convincing tactics are particularly important. Since many US-American negotiators negotiate hardball, pressuring tactics (esp. time based) and also deceiving tactics are very common (see further below under the topic lists). Even exerting personal pressure on one individual negotiator is part of the negotiation repertoire.

4.3.6 Negotiation Preparation

Proper preparation is generally very important in the USA, even if the pressure of routine tasks often causes practical deficits in the preparation for negotiators all over the world. For important negotiations in the US, mock negotiations are practised as part of the negotiation preparation. Law firms sometimes even have a pseudo courtroom to practice the situation of the court hearing more realistically.

4.3.7 Place, Time and Composition of the Own Negotiation Team

Negotiations often take place at the premises of the US host. If practical arguments suggest it would be wise to use other rooms, e.g. in a hotel, these will be booked. As US-American negotiators appreciate short negotiations, there is usually a distinct temporal forerun before bigger negotiations. If high business chances are at stake, negotiations are also planned for the short term. Negotiation time is thus very valuable. Once established, negotiation plans are accordingly generally very tight and binding. In global comparison, US-negotiation teams are relatively small. In contrast to the latter, legal negotiation teams—especially those charged with concretising the basic contractual agreement—are generally quite large.

4.3.8 Small Talk

As already mentioned above, → *small talk* is only of limited relevance in the USA. When striving for a quick, efficient negotiation, small talk merits little to no attention. It is, however, a different story at social events connected to the actual negotiation. Business, traveling, global events, sports (particularly popular sports such as baseball, American football, basketball, golf and tennis) and, in country regions, hunting and fishing are popular topics for small talk. US-Americans also talk about politics and religion (at least more than is the case in Germany). Due to the strong political tensions in the USA, foreign negotiators are advised to stick to → *active listening* regarding these topics. Even if a US-American negotiator happens to make critical statements regarding the current political situation in his/her country, it is strongly advisable not to criticise the USA. The general bond between US-citizens and their country is very strong. Attacking the USA with negative statements as well as criticising their values and traditions is often perceived as a personal attack.

4.3.9 Strategies and Tactics

In view of the advanced status of education with regard to negotiations, it is unsurprising that the use of strategies and tactics is very common. The enormous diversity of tactics makes it impossible to address even all the essential ones. As a general recommendation, good negotiators should endeavour to shift the → *burden of justification* to the other side, since it becomes much more difficult for the person obliged to justify arguments to enforce demands.[15] Pressure tactics and tactics using deception are very popular among US-American negotiators and often take the form of → *deadlines* or → *take it or leave it* offers. Even though the style of communication is open, the use of indirect pressure is predominant. Many US-American negotiators favour the combination of indirect pressure and presenting a feasible alternative over simply exerting pressure. This approach increases the probability of a successful compromise, as the other party does not simply yield to imposed demands.

Personal relationships are generally not a priority for US-negotiators. According to hearsay, US-American negotiators often attempt to exert personal pressure on individual negotiators.[16] In addition to numerous negotiators who use the tactical knowledge they gain as a "recipe" to be applied, there are most certainly other negotiators who use a deliberately planned tactical approach. In this regard, knowledge on combining auctions with negotiations (→ *negotiauction*) is utilised in the purchasing department. Potential suppliers are in close proximity and make offers in the certain knowledge that there are other competitors, although their respective

[15] Cf. Solomon and Quinney (2010), p. 41, here with the term of burden of proof.

[16] Cf. Solomon and Quinney (2010), p. 55.

offers are not known. What's more, suppliers are given performance parameters, for which individual offers are invited. This serves to enable → *cherry picking*: it is generally expected that price concessions can be elicited from the overall most cost-effective supplier in those sections where he/she demands higher prices. In this way, there is a tactical non-disclosure of the fact that he/she is already the most cost-effective supplier.

Topic Lists

The hereinafter listed topics are intended to facilitate the comprehension of the discussed topics. By means of these lists, the reader can familiarise her/himself with specific aspects of negotiations.

Due to the thematical overlap of certain aspects, some key terms may be listed more than once. In order to reduce overlapping areas, some of the thematic lists are confined to specific aspects.

The list of topics contains only the bold printed generic terms. Other key terms that are discussed within a generic term are generally not listed in order to keep the topic lists concise. Since topic lists can be related to each other, some of them are summarised under more general terms. For example, there is the general term "communication techniques" which comprises lists of topics such as "answering techniques" and "question techniques".

Auxiliary Means

Auxiliary means are actual or legal instruments, which are required within certain techniques and are thus also needed for specific tactics or strategies or serve to avert them.

In the following, terms relating to negotiators (see under involved parties), and auxiliary means that are primarily used in the preparation of negotiations (see under preparation) are excluded:

Actual Auxiliary Means

Besides legal auxiliary means, negotiations include various actual auxiliary means. The key terms in this context are listed as follows:

S. Jung, P. Krebs, *The Essentials of Contract Negotiation*,
https://doi.org/10.1007/978-3-030-12866-1

- Agenda
- Annotations
- Aspiration point
- BATNA (best alternative to a negotiated agreement)
- Body language
- Change the standards
- Deadline
- Deal-breaker
- Interim results
- Negotiation pause
- Prenegotiation plan
- Principle of dual control
- Protocols
- Reference point
- Retracking the deal
- SMART
- SWOT-analysis
- Traffic light systems

Legal Means

In addition to general auxiliary means, negotiations in particular also include legal auxiliary means. They are mainly (but not only) applied in the concrete drafting of contracts. However, not generally listed hereinafter are legal framework conditions.

- Annotations
- Bargaining in the shadow of the law
- Boilerplates
- Negotiation clause
- Presenting a false legal opinion
- Single text negotiation

Behavioural Economics and Psychological Effects

Findings from the field of behavioural economics and psychological effects often form the basis for special tactics and techniques (for this see further under tactics and techniques and their according effects). In the following all relevant terms from this field are listed.

Effects

Findings of behavioural economics and psychological effects that may be relevant in the context of contract negotiations are listed here.

- Availability bias
- Backlash effect
- Behavioural economics
- Bias
- Electronic multitasking
- Endowment effect
- Framing
- Gender
- Halo effect
- Impression (first and last)
- Incompatibility bias
- Norm of reciprocity
- Optimism bias
- Path dependency
- Reactive devaluation
- Reference point
- Similar-to-me-effect
- Status quo bias
- Sunk cost bias

Tactics, Techniques and Their Underlying Effects

Here follows an exemplary list of some tactics and techniques based on effects of behavioural economics or psychological effects. These effects are listed in brackets after the respective tactic or technique.

- Ambitious target price setting (self-fulfilling prophecy)
- Anchor discreditation (anchoring effect)
- Better than that (anchoring effect)
- Door-in-the-face tactic (anchoring effect, norm of reciprocity)
- First offer (anchoring effect)
- Foot-in-the-door technique (escalation of commitment effect)
- Ostensible connexity (Halo effect)
- Salami tactic (endowment effect)
- Several small consessions (hedonic framing)
- Similar-to-me-tactic (similar-to-me-effect)
- Tactic of small quantities (bandwagon effect, scarcity effect)

Communication Techniques

As negotiating means communicating, this book describes various communication techniques. The following topic lists include all relevant terms in this field:

Answering Techniques

The following is a compilation of key terms in reference to answering techniques (but not to argumentation techniques)

- But-yes answer
- Considered response
- Not happy
- Silence
- Yes, but-answer

Argumentation Techniques

In negotiations, argumentation techniques are used to convince the negotiating partner of the own point of view. Both rational as well as irrational techniques are used in negotiations. In a broader sense these techniques include:

- Better offer
- Burden of justification
- Change the standards
- Conclusion by analogy
- Exception argument
- Fewer, convincing arguments
- Floodgate argument
- FOG
- Ostensible connexity
- Pareto optimum
- Precedent
- Presenting a false legal opinion
- TINA

Further Communication Techniques

Besides question (see under list question techniques), answer (see under answering techniques), and argumentation techniques (see under argumentation techniques), and terms related to listening (see under listening), there are further aspects linked to communication in negotiations. In particular, these aspects include points from the field of nonverbal communication. The corresponding techniques can be listed as followed:

- 7-38-55-rule
- Body language
- Chit-chat
- DAD approach
- E-mail
- Empathy
- Hide your glee
- Impression (first and last)
- Misunderstandings
- Negotiation pause
- Refusal to communicate
- Sharing information
- Signalling
- Wince

Listening

Listening is crucial for obtaining information. Furthermore, listening is essential for building a good relationship with the negotiating partner, since attentive listening also signals interest and respect.

- 70-30-rule
- Active listening

Questioning Techniques

- A-not-A question
- Closed questions
- Columbo
- Open questions
- Premise questions
- Questions
- What-if question
- Yes/No questions

Competitive Negotiating

Not all negotiators negotiate cooperatively. Competitively-oriented negotiations are still standard practice, using pressure, threats and fraud. The following topic lists regard these aspects.

Deceptions

In the following list all terms linked to deceptions in negotiations are summarised. For instance, many tactics base upon deceptions and misleading the negotiating partner.

- All I‘ve got
- Better offer
- Budget limitation
- Cunning deception
- EANT (ethically ambiguous negotiation tactics)
- Empty promise
- False deadline
- Foggy recall
- Knocking on the bush
- Ostensible connexity
- Padding
- Presenting a false legal opinion
- Similar-to-me-effect
- Strategic misrepresentation
- Tactic of small quantities

Pressure and Threats

Pressure and threats are a common means to force the negotiating partner to make concessions or to provoke mistakes on the opposing side. The following is a compilation of all the terms associated with pressure and threats in negotiations.

- (Aggressive) Claim-Management (Claim or Claims Management)
- BAFO (Best and final offer)
- Big fish
- Brinkmanship
- Calling a higher authority
- Cherry picking
- Chicken

- Creating facts
- Credible threat
- Deadline
- EANT (ethically ambiguous negotiation tactics)
- Entanglement tactic
- False deadline
- Refusal to communicate
- Russian front
- See you in court
- Take it or leave it
- This will hurt you more than it will hurt me
- Warning instead of threatening

Cooperative Negotiating

The following is a list of all terms that are linked to negotiating cooperatively in a broader sense. There are certain overlapping areas with negotiation strategies (see under tactics), since cooperative negotiation is a negotiation strategy in itself.

Cooperative Negotiating

This section starts with a list of all terms related to cooperative negotiating, under the exclusion of all terms linked to trust (see specifically under trust).

- Developing the negotiation partners' ideas
- Harvard negotiation concept
- Negotiation pie
- Orange example
- Pareto optimum
- Soft bargaining
- Win-win strategy

Mutual Trust

Trust is an essential factor for the success of negotiations. Related terms are listed below. In order to reduce the overlapping areas, terms that are primarily discussed under general term of cooperative negotiations are excluded (see further under cooperative negotiations).

- Building a golden bridge
- Change the negotiator
- Chit-chat
- Permanent business relation
- Respect

Economic Concepts and Terms

The following is a list of basic economic concepts and terms as the essential background know-how for contract negotiations.

- Akerlof Market
- Behavioural economics
- Moral hazard
- Negotiator's dilemma
- Pareto optimum
- Principal-agent-problem

Emotions

Despite the fact that the Harvard negotiation concept recommends that people and problems be considered separately, emotions play a significant role in contract negotiations in practice. The keywords in this regard are listed below.

- Building a golden bridge
- Chit-chat
- Core concerns framework
- Emotions
- Empathy
- Hide your glee
- Impression (first and last)
- Negotiation levels
- Not happy

Gaining Information

Gathering information is an essential task in the course of contract negotiations. In particular, questioning techniques (for details see under questioning techniques) can be used to obtain relevant information. Here, all key terms in the context of gaining information, with the exception of questioning techniques, are listed:

- 70-30-rule
- Active listening
- Analyst
- Body language
- Emotions
- FOG
- Information control
- Information demand analysis
- Information procurement
- Knocking on the bush
- Negotiator's dilemma
- Questions

Improving Negotiation Skills

Skilful negotiating can be learned. In the following, all key terms within this field are listed. There is a large overlap with the preparation of negotiations (see further under preparation), since the improvement of the own negotiation skills is an essential part of preparation for negotiations.

- ACBD-rule
- Adopt an outsider lens
- Advocatus diaboli
- Misunderstandings
- WWW
- WWYDD

Negotiation Types

Negotiations can be designed in various ways. The exact type of negotiations depends on various factors, such as the negotiation subject, the importance of the potential conclusion of the contract and the parties involved in the negotiation. Certain reiterations of terms with the list of negotiation tactics (for more detail see under negotiation tactics) may occur

- Auction
- Electronic multitasking
- E-mail
- Face-to-face
- Negotiauction
- Renegotiations

Negotiators (People/Parties)

Negotiations can either directly or indirectly involve various people with different tasks, authorisations, skills and interests. The following list includes all relevant terms.

Qualities

People involved in negotiations have different characteristics. Negotiations should thus be aware of these traits and have the ability to recognize the traits of other negotiators in order to adjust their tactics and strategies accordingly. Sometimes these qualities are closely linked to certain emotions (which can be found in a separate list):

- Assertiveness
- Empathy
- Gender
- Respect
- Unpredictability

Role

In the course of a negotiation, people can take on different positions and thus perform different tasks. The following list includes all relevant key terms for the distribution of roles.

- Advocatus diaboli
- Analyst
- Back office
- Chief negotiator
- Decision-maker
- Driver
- Good guy/bad guy
- Organiser
- Recording clerk (*see under* protocols)
- Two negotiators

Negotiation Strategies

Strategies are guiding principles for actions and are designed for the whole negotiation or at least large parts thereof. They are usually formulated in general terms so that they require further development by means of adequate tactics to be applied in negotiations. The Harvard negotiation concept is a comprehensive and general concept and accordingly summarises various strategies.

- Blockade strategy
- Boulwarism
- Generous tit for tat (GTFT)
- Negotiauction
- Soft bargaining
- This will hurt you more than it will hurt me
- Win-lose strategy
- Win-win strategy

Preparation of Negotiations

Good preparation is essential for the success of negotiations. The corresponding key notions are listed in the following overview. Negotiation exercises (see under improving negotiation skills) are also part of the negotiation preparation process and likewise certain auxiliary means (see under auxiliary means), e.g. determining the BATNA. Repetitions in the lists occur due to the fact that certain steps in the preparation procedure, e.g. gathering of information, are not only conducted in the preparation of the negotiation, but rather play an important role throughout the whole negotiation.

- 80-20-rule
- Advocatus diaboli
- Agenda
- Ambitious target price setting
- Annotations
- Aspiration point
- Back office
- BATNA (best alternative to a negotiated agreement)
- Chit-chat
- Cui bono
- Deal-breaker
- Information demand analysis
- Information procurement
- Know your target

- Missing the big picture
- Multi-person BATNA
- Negotiation phases
- Traffic light systems

Solutions and Compromises

Finding common solutions and compromises is an essential part of negotiations. There is a certain overlap with the terms listed under negotiation techniques (see under negotiation techniques), which is why the iterated terms are not included in the following list.

- BAFO (Best and final Offer)
- Building a golden bridge
- Change the negotiator
- DDD approach
- FC approach
- Final offer arbitration (FOA)
- Flip a coin
- Developing the negotiation partners' ideas
- Incomplete solutions
- Logrolling
- MESO
- Negotiation pie
- Non-linear-compromises
- Orange example
- Pareto optimum
- Split the difference
- ZOPA (Zone of possible agreement)

Time

Time is an essential factor in negotiations. For example, diverse tactics rely on time-related factors. Hereinafter all relevant terms broadly linked to the factor time, are listed:

- Agenda
- Calculated delay
- Change the negotiator
- Deadline
- False deadline
- Go for a walk

- Negotiation pause
- Refusal to communicate
- Silence
- SMART goal formulation technique
- Tactic of small quantities

Bibliography

Acuff, Frank L.: How to Negotiate Anything with Anyone Anywhere Around the World, 3. Ed., New York 2008.
Adamczyk, Gregor: Storytelling – Mit Geschichten überzeugen, Freiburg 2014.
Adelson, Rachel: Detecting deception, Monitor on Psychology 35 (2004), p. 70.
Aderhold, Lutz/Koch, Raphael/Lenkaitis, Karlheinz: Vertragsgestaltung, 2. Ed., Baden-Baden 2015.
Adler, Rachel F./Benbunan-Fich, Raquel: Juggling on a high wire: Multitasking effects on performance, International Journal of Human-Computer Studies 70 (2012), pp. 156–168.
Adler, Rachel F./Benbunan-Fich, Raquel: The Effects of Task Difficulty and Multitasking on Performance, Interacting with Computers 27 (2015), pp. 430–439.
Adler, Robert S./Silverstein, Elliot M.: When David meets Goliath: Dealing with power differentials in negotiations, Harvard Negotiation Law Review 2000, pp. 1–77.
Akerlof, George A.: The Market for "Lemons": Quality Uncertainty and the Market Mechanism, Quarterly Journal of Economics, 3 (1970), pp. 488–500.
Allert, Arnd: Erfolgreich verhandeln bei M&A-Transaktionen im Mittelstand, Lampertheim 2014.
Allpart, Gordon W./Ordbert, Henry S.: Trait-Names: a Psycho-Lexical Study Psychological Monographs 211 (1936), pp. 1–38.
Amanatullah, Emily T./Tinsley, Catherine H.: Punishing female negotiators for asserting too much…or not enough: Exploring why advocacy moderates backlash against assertive female negotiators, Organizational Behavior and Human Decision Processes 120 (2013), pp.110–122.
Andrade, Jackie: What does doodling do?, Applied Cognitive Psychology 1 (2009), pp.100–106.
Ariely, Dan: Predictably Irrational: The Hidden Forces that Shape Our Decisions, New York 2008.
Atkin, Thomas S./Rinehart Lloyd M.: The Effect of Negotiation Practices on the Relationship between Suppliers and Customer, Negotiation Journal 22 (2006), pp. 47–65.
Audebert, Patrick: Bien négocier, 3. Ed., Paris 2005.
Axelrod, Robert: The Evolution of Cooperation, 1. Ed., New York 1984, 2. Ed., New York 2006.
Babcock, Linda/Laschever, Sara: Why Women Don't Ask, 1. Ed., Princeton 2007.
Bacharach, Samuel B./Lawler, Edward J.: Power and tactics in bargaining, Industrial and Labor Relations Review 34 (1981), pp. 219–233.
Baird, Douglas G./Gertner, Robert H./Picker Randal C.: Game Theory and the Law, 1. Ed., Cambridge (Mass.) 1998.
Baker, James A. III: Work Hard, Study…and keep out of politics, 1. Ed., Evanston 2006.
Balachandra, Laksshmi/Bordone, Robert C./Menkel-Meadow, Carrie/Ringstorm, Philip/Sarath, Edward: Improvisation and Negotiation: Expecting the Unexpected, Negotiation Journal 21 (2005), pp. 415–423.

S. Jung, P. Krebs, *The Essentials of Contract Negotiation*,
https://doi.org/10.1007/978-3-030-12866-1

Banaji, Mahzarin/Greenwald, Anthony G.: Blindspot: Hidden Biases of Good People, New York 2013.
Barisch, Sina: Optimierung von Verhandlungsteams – Der Einflussfaktor Hierarchie, Wiesbaden 2011.
Barrett, Frank J.: Critical Moments as "Change" in Negotiation, Negotiation Journal 20 (2004), pp. 213–219.
Bazerman, Max H./Curhan Jared R./Moore, Don A./Valley, Kathleen L.: Negotiation, Annual Reviews 1 (2000), pp. 279–314.
Bazerman, Max H./Moore, Don A./Gillespie, James J.: The Human Mind as a Barrier to Wiser Environmental Agreements, American Behavioral Scientist 42 (1999), pp. 1277–1300.
Bazerman, Max H./Neale, Magaret A.: Negotiator Judgement a Critical Look at the Rationality Assumption, American Behavioral Scientist 2 (1983), pp. 211–228.
Bazerman, Max H./Neale, Magaret A.: Negotiating Rationally, New York 1992.
Bazerman, Max H./Watkins, Michael D.: Predictable Surprises – The Disasters You Should Have Seen Coming and How to Prevent Them, Boston, (Massachusetts) 2004.
Beam, Carrie/Segev, Arie: Automated Negotiations: A Survey of the State of the Art, Wirtschaftsinformatik 3/97, pp. 263–267.
Bear, Julia B.: "Passing the buck": Incongruence between gender role and topic leads to avoidance of negotiation, Negotiation and Conflict Management Research 4 (2011), pp. 47–72.
Bear, Julia B./Babcock, Linda: Negotiation topic as a moderator of gender differences in negotiation, Psychological Science 23 (2012), pp. 743–744.
Beck, Hanno: Behavioral Economics – Eine Einführung, Wiesbaden 2014.
Becker, Tatjana: Festsetzung und Durchsetzung von Verhandlungszielen, Hamburg 2016.
Beck'sches Formularbuch: Handels- und Wirtschaftsrecht, 11. Ed., München 2013.
Bender, Rolf/Nack, Armin/Treuer, Wolf D.: Tatsachenfeststellung vor Gericht – Glaubhaftigkeits- und Beweislehre, Vernehmungslehre, 4. Ed., München 2014.
Benton, Alan A./Kelley, Harold H./Liebling, Barry: Effects of extremity of offers and concession rate on the outcomes of bargaining, Journal of Personality and Social Psychology 1 (1972), pp. 73–83.
Berger, Klaus P.: Private Dispute Resolution in International Business: Negotiation, Mediation, Arbitration, 3. Ed., Alphen aan den Rijn 2015.
Bernhardt, Madeleine: Effektive Befragungsstrategien für Juristen in unternehmensinternen Untersuchungen, 1. Ed., Hamburg 2015.
Berz, Gregor: Spieltheoretische Verhandlungs- und Auktionsstrategien – Mit Praxisbeispielen von Internetauktionen bis Investmentbanking, Freiburg 2007.
Bittner, Gerhard/Schwarz, Elke: Emotion Selling – Messbar mehr verkaufen durch neue Erkenntnisse der Neurokommunikation, Wiesbaden 2010.
Bohnet, Iris/Bowles, Hannah R.: Special Section: Gender in Negotiation: Introduction, Negotiation Journal 24 (2008), pp. 389–392.
Borbonus, René: 30 Minuten – Sich durchsetzen, Offenbach 2014.
Bordone, Robert C./Carr, Chad M.: Critical Decisions in Negotiation: A New Video Resource for Teaching Negotiation, Negotiation Journal 29 (2013), pp. 463–476.
Bowles, Hannah Riley: Psychological Perspectives on Gender in Negotiation, Harvard Kennedy School, Working Paper Series 2012, pp. 1–42.
Bowles, Hannah Riley/Babcock, Linda/McGinn, Kathleen L.: Constraints and Triggers: Situational Mechanics of Gender in Negotiation, Journal of Personality and Social Psychology 89 (2005), pp. 951–965.
Bowles, Hannah Riley/Babcock, Linda/Lai, Lei: Social incentives for gender differences in the propensity to initiate negotiations: Sometimes it does hurt to ask, Organizational Behavior and Human Decision Processes 103 (2007), pp. 84–103.
Bowles, Hannah Riley/Kray, Laura J.: Negotiation is a Man's Game – ultimate truth or Enduring Myth?, Harvard Business School 2013, pp. 1–11.
Boyce, Tim: Succesful Contract Negotiation, London 1996.

Brahm, Laurence J.: Doing Business in China – The Sun Tzu Way, 2004.

Brahm, Laurence J.: When yes Means No! (or yes or maybe) – How to negotiate a deal in China, 2005

Braun, Gerold: Verhandeln in Einkauf und Vertrieb, 2. Ed., Wiesbaden 2013.

Breslin, William J./Rubin, Jeffrey Z. (Eds.).: Negotiation Theory and Practice, 3. Ed., Cambridge (Mass.) 1995.

Brett, Jeanne M.: Negotiating Globally: How to Negotiate Deals, Resolve Disputes, and Make Decisions Across Cultural Boundaries, 3. Ed., San Francisco 2014.

Brewer, Neil/Williams, Kipling D.: Psychology and Law: An Empirical Perspective, New York 2007.

Brinkman, Rick/Kirschner, Rick: Dealing with People You Can't Stand – How to Bring Out the Best in People at Their Worst, 3. Ed., New York, Chicago 2012.

Bruno, Tiziana/Adamczyk, Gregor/Gessner, Martina: Menschen einschätzen und überzeugen, Freiburg 2012.

Bühring-Uhle, Christian/Eidenmüller, Horst/Nelle, Andreas: Verhandlungsmanagement – Analyse – Werkzeuge – Strategien, München 2009.

Burkhardt, Nina/Lamb, Berton L./Taylor, Jonathan G.: Power distribution in complex environmental negotiations: Does balance matter?, Journal of Public Administration Research and Theory 7 (1997), pp. 247–275.

Butt, Arif N./Choi, Jin N./Jaeger, Alfred M.: The effects of self-emotion, counterpart emotion, and counterpart behavior on negotiator behavior: a comparison of individual-level and dyad-level dynamics, Journal of Organizational Behavior 6 (2005), pp. 681–704.

Cahen, Phillipe: Signaux faibles, mode d'emploi – Déceler les tendances, anticiper les ruptures, Paris 2011.

Camerer, Colin/Loewenstein, George/Weber, Martin: The Curse of Knowledge in Economic Setting: An Experimental Analysis, The Journal of Political Economy 97 (1989), pp. 1232–1254.

Camp, James R.: No: The Only Negotiating System You Need for Work and Home, New York 2007.

Campbell, Joseph: The Hero with a Thousand Faces, New York, 1949.

Campbell, Keith E./Kleim, David M./Olson, Kenneth R.: Conversational Activity and Interruptions among Men and Women, The Journal of Social Psychology 132 (1992), pp. 419–421.

Carnevale, Peter J. D./Lawler, Edward J.: Time Pressure and the development of integrative agreements in bilateral negotiations, Journal of Conflict Resolution 30 (1986), pp. 636–659.

Carney, Dana R./Cuddy, Amy J. C./Jap, Andy J.: Power Posing – Brief Nonverbal Displays Affect Neuroendocrine Levels and Risk Tolerance, Journal of Applied Psychology 4 (2015), pp. 1–10.

Chartrand, Tanya L./Bargh, John A.: The Chameleon Effect: The Perception-Behavior Link and Social Interaction, Journal of Personality and Social Psychology 76 (1999), pp. 893–910.

Chie, Steve Shu-Cheng/Friedman, Raymond A./Shih, Huei-Lin: Beyond Offers and Counteroffers – The Impact of Interaction Time and Negotiator Job Satisfaction on Subjective Outcomes in Negotiation, Negotiation Journal 29 (2013), pp. 39–60.

Churchman, David: Negotiations – Process, Tactics, Theory, 2. Ed., Boston, 1995.

Cialdini, Robert B./Vincent, Joyce E./Lewis, Stephen K./Catalan, José/Wheeler, Diane/ Darby, Betty L.: Reciprocal Concessions Procedure for Inducing Compliance. The Door-in-the-Face Technique, Journal of Personality and Social Psychology 2 (1975), pp. 206–215.

Cialdini, Robert B.: Influence – Science and Practice, 5. Ed., Boston 2008.

Clausewitz, Carl von: Vom Kriege – vollständige Ausgabe, 7. Ed., Hamburg 2014 (Originally published in 1832).

Cohen, Herb: You Can Negotiate Anything: The World's Best Negotiator Tells You How to get What You Want, 1. Ed., New York, Toronto 1982.

Cohen, Jonathan R.: When people are the means: Negotiating with respect, Georgetown Journal of Legal Ethics 14 (2001), pp. 739–802.

Cohen, Raymund: Negotiating Across Cultures. International Communication in an independent World, 2. Ed., Washington DC 2004.

Collins, Patrick: Negotiate to Win! Talking Your Way to What You Want, New York 2009.

Combalbert, Laurent: Négocier en situations complexes – Résoudre les situations difficiles par la négociation influente, Paris 2012.

Craver, Charles B.: The inherent tension between value creation and value claiming during bargaining interactions, Cardozo Journal of Conflict Resolution 12 (2010), pp. 101–118.

Craver, Charles B.: Skills & Values – Legal Negotiating, Dayton 2012.

Craver, Charles B./Barnes, David W.: Gender, Risk Taking, and Negotiation Performance, Michigan Journal of Gender and Law 5 (1999), pp. 299–352.

Croson, Rachel/Gneezy, Uri: Gender Differences in Preferences, Journal of Economic Literature 47 (2009), pp. 1–27.

Csikszentmihalyi, Mihaly/Csikszentmihalyi, Isabella S.: Optimal Experience –Psychological Studies of Flow in Consciousness, 1. Ed., Cambridge (Mass.) 1988.

Cuddy, Amy J. C./Fiske, Susan T./Glick, Peter/Xu, Jun: A model of (often mixed) stereotyp content: Competence and warmth respectively follow perceived status and competition, Journal of Personality and Social Psychology 82 (2002), pp. 878–902.

Cummins, Tim/David, Mark/Kawamoto, Katherine: Contract and Commercial Management – The Operational Guide, 1. Ed., Zaltbommel 2011.

Curhan, Jared R./Elfenbein, Hillary A./Eisenkraft, Noah: A Multi-Round Negotiation Study, Journal of Applied Social Psychology 40 (2010), pp. 690–709.

Cutcher-Gershenfield, Joel/Watkins, Michael: Towards A Theory of Representation in Negotiation, in: Mnookin, R.H./Susskind, L.E. (Eds.): Negotiating on Behalf of Others, Thousand Oaks (California) 1999, pp. 23–51.

Daigneault, Edward W.: Drafting International Agreement in Legal English, 2. Ed., Vienna 2009.

Dall, Martin: Der Verhandlungsprofi – Besser verhandeln – mehr erreichen, Wien 2011.

Däubler, Wolfgang: Verhandeln und Gestalten – Der Kern der neuen Schlüsselqualifikationen, Munich 2003.

David, Patrick: La négociation commerciale en practique, 7. Ed., Paris 2015.

Dawson, Roger: Secrets of Power Negotiating – Inside Secrets from a Master Negotiator, 3. Ed. (15th Ann. Ed.), New Jersey 2011.

De Cozar, Éric/Fréderic, Vendeuvre: Négocier plus, Négocier mieux – Savoir créer et partager la valeur, Paris 2013.

DePaulo, Bella M./Malone Brian E./Lindsay, James J./Muhlenbruck, Laura/Charlton, Kelly/Cooper, Harris: Cues to Deception, Psychological Bulletin 129 (2003), pp. 74–118.

Diamond, Stuart: Getting More – You are always negotiating. Get what you want every day, London 2011.

Diekmann, Kristina A./Tenbrunsel, Ann E./Galinsky, Adam D.: From self-prediction to self-defeat: behavioral forecasting, self-fulfilling prophecies, and the effect of competitive expectations, Journal of Personality and Social Psychology 85 (2003), pp. 672–683.

Dindia, Kathryn: The Effects of Sex of Subject and Sex of Partner on Interruptions, Human Communication Research 13 (1987), 345–371.

Dixit, Avinash, K./Barry, Nalebuff J.: The Art of Strategy – A Game Theorist's Guide to Success in Business and Life, New York, London 2008.

Dixit, Avinash K./Skeath, Susan/Reiley, David H.: Games of Strategy, 3. Ed., New York 2009.

Dobelli, Rolf: Die Kunst des klaren Denkens – 52 Denkfehler die Sie besser anderen überlassen, Munich 2011.

Dobelli, Rolf: Die Kunst des klugen Handelns – 52 Irrwege die Sie besser anderen überlassen, Munich 2012.

Donaldson Michael C.: Erfolgreich Verhandeln für Dummies, 4. Ed., Weinheim 2008.

Donohue, William A.: Critical Moments as "Flow" in Negotiation, Negotiation Journal 20 (2004), pp. 147–151.

Donohue, William A./Taylor, Paul J.: Role Effects in Negotiation: The One-Down Phenomenon, Negotiation Journal 23 (2007), pp. 307–331.
Doran, George T.: There's a S.M.A.R.T. way to write management's goals and objectives, Management Review 11 (1981), pp. 35–36.
Druckman, Daniel: Departures in Negotiation: Extensions and New Directions, Negotiation Journal 20 (2004), pp. 185–204.
Druckman, Daniel: Intuition or Counterintuition? The Science behind the Art of Negotiation, Negotiation Journal 25 (2009), pp. 431–448.
Druckman, Daniel/Olekalns, Mara/Smith, Phillip L.: Interpretive Filters: Social Cognition and the Impact of Turning Points in Negotiation, Negotiation Journal 25 (2009), pp. 13–40.
Dunning, David/Kruger, Justin: Unskilled and Unaware of It: How Difficulties in Recognizing One's Own Incompetence Lead to Inflated Self-Assessments, Journal of Personality and Social Psychology 77 (1999), pp. 1121–1134.
Dupont, Christophe: La Négociation, Paris 1994.
Eckel Catherine C./Grossmann, Philip J.: Forecasting Risk Attitudes: An Experimental Study of Actual and Forecast Risk Attitudes of Women and Men, Journal of Economic Behaviour and Organization 68 (2008), pp. 1–17.
Edmüller, Andreas/Wilhelm, Thomas: Manipulationstechniken – Erkennen und abwehren, Freiburg 2010.
Effron, Daniel/Bryan, Christopher/Murninghan, Keith: Cheating at the end to avoid regret, Journal of Personality and Social Psychology 109 (2015), pp. 395–414.
Eidenmüller, Horst: Exerting Pressure in Contractual Negotiations, European Review of Contract Law 3 (2007), pp. 21–40.
Ellis, Yvonne/Daniels, Bobbie/Jauregui, Andres: The effect of multitasking on the grade performance of business students, Research in Higher Education Journal 8 (2010), pp. 1–10.
Engel, Martin: Collaborative Law, Tübingen 2010.
Englich, Birte/Mussweiler, Thomas/Strack, Fritz: Playing Dice with Criminal Sentences: The Influence of Irrelevant Anchors on Experts' Judicial Decision Making, Personality and Social Psychology Bulletin 2 (2006), pp. 188–200.
Epley, Nicholas/Whitchurch, Erin: Mirror, Mirror on the Wall: Enhancement in Self-Recognition, Personality and Social Psychology Bulletin 34 (2008), pp. 1159–1170.
Erbacher, Christian E.: Grundzüge der Verhandlungsführung, 3. Ed., Zürich 2010.
Eriksson, Karin H./Sandberg, Anna: Gender Differences in Initiation of Negotiation: Does the Gender of the Negotiation Counterpart Matter?, Negotiation Journal 28 (2012), pp. 407–428.
Eskine, Kendalle J./Kacinik, Natalie A./Prinz Jesse: A bad taste in the mouth: gustatory disgust influences moral judgment, Psychological Science 3 (2011), pp. 295–299.
Faludi, Susan: Backlash: The Undeclared War against American Women, New York 1991.
Fang, Tony: Chinese Business Negotiating Style, Thousand Oaks 1999.
Fang, Tony: Negotiation: The Chinese Style, Journal of Business & Industrial Marketing 21 (2006) (1), pp. 50–60.
Faure, Guy O.: Dumb Barter: A Seminal Form of Negotiation, Negotiation Journal 27 (2011), pp. 403–418.
Fischhoff, Baruch: Hindsight is not equal to foresight: The effect of outcome knowledge on judgment under uncertainty, Journal of Experimental Psychology: Human Perception and Performance 1 (1975), pp. 288–299.
Fisher, Roger/Brown, Scott: Getting Together – Building Relationships as We Negotiate, 1. Ed., Boston 1988.
Fisher, Roger/Ury, William: Getting to Yes – Negotiating an agreement without giving in, New York 1981.
Fisher, Roger/Ury, William/Patton, Bruce: Das Harvard-Konzept – Der Klassiker der Verhandlungstechnik, 22. Ed., Frankfurt 2006.
Fisher, Roger/Shapiro, Daniel: Beyond Reason – Using Emotions as You Negotiate, 1. Ed., London 2005.

Fleck, Denise/Volkema, Roger/Pereira, Sergio/Levy, Barbara/Vaccari, Lara: Neutralizing Unethical Negotiating Tactics: An Empirical Investigation of Approach Selection and Effectiveness, Negotiation Journal 30 (2014), pp. 23–48.

Forgas, Joseph P.: On feeling good and getting your way: Mood effects on negotiator cognition and behavior, Journal of Personality and Social Psychology 3 (1998), pp. 565–577.

Freedman, Jonathan/Fraser, Scott: Compliance Without Pressure: The Foot-In-The-Door Technique, Journal of Personality and Social Psychology 2 (1966), pp. 195–202.

Fried, Charles: Contract as Promise – A Theory of Contractual Obligation, Cambridge (Mass.) 1981.

Fritzsche, Thomas: Soverän verhandeln – Psychlogische Strategien und Methoden, 2. Ed., Bern 2016.

Froman, Lewis A./Cohen, Michael D.: Compromise and logroll: Comparing the efficiency of two bargaining processes, Behavioral Sciences 2 (1990), pp. 180–183.

Galinsky, Adam G./Mussweiler, Thomas: First Offers as Anchors: The Role of Perspective-Taking and Negotiator Focus, Journal of Personality and Social Psychology 4 (2001), pp. 657–669.

Geraghty, Michael: Anybody Can Negotiate – Even You: How to Become a Master Negotiator, New York u. a. 2006.

Gibson, Kevin: Making Sense of the Sacred, Negotiation Journal 27 (2011), pp. 477–492.

Gilbert, Daniel T./Morewedge, Carey K./Risen, Jane L./Wilson, Timothy D.: Looking Forward to Looking Backward – The Misprediction of Regret, Psychological Science 15 (2004), pp. 346–350.

Gino, Francesca/Moore, Don A.: Using final deadlines strategically in negotiation, Negotiation and Conflict Management Research 4 (2008), pp. 371–388.

Glenn, Phillip/Susskind, Lawrence: How Talk Works: Studying Negotiation Interaction, Negotiation Journal 26 (2010), pp. 117–123.

Goh, Cee Chen: Negotiating with the Chinese, Brookfield 1996.

Golann, Dwight: Death of a Claim: The Impact of Loss Reactions on Bargaining, Negotiation Journal 20 (2004), pp. 539–553.

Goldman, Barry M./Shapiro, Depra L. (Eds.): The Psychology of Negotiations in the 21st Century Workplace – New Challenge and New Solutions, New York 2012.

Gordon, Colin (Ed.): Power/Knowledge: Selected Interviews & Other Writings by Michel Foucault 1972 – 1977, Brighton 1980.

Graham, John L./Lam, N. Mark: The Chinese Negotiatiation, Harvard Business Review (2003) (10), pp. 1–17.

Greig, Fiona: Propensity to Negotiate and Career Advancement: Evidence from an Investment Bank that Women are on a "Slow Elevator", Negotiation Journal 24 (2008), pp. 495–508.

Greiter, Ivo/Schweizer, Adrian/Ponschab, Rainer: Schlüsselqualifikationen – Kommunikation – Mediation – Rhetorik – Verhandlung – Vernehmung, Köln 2008.

Gigerenzer, Gerd/Seiten, Reinhard: Bounded Rationality, Cambridge (Mass.) 2001.

Guedj, Jean-Paul: Négocier avec succès, Levallois-Perret 2015.

Guth, Stephen R.: The Contract Negotiation Handbook: An Indispensable Guide for Contract Professionals, Morrisville (North Carolina) 2008.

Haft, Fritjof: Juristische Rhetorik, 8. Ed., Freiburg 2009.

Haft, Fritjof: Verhandlung und Mediation – Die Alternative zum Rechtsstreit, 2. Ed., München 2000.

Haft, Fritjof/Schlieffen, Katharina Gräfin von (Eds.): Handbuch Mediation, 3. Ed., München 2016.

Hägg, Göran: Die Kunst, überzeugend zu reden – 44 Kleine Lektionen in praktischer Rhetorik, Munich 2003.

Hagger, Martin S.: Ego Depletion and the Strength Model of Self Control: A Meta – Analysis, Psychological Bulletin 136 (2010), pp. 495–525.

Hameiri, Boaz/Porat, Roni/Bar-Tal, Daniel/Bieler, Atara/Halperin, Eran: Paradoxical thinking as a new avenue of intervention to promote peace, Proceedings of the National Academy of Sciences of the United States of America 111 (2014), pp. 10996–11001.

Hamilton, David L./Katz, Lawrence B./Leirer, von O.: Cognitive representation of personality impressions – Organisational processes in first impression formation, Journal of Personality and Social Psychology 4 (1980), pp. 1050–1063.

Harding, Chet: Improvisation and Negotiation: Making It Up as You Go Along, Negotiation Journal 20 (2004), pp. 205–212.

Harper, Richard/Randall, Dave/Sharrock, Wes: Choice: The Sciences of Reason in the 21st Century: A Critical Assessment, Cambridge 2016.

Harrington, Joseph E.: Games, Strategies and Decision Making, 2. Ed., New York 2015.

Harrison, Albert A./Hwalek, Melanie/Raney, David F./Fritz, James G.: Cues to Deception in an Interview Situation, Social Psychology 41 (1979), pp. 156–161.

Heeper, Astrid/Schmidt, Michael F.: Erfolgreich Verhandeln – Sich gut vorbereiten – gekonnt abschließen, 4. Ed., Berlin 2013.

Hernandez Requejo, William/Graham, John L.: Global Negotiation. The New Rules, New York, 2008.

Heussen, Benno/Pischel, Gerhard (Eds.): Handbuch Vertragsverhandlung und Vertragsmanagement, 4. Ed., Cologne 2014.

Hoeppner, Sven: The unintended consequence of doorstep consumer protection: surprise, reciprocation, and consistency, European Journal of Law and Economics 38 (2014), pp. 247–276.

Hofstede, Geert/Hofstede, Gert Jan/Minkov, Michael: Cultures and Organizations – Software of the Mind, Intercultural Cooperation and Its Importance for Survival, 3. Ed., New York 2010.

Honeyman, Christopher/Coben, James/De Palo, Giuseppe: Rethinking Negotiation Teaching – Innovations for Context and Culture, Saint Paul 2009.

Insko, Chester A. et al.: Interindividual-Intergroup Discontinuity in the Prisoner's Dilemma Game, Journal of Conflict Resolution 38 (1994), pp. 87–116.

Insko, Chester A. et al.: Individual-group discontinuity as a function of fear and greed, Journal of Personality and Social Psychology 58 (1990), pp. 68–79.

Irving, Janis L.: Groupthink – Psychological Studies of Policy Decisions and Fiascoes, 2. Ed., Boston 1982.

Jensen, Michael C./Meckling, William H.: Theory of the firm: Managerial behavior, agency costs and ownership structure, Journal of Financial Economics 4 (1976), pp. 305–360.

Jex, Steve M./Britt, Thomas W.: Organizational Psychology – A Scientist-Practitioner Approach, 3. Ed., Hoboken 2014.

Jhering, Rudolf von: Culpa in contrahendo oder Schadensersatz bei nichtigen oder nicht zur Perfection gelangten Verträgen, Jherings Jahrbücher 4 (1861), pp. 1–112.

Jung, Stefanie/Krebs, Peter: Die Vertragsverhandlung – Taktische, strategische und rechtliche Elemente, Wiesbaden 2016.

Kahneman, Daniel: Thinking fast and slow, New York 2011.

Kahneman, Daniel/Knetsch, Jack L./Thaler, Richard H.: Anomalies: The Endowement Effect, Loss Aversion, and Status Quo Bias, The Journal of Economic Perspectives 1 (1991), pp. 193–206.

Kahneman, Daniel/Slavic, Paul/Tversky, Amos: Judgement under uncertainty: Heuristics and Biases, Cambridge (Mass.) 1982.

Kahneman, Daniel/Tversky, Amos: Prospect Theory: An Analysis of Decision under Risk, Econometrica 2 (1979), pp. 263–291.

Kahneman, Daniel /Tversky, Amos: Choices, Values, and Frames, American Psychologist 4 (1984), pp. 341–350.

Kahneman, Daniel /Tversky, Amos: Advances in Prospect Theory: Cumulative Representation of Uncertainty, Journal of Risk and Uncertainty 5 (1992), pp. 297–323.

Kahneman, Daniel/Tversky, Amos: Choices, Values and Frames, Cambridge 2000.

Karrass, Chester L.: Give and Take: The Complete Guide to Negotiating Strategies and Tactics, New York 1993.

Katz, Guy: Intercultural Negotiation – The unique case of Germany and Israel, Norderstedt 2011.

Kay, Ketty/Shipman, Claire: The Confidence Code – The Science and Art of Self-Assurance – What Women Should Know, New York 2014.

Kemmerling, Birte C.: The Impact of Concession Strategies on Negotiation Performance, Hamburg 2016.

Kirgis, Paul F.: Hard bargaining in the classroom, Negotiation Journal 28 (2012), 93–115.

Kirgis, Paul F.: Bargaining with consequences: Leverage and coercion in negotiation, Harvard Negotiation Law Review 1 (2014), pp. 69–128.

Kittel, Frank: Verhandeln, Freiburg 2015.

Klucharev, Vasily/Smidts, Ale/Fernández, Guillén: Brain mechanisms of persuasion: how 'expert power' modulates memory and attitudes, Social Cognitive and Affective Neuroscience 4 (2008), pp. 353–366.

Knapp, Mark L./Hall Judith A./Horgan Terrance G.: Nonverbal Communication in Human Interaction, 8. Ed., Boston 2013.

Knapp, Peter/Novak, Andreas: Effizientes Verhandeln – Konstruktive Verhandlungstechniken in der täglichen Praxis, 3. Ed., Frankfurt a.M. 2010.

Kolb, Deborah M.: Too Bad for the Women or Does It Have to Be? Gender and Negotiation Research over the Past Twenty-Five Years, Negotiation Journal 25 (2009), pp. 515–531.

Kolb, Deborah M./Porter, Jessica L.: Negotiating at Work: Turn Small Wins into Big Gains, New York 2015.

Kolb, Deborah M./Williams, Judith: Everyday Negotiation – Navigating the Hidden Agendas in Bargaining, San Francisco 2003.

Köster, Ralf: Die Anwendung von Strategemen in der Verhandlungskultur, Wiesbaden, 2009.

Kramer, Roderick M./Pommerenke, Pamela L./Newton. Elizabeth: The social context of negotiation: Effects of social identity and accountability on negotiator judgement and decision making, Journal of Conflict Resolution 3 (1993a), pp. 633–656.

Kramer, Roderick M./Newton, Elizabeth/Pommerenke, Pamela L.: Self-enhancement biases and negotiator judgement: Effects of self-esteem and mood, Organizational Behavior and Human Decision Processes 1 (1993b), pp. 110–133.

Kray, Laura/Kennedy, Jessica A./van Zant, Alex: Not competent enough to know the difference? Gender stereotypes about women's ease of being misled predict negotiator deception, Organizational Behavior and Human Decision Processes 2 (2014), pp. 61–72.

Kray, Laura J./Locke, Connson C./Van Zant, Alex B.: Feminine Charm: An Experimental Analysis of Its Costs and Benefits in Negotiations, Personality and Social Psychology Bulletin 38 (2012), pp. 1343–1357.

Krebs, Peter: Die Begründungslast, Archiv für die civilistische Praxis 195 (1995), pp. 171–211.

Krebs, Peter: Sonderverbindung und außerdeliktische Schutzpflichten, München 2000.

Kremenyuk, Victor A.: International Negotiation. Analysis, Approaches, Issues, 2. Ed., San Francisco, 2002.

Krishnan, Alparna/Kurtzberg, Terri R./Naquin, Charles E.: The Curse of the Smartphone: Electronic Multitasking in Negotiations, Negotiation Journal 30 (2014), pp. 191–208.

Krüger, Christoph/Kensok, Peter: Das neue Verhandeln: Vom Schlachtfeld zum Verhandlungstisch, Göttingen 2012.

Kumar, Rajesh/Worm, Verner: International Negotiation in China and India, London 2011.

Kupfer Schneider, Andrea/Honeyman, Christopher (Eds.): The Negotiator's Fieldbook, Washington 2006.

Kyprianou, Alexis: La Bible de la négociation – 75 fiches pour utiliser et contrer les techniques des meilleurs négociateurs, Paris 2013.

Hannah R./Babcock, Linda: Social Costs of Setting High Aspirations in Competitive Negotiation, Negotiation and Conflict Management 1 (2013), pp. 1–12.

Langers, Ellen: The illusion of Control, Journal of Personality and Social Psychology 2 (1975), pp. 311–328.

Lai, Lei/Bowles, Hannah R./Babcock, Linda: Social Costs of Setting High Aspirations in Competitive Negotiation, Negotiation and Conflict Management 1 (2013), pp. 1–12.

Lakhani, Avnita: The truth about lying as a negotiation tactic: Where business, ethics, and law collide ... or do they?, ADR Bulletin 9 (2007), pp. 1–9.

Lax, David: When Auctions Met Negotiations, Negotiation Journal 26 (2010), pp. 357–366.

Lax, David/Sebenius, James K.: The Manager as Negotiator. Bargaining for Cooperation and Competitive Gain, New York 1986.

Lax, David A./Sebenius, James K.: 3-D Negotiation – Powerful Tools to Change the Game in Your Most Important Deals, 1. Ed., Cambridge (Mass.) 2006.

Leal, Sharon/Vrij, Aldert: Blinking During and After Lying, Journal of Nonverbal Behavior 32 (2008), pp. 187–194.

Leary, Kimberlyn: Critical Moments in Negotiation, Negotiation Journal 20 (2004), pp. 143–145.

Lenzing, Aline: Nachverhandlungen in Geschäftsbeziehungen – Relevanz, Analyse und Implikationen, Hamburg 2016.

Levin, Irwin P./Schneider Sandra L./Gaeth, Gary J.: All Frames are Not Created Equal: A Typology and Critical Analysis of Framing Effects, Organisational Behavior and Human Decision Processes 2 (1998), pp. 149–188.

Lewicki, Roy J./Barry, Bruce/Saunders, David M.: Negotiation – Reading, Exercises, and Cases, 5. Ed., New York 2007.

Lewis, Richard D.: When Cultures Collide – Leading Across Cultures, 3. Ed., Boston, London 2006.

Lighthall, Nichole R./Mather, Mara/Gorlick, Marissa A.: Acute Stress Increases Sex Differences in Risk Seeking in the Balloon Analogue Risk Task, PLOS ONE 4 (2009), pp. 1–6.

Locke, Edwin A./Shaw, Karyll N./Saari, Lise M./Latham, Gary P.: Goal Setting and Task Performance: 1969–1980, Psychological Bulletin 90 (1981), pp. 125–152.

Luce, Robert Duncan/Raiffa, Howard: Games and Decisions – Introduction and Critical Survey, New York 1957.

Lytle, Anne L./Brett, Jeanne M./Shapiro, Debra L.: The Strategic Use of Interests, Rights, and Power to Resolve Disputes, Negotiation Journal 15 (1999), pp. 31–52.

Macduff, Ian: Using Blogs in Teaching Negotiation: A Technical and Intercultural Postscript, Negotiation Journal 28 (2012), pp. 201–215.

Machiavelli, Niccolò: Der Fürst, Neuenkirchen 2007 (First published under the title Il Principe 1532).

Malhotra, Deepark/Bazerman, Max H.: Negotiation Genius – How to Overcome Obstacles and Achieve Brilliant Results at the Bargaining Table and Beyond, New York 2007a.

Malhotra, Deepark/Bazerman, Max H.: Investigative Negotiation, Harvard Business Review 85 (2007b), pp. 72–78.

Malhotra, Deepark/Gino, Francesca: The Pursuit of Power Corrupts – How Investing in Outside Options Motivates Opportunism in Relationships, Administrative Science Quarterly 56 (2011), pp. 559–592.

Manhart, Ulrike: Höre! Rede! Siege! Leitfaden für erfolgreiches Verhandeln, 2. Ed., Vienna 2014.

Marcus, Leonard J./Dorn, Barry C./McNulty, Eric J.: The Walk in the Woods: A Step-by-Step Method for Facilitating Interest-Based Negotiation and Conflict Resolution, Negotiation Journal 28 (2012), pp. 337–349.

Mastenbroek, Willem F.: Verhandeln – Strategie, Taktik, Technik, 1. Ed., Wiesbaden 1992.

Maynard, Douglas W.: Demur, Defer, and Deter: Concrete, Actual Practices for Negotiation in Interaction, Negotiation Journal 26 (2010), pp. 125–143.

McCloskey, Henry J.: Coercion: Its nature and significance, The Southern Journal of Philosophy 3 (1980), pp. 335–351.

McGinn, Kathleen L./Nöth, Markus: Communicating Frames in Negotiations, in: Bolton, Gary E./Croson, Rachel T.A. (Eds.), Oxford Handbook of Economic Conflict Resolution, Oxford 2012, pp. 61–75.

McJohn, Stephen M.: Default rules in contract law as response to status competition in negotiation, Suffolk University Law Review 39 (1997), pp. 1–21.

McMillan, Julie R./Clifton, A. Kay/McGrath, Diane/Gale, Wanda S.: Women's language: Uncertainty or Interpersonal Sensitivity and Emotionality?, Sex Roles 3 (1977), pp. 545–554.

Mehrabian, Albert: Silent Messages: Implicit Communication of Emotions and Attitudes, 2. Ed., Wadsworth, Belmont 1971.

Mehring, Florian W.: Die Hohe Schule der Kriegskunst bei Geschäftsverhandlungen. Kommentierte Übersetzung eines an Chinesen gerichteten Ratgebers des Verhandlungsforschers Liu Biron, Hamburg 2017.

Merchant, Karima: How Men and Women differ: Gender Differences in Communication Styles, Influence Tactics, and Leadership Styles, CMC Senior Theses (2012), pp. 1–62.

Mery, Marwan: Manuel de négociation complexe – Menaces, mensonges, insultes….méthodes et techniques pour faire face à toute situation, Paris 2013.

Micholka-Metsch, Jutta/Metsch, Marc-Christopher: Strategien für die deutsch – chinesische Geschäftsbeziehung. Erfolgreich verhandeln und Konflikte lösen, Wiesbaden 2015.

Miles, Edward W.: Developing Strategies for Asking Questions in Negotiation, Negotiation Journal 29 (2013), pp. 383–412.

Miller, George A.: The Magical Number Seven, Plus or Minus Two: Some Limits on Our Capacity for Processing Information, Psychological Review 2 (1955), pp. 343–352.

Mnookin, Robert H.: Bargaining With the Devil, New York 2010.

Mnookin, Robert H./Peppet, Scott R./Tulumello, Andrew S.: Beyond Winning: Negotiating to Create Value in Deals and Disputes, Cambridge (Mass.) 2004.

Mnookin, Robert H./Susskind, Lawrence E. with Foster, Pacey C. (Eds.): Negotiating on Behalf of Others, Thousand Oaks (Ca.) 1999.

Moal-Ulvoas, Gaëlle: Business Negotiation, 1. Ed., Louvain-la-Neuve 2014. Modler, Peter: Das Arroganz-Prinzip, Dortmund 2009.

Moffitt, Michael, L./Bordone, Robert C.: The Handbook of Dispute Resolution, 2. Ed., San Francisco 2005.

Movius, Hallam/Susskind, Lawrence: Built to Win, Boston (Mass.) 2009.

Movius, Hallam/Wilson, Timothy D.: How We Feel about the Deal, Negotiation Journal 27 (2011), pp. 241–250.

Müllerschön, Albrecht: Anhang: Erfolgreiche (Vergütungs-)Verhandlungen in: Mayer/Kroiß, Rechtsanwaltsvergütungsgesetz, 6. Ed., Baden-Baden 2013.

Muraven, Mark/Tice, Dianne F./Baumeister, Roy F.: Self-Control as a Limited Ressource: Regulatory Depletion Patterns, Journal of Personality and Social Psychology 74 (1998), pp. 774–798.

Nadler, Janice: Rapport in Legal Negotiation: How Small Talk Can Facilitate E-Mail Dealmaking, Harvard Negotiation Law Review 9 (2004), pp. 223–253.

Nash, John: Equilibrium Points in n-Person Games, Proceedings of the Natural Academy of Sciences 1 (1950a), pp. 48–49.

Nash, John: The Bargaining Problem, Econometrica 2 (1950b), pp. 155–162.

Nasher, Jack: Durchschaut – Das Geheimnis, kleine und große Lügen zu entlarven, 2. Ed., Munich 2010.

Nasher, Jack: DEAL! Du gibst mir, was ich will, 1. Ed., Munich 2015.

Neisser, Ulric: The Concept of Intelligence, Intelligence 3 (1979), pp. 217–227.

Nelson, Noa/Albeck-Solomon Rivka/Ben-Ari, Rachel: Are Your Disputants Insecure and Does it Matter? Attachment and Disputants' Speech during Mediation, Negotiation Journal 27 (2011), pp. 45–68.

Newman, Matthew L./Pennebaker, James W./Berry, Diane S./Richards, Jane M.: Lying Words: Predicting Deception From Linguistic Styles, Personality and Social Psychology Bulletin 29 (2003), pp. 665–675.

Niederle, Muriel/Vesterlund, Lise: Gender Differences in Competition, Negotiation Journal 24 (2008), pp. 447–463.

Nierenberg, Gerard I./Calero, Henry H./Grayson, Gabriel: How to Read a Person Like a Book. Observing Body Language to Know What People Are Thinking, 1. Ed., New York 2010.

Olekalns, Mara/Adair, Wendi L. (Eds.): Handbook of Research on Negotiation, 1. Ed., Cheltenham 2013. Olekalns, Mara/Druckman, Daniel: With Feeling: How Emotions Shape Negotiation, Negotiation Journal 30 (2014), pp. 455–478.

Opresnik, Marc: Die Geheimnisse erfolgreicher Verhandlungsführung – Besser verhandeln – in jeder Beziehung, 2. Ed., Berlin, Heidelberg 2014.

Ott, Edward E.: 50 dialektische Argumentationsweisen und Kunstgriffe, um bei rechtlichen Auseinandersetzungen Recht zu behalten, 1. Ed., Basel 1990.

Paddock, Elizabeth L./Kray, Laura J.: The Role of Gender in Negotiation in: Michael Benoliel (Ed.), Negotiation Excellence: Successful Deal Making, 2. Ed., Singapur 2015, 209–226.

Parlamis, Jennifer D./Mitchell, Lorianne D.: Teaching Negotiations in the New Millennium: Evidence – Based Recommendations for Online Course Delivery, Negotiation Journal 30 (2014), pp. 93–113.

Pesic, Martina: Emotionen in Verhandlungen, 1. Ed., Hamburg 2016.

Picker, Randal C./Gertner, Robert H./Baird, Douglas G.: Game Theory and the Law, 1. Ed., Cambridge (Mass.) 1994.

Pinet, Angelique: The Negotiation Phrase Book, 1. Ed., Avon (Mass.) 2011.

Ponschab, Reiner/Schweizer, Adrian: Schlüsselqualifikationen: Kommunikation – Mediation – Rhetorik – Verhandlung – Vernehmung, 1. Ed., Cologne 2008.

Pratsch, Stephanie: The Role of Aspirations in Negotiation, 1. Ed., Hamburg 2016.

Protner, Jutta: Besser Verhandeln – Das Trainingsbuch, 1. Ed., Offenbach 2010.

Purdy, Jill M./Nye, Pete: The Impact of Communication Media on negotiation outcomes, The International Journal of Conflict Management 2 (2000), pp. 162–187.

Putman, Robert D.: Diplomacy and domestic politics: the logic of two-level games, International Organization 3 (1988), pp. 427–460.

Püttjer, Christian/Schnierda, Uwe: Die heimlichen Spielregeln der Verhandlung – So trainieren Sie ihre Überzeugungskraft. 1. Ed., Frankfurt a.M. 2010.

Rackham, Neil/Carlisle, John: The Effective Negotiator – Part I: The Behavior of Successful Negotiators, Journal of European Industrial Training 6 (1978a), pp. 6–11.

Rackham, Neil/Carlisle, John: The Effective Negotiator – Part I: Planning for Negotiations, Journal of European Industrial Training 6 (1978b), pp. 2–5.

Raiffa, Howard: The Art and Science of Negotiating, 1. Ed., Cambridge (Mass.) 1982.

Raiffa, Howard/Richardson, John/Metcalfe, David: Negotiation Analysis – The Science and Art of Collaborative Decision Making, 1. Ed., Cambridge (Mass.) 2007.

Ranehill, Eva et al.: Assessing the Robustness of Power Posing: No Effect on Hormones and Risk Tolerance in Large Sample of Men and Women, Psycological Science 26 (2015), pp. 653–656.

Rapoport, Anatol/Chammah, Albert M.: Prisoner's Dilemma – A Study in Conflict and Cooperation, 1. Ed., Ann Arbor (Michigan) 1965.

Requejo, William Hernandez/Graham, John L.: Global Negotiation. The New Rules, New York 2008.

Rhodo, Alexander/Schönbohm, Avo/van Vliet, Jacobus: The Tactical Utilization of Cognitive Biases in Negotiation, Working Paper of the Institute of Management, Berlin 2014, paper no. 80.

Rizzo, Mario/Whitman, Glen: The Camel's Nose is in the Tent: Rules, Theories and Slippery Slopes, University of California, Los Angeles (UCLA) Law Review 51 (2003), pp. 539–592.

Robinson, Lauar F./Reis, Harry T.: The Effects of Interruption, Gender, and Status on Interpersonal Perceptions, Journal of Nonverbal Behavior 13 (1989), pp. 141–153.

Rosette, Ashleigh Shelby/Kopelman, Shirli/Abbott, JeAnna Lanza: Good Grief! Anxiety Sours the Economic Benefits of First Offers, Group Decision and Negotiation 3 (2014), pp. 629–647.

Rosner, Siegfried/Winheller, Andreas: Mediation und Verhandlungsführung – Theorie und Praxis des wertschöpfenden Verhandelns nicht nur in Konflikten, 1. Ed., Munich 2012.

Ross, Lee/Stillinger, Constance: Barriers to conflict resolution, Negotiation Journal 7 (1991), pp. 389–404.

Rubin, Jeffrey, Z./Brown, Bert R.: The Social Psychology of Bargaining and Negotiation, 1. Ed., New York 1975.

Rubinstein, Ariel: Perfect Equilibrium in a Bargaining Model, Econometrica 1 (1982), pp. 97–110.

Rudman, Laurin A./Moss-Racusin, Julie E./Nauts, Phelan S.: Status incongruity and backlash effects: Defending the gender hierarchy motivates against female leaders, Journal of Experimental Social Psychology 1 (2012), pp. 165–179.

Salacuse, Jeswald W.: The Global Negotiator, 1. Ed., New York 2003.

Samuelson, William/Zeckhauser, Richard: Status Quo Bias in Decision Making, Journal of Risk and Uncertainty 1 (1988), pp. 7–59.

Sears, Greg J./Rowe, Patricia M.: A personality based similar-to-me effect in the employment interview: Conscientiousness, affect versus competence-mediated interpretations and the role of the job relevance, Canadian Journal of Behavioral Science/Revue Canadienne des Sciences du Comportement 35 (2003), pp. 13–24.

Schelling, Thomas: The Strategy of Conflict, 1. Ed., Cambridge (Mass.) 1960.

Schleichert, Hubert: Wie man mit Fundamentalisten diskutiert, ohne den Verstand zu verlieren – Anleitung zum subversive Denken, 7. Ed., Munich 2012.

Schlösser, Tim: Druckausübung in Vertragsverhandlungen – Eine ökonomische Analyse zum allgemeinen Zivilrecht, 1. Ed., Munich 2014.

Schmitz, Raimund/Spilker, Ulrich/Schmelzer, Josef A.: Strategische Verhandlungsvorbereitung – Ein Leitfaden mit Arbeitshilfen, wie Sie Ihre Ziele in 5 Schritten sicher erreichen, 1. Ed., Wiesbaden 2006.

Smyser, W. R.: How Germans Negotiate, Washington, D. C. 2003.

Schneider, Andrea K./Tinsley, Catherine H./Cheldelin, Sandra/Amanatullah, Emily T.: Likeability v. Competence: The Impossible Choice Faced by Female Politicians, Attenuated by Lawyers, Duke Journal Of Gender Law & Policy 17 (2010), pp. 363–384.

Schopenhauer, Arthur: Eristische Dialektik oder die Kunst, Recht zu behalten in 38 Kunstgriffen dargestellt, 7. Ed., Frankfurt a.M. 2009 (Manuskript ca. 1830).

Schott, Barbara/Troczynski, Peter: Verhandeln, 1. Ed., Freiburg 2012.

Schranner, Matthias: Teure Fehler – Die 7 größten Irrtümer in schwierigen Verhandlungen, 2. Ed., Berlin 2009.

Schranner, Matthias: Verhandeln im Grenzbereich, 11. Ed., Munich 2014.

Schroevers, Sander M./Lewis, Ian R.: Negotiations in English, 1. Ed., Freiburg 2010.

Schulze, Reiner/Zoll, Fryderyk: Europäisches Vertragsrecht, 1. Ed., Baden-Baden 2015.

Schweitzer, Maurice/Croson, Rachel T. A.: Curtailing Deception: The Impact of Direct Questions on Lies and Omissions, International Journal of Conflict Management 3 (1999), pp. 225–248.

Sebenius, James K.: Level Two Negotiations: Helping the Other Side Meet Its "Behind-the-Table" Challenges, Negotiation Journal 29 (2013), pp. 7–21.

Senger, Harro von: Strategeme, Lebens- und Überlebenslisten der Chinesen – die berühmten 36 Strategeme aus drei Jahrtausenden, 4. Ed., Bern 1988.

Shaughnessy, Brooke/Mislin, Alexandra/Hentschel, Tanja: Should He Chitchat? The Benefits of Small Talk for Male Versus Female Negotiators, Basic and Applied Social Psychology 37 (2015), pp. 105–117.

Shell, Richard G.: When Is it legal to lie in Negotiations, Sloan Management Review Spring 1991, pp. 93–101.

Shefrin, Hersh M./Thaler, Richard H.: The behavioral life cycle hypothesis, Economic Inquiry 4 (1988), pp. 609–643.

Shonk, Katherine: The "Sandberg Effect": Why Women Are Asking for More, Program on negotiation, Negotiation Strategies for Women, Program on Negotiation 11 (2013a), pp. 7–10.

Shonk, Katherine: Women Negotiators: Focus on the Power and Status, Program on negotiation, Business Negotiation Strategies for Women, Program on Negotiation 11 (2013b), pp. 12–16.

Simon, Herbert A.: Models of Bounded Rationality: Empirically grounded economic reason, 1. Ed., Cambridge (Mass.) 1997.

Small, Deborah A./Gelfand, Michele/Babcock, Linda/Gettmann, Hilary: Who goes to the Bargaining Table? The Influence of Gender and Framing on the Initiation of Negotiation, Journal of Personality and Social Psychology 93 (2007), pp. 600–613.

Smith, Thomas H.: Metaphor for Navigating Negotiations, Negotiation Journal 21 (2005), pp. 343–364.

Smyth, Leo F.: Escalation and Mindfulness, Negotiation Journal 28 (2012), pp. 45–72.

Solnick, Sara J.: Gender differences in the ultimatum game, Economic Inquiry 29 (2001), pp. 189–200.

Solomon, Richard H./Quinney, Nigel (Eds.): American Negotiating Behavior: Wheeler-Dealers, Legal Eagles, Bullies, and Preachers, Washington, D.C., 2010.

Staw, Barry M.: Knee-Deep in the Big Muddy: A Study of Escalating Commitment to a Chosen Course of Action, Organizational Behavior and Human Performance 1 (1976), pp. 27–44.

Steedman, Ian: Reservation Price and Reservation Demand, in: The New Palgrave. A Dictionary of Economics, London 1987, pp. 158–159.

Stelmach, Jerzy/Brozek, Bartosz: Theorie der juristischen Verhandlungen, 1. Ed., Baden-Baden 2014.

Stern, Patrice/Mouton, Jean: La Boîte à outils de la Négociation, 2. Ed., Paris 2014.

Stone, Douglas/Heen, Sheila: Thanks for The Feedback – The Science and Art of Receiving Feedback Well, 1. Ed., New York 2014.

Stone, Douglas/Patton, Bruce/Heen, Sheila: Difficult Conversations – Your Boss, Your Spouse, Your Friends, Your Kids, Your Clients, 1. Ed., London 2000.

Strack, Fritz/Mussweiler, Thomas: Explaining the Enigmatic Anchoring Effect: Mechanisms of Selective Accessibility, Journal of Personality and Social Psychology 3 (1997), pp. 437–446.

Straker, David: Changing Minds – in Detail, 2. Ed., Crowthrone 2010.

Strempel, Ilse: Das Auge – Spiegel der Seele, Marburger UniJournal 19 (2004), pp. 36–39.

Stuart, Harborne W. Jr.: Surprise Moves in Negotiation, Negotiation Journal 20 (2004), pp. 239–251.

Stuhlmacher, Alice F./Citera, Maryalice/Willis, Toni: Gender Differences in Virtual Negotiation: Theory and Research, Sex Roles 57 (2007), pp. 329–339.

Subramanian, Guhan: Negotiauctions: New Dealmaking Strategies for a competitive Marketplace, 1. Ed., New York 2010.

Sun Tzu: Die Kunst des Krieges, 14. Ed., Hamburg 2015 (benannt nach Sunzi ca. 500 v. Chr.).

Susskind, Lawrence E.: The Siting Puzzle – Balancing Economic and Environmental Gains and Losses, Environmental Impact Assessment Review 5 (1985), pp. 157–163.

Susskind, Lawrence E.: Ten Propositions Regarding Critical Moments in Negotiation, Negotiation Journal 20 (2004), pp. 339–340.

Susskind, Lawrence E.: Good for you – Great for Me: Finding the Trading Zone and Winning at Win-Win Negotiation, 1. Ed., Philadelphia 2014.

Sutter, Matthias/Bosman, Ronald/Kocher, Martin/van Windern, Frans: Gender pairing and bargaining: Beware the same sex!, Working Papers in Economics and Statistics 27 (2008), pp. 1–27.

Sydow, Jörg/Schreyögg, Georg/Koch, Jochen: Organisational Path Dependence: Opening the black box, Academy of Management Review 4 (2009), pp. 689–702.

Sydow, Jörg/Duschek, Stephan: Netzwerkzeuge – Tools für das Netzwerkmanagement, 1. Ed., Wiesbaden 2013.

Thaler, Richard H.: Mental Accounting Matters: Journal of Behavioral Decision Making 3 (1999), pp. 183–206.

Thaler, Richard H./Sunstein, Cass R.: Nudge Improving Decisions about Health, Wealth and Happiness, 1. Ed., New Haven 2008.

Thiele, Albert: Die Kunst zu überzeugen – Faire und unfaire Dialektik, 8. Ed., Berlin 2006.

Thomas, Kenneth W./Kilmann, Ralph H.: Conflict Mode Instrument, 1. Ed., New York 1974.

Thompson, Leigh L./Hastie, Reid: Social Perception in Negotiation, Organizational Behavior and Human Decision Processes 1 (1990), pp. 98–123.

Thompson, Leigh L./Valley, Kathleen/Kramer, Roderick M.: The Bittersweet Feeling of Success: An Examiniation of Social Perception in Negotiation, Journal of Experimental Social Psychology 31 (1995), pp. 467–492.

Thompson, Leigh L. (Ed.): Negotiation Theory and Research, 1. Ed., New York 2006.

Thompson, Leigh L.: The Mind and Heart of the Negotiatior, 6. Ed., Harlow 2014.

Thorndike, Edward. L.: A Constant Error in Psychological Ratings, Journal of Applied Psychology 1 (1920), pp. 25–29.

Tinsley, Catherine H./Amanatullah, Emily T.: Backlash: Who Does it, When and Why?, IACM 21st Annual Conference Paper, 2008, pp. 1–35.

Trebilcock, Michael J.: The Limits of Freedom of Contract, 1. Ed., Cambridge (Mass.) 1993.

Tu, Jung-Tsung: Impact of Culture on International Business Negotiation, 2007.

Tversky, Amos/Kahneman, Daniel: Availability: A Heuristic for Judging Frequency and Probability, Cognitive Psychology 2 (1973), pp. 207–232.

Tversky, Amos/Kahneman, Daniel: Judgement Under Uncertainty: Heuristics and Biases, Science 4157 (1974), pp. 1124–1131.

Tversky, Amos/Kahneman, Daniel: The Framing of Decisions and the Psychology of Choice, Science 4481 (1981), pp. 453–458.

Uher, Thomas E./Davenport, Philip: Fundamentals of Building Contract Management, 2. Ed., Sydney 2009.

Urlacher, Brian R.: Groups, Decision Rules, and Negotiation Outcomes: Simulating the Negotiator's Dilemma, Negotiation Journal 30 (2014), pp. 5–22.

Ury, William: Getting to Yes With Yourself and Other Worthy Opponents, 1. Ed., New York 2015.

Ury, William: Must We Fight? From the Battlefield to the Schoolyard – A New Perspective on Violent Conflict and Its Prevention, 1. Ed., San Francisco 2002.

Ury, William: The Third Side: How We Fight and How We Can Stop, 2. Ed., New York 2000.

Van Kleef, Gerben A./Côté, Stéphane: Expressing anger in conflict: When it helps and when it hurts, Journal of Applied Psychology, 92 (2007), pp. 1557–1569.

Voeth, Markus/Herbst, Uta: Verhandlungsmanagement – Planung, Steuerung und Analyse, 2. Ed., Stuttgart 2015.

Von der Heyde, Anke/Von der Linde, Boris: Gesprächstechniken für Führungskräfte – Methoden und Übungen zur erfolgreichen Kommunikation, 3. Ed., Planegg 2009.

Vrij, Aldert/Mann, Samantha: Detecting Deception: The Benefit of Looking at a Combination of Behavioral, Auditory and Speech Content Related Cues in a Systematic Manner, Group Decision and Negotiation 13 (2004), pp. 61–79.

Vuorela, Taina: Laughing Matters: A Case Study of Humor in Multicultural Business Negotiations, Negotiation Journal 21 (2005), pp. 105–130.

Wachs, Friedhelm: Faktor V – Die fünf Phasen erfolgreichen Verhandelns, 1. Ed., Weinheim 2012.

Walters, Amy E./Stuhlmacher, Alice F./Meyer, Lia L.: Gender and Negotiator Competitiveness: A meta analysis, Organizational Behaviour and Human Decision Processes 76 (1998), pp. 1–29.

Walz, Robert: Verhandlungstechniken für Notare, 1. Ed., Munich 2003.

Wannenwetsch, Helmut: Erfolgreiche Verhandlungsführung in Einkauf und Logistik, 3. Ed., Berlin, Heidelberg 2009.

Ward, Andrew/Disston, Lauren G./Brenner L./Ross L.: Acknowledging the Other Side in Negotiation, Negotiation Journal 24 (2008), pp. 269–285.

Watkins, Michael: Breakthrough in Business Negotiations: A Toolbox for Managers, 1. Ed., San Francisco 2002.

Watzenberg, Anja: Der Homo Oeconomicus und seine Vorurteile: Eine Analyse des zivilrechtlichen Benachteiligungsverbots, 1. Ed., Berlin, Boston 2014.
Wendler, Axel/Hoffmann, Helmut: Technik und Taktik der Befragung, 2. Ed., Stuttgart 2015.
Wheeler, Michael: The Fog of Negotiation: What Negotiators Can Learn from Military Doctrine, Negotiation Journal 29 (2013a), pp. 23–38.
Wheeler, Michael: The Art of Negotiation. How to Improve in a Chaotic World, 1. Ed., New York 2013b.
White, S./Neale, Margaret A.: The role of negotiator aspirations and settlement expectancies in bargaining outcomes, in: Organizational Behaviour and Human Decision Processes 57 (1994), pp. 303–317.
Wiesner, Donald A./Glaskowsky, Nicholas A.: Illustrated Negotiator's Glossary, 1. Ed., Coral Gables 2001.
Williams, Gerald A./Craver, Charles: Legal negotiating, 1. Ed., St. Paul 2007.
Williamson, Oliver E.: The Economics of Organization: The Transaction Cost Approach, The American Journal of Sociology 87 (1981), pp. 548–577.
Williamson, Oliver E.: The Economic Institutions of Capitalism, 1. Ed., New York, 1985.
Williamson, Oliver E.: Transaction Costs Economics, in: Schmalensee/Willig, Handbook of Industrial Organization, Vol. I, 1. Ed., Amsterdam 1989.
Wilson, Paul R.: Perceptual Distortion of Height as a Function of Ascribed Academic Status, The Journal of Social Psychology 1 (1968), pp. 97–102.
Wilson, Timothy D./Dunn, Dana S./Bybee, Jane A./Hyman, Diane B./Rotondo, John A.: Effects on Analysing Reasons on Attitude-Behavior Consistency, Journal of Personality and Social Psychology 47 (1984), pp. 5–16.
Wilson, Timothy D./Houston, Christopher E./Etling, Kathryn M./Brekke, Nancy: A New Look at Anchoring Effects. Basic Anchoring and Its Antecedents, Journal of Experimental Psychology General 4 (1996), pp. 387–402.
Young, Mark/Schlie, Erik: The Rhythm of the Deal: Negotiation as a Dance, Negotiation Journal 27 (2011), pp. 191–203.
Zamir, Eyal/Teichman, Doron (Eds.): The Oxford Handbook of Behavioral Economics and the Law, 1. Ed., Oxford 2014.
Zimmermann, Don H./West, Candace: Sex Roles, Interruptions and Silences in Conversation, Language and Sex: Difference and Dominance, in: Thorne, Barrie/Henley, Nancy (Eds.), Language and Sex. Difference and Dominance, 1. Ed., Rowley (MA.) 1975, pp. 105–129.
Zhang, Quiang/Zhong, Zheng/Yang, Mingna/Fu, Jianbo: Shangwu Tanpan (Business Negotiations), 3. Ed., Beijing 2018.

Further Literary Resources

Baker&McKenzie/PILPG: The International Negotiations Handbook – Success through Preparation, Strategy and Planning, 2007. (available under: http://www.bakermckenzie.com)
Harvard Law School: BATNA Basics: Boost your Power at the Bargaining Table, Program on negotiation, Cambridge (Mass.) 2012a, pp. 1–8.
Harvard Law School: Crisis Communication – How to Avoid Being Held Hostage by Crises Negotiations, Program on negotiation, Cambridge (Mass.) 2012b, pp. 1–8.
Harvard Law School: Dealing with Difficult People, Free Report, Cambridge (Mass.) 2013a, pp. 1–17.
Harvard Law School: How to Negotiate Better Business Deals, Program on negotiation, Cambridge (Mass.) 2014a, pp. 1–15.
Harvard Law School: Negotiation Strategies and Negotiation Techniques to Help you Become a Better Negotiator, Program on negotiation, Cambridge (Mass.) 2014b, pp. 1–17.

Harvard Law School: Negotiation Strategies For Women – Secrets to Success, Program on negotiation, Cambridge (Mass.) 2013b, pp. 1–25.

Harvard Law School: Real Leaders Negotiate – Understanding the Difference between Leadership and Management, Free Report, Cambridge (Mass.) 2015, pp. 1–31.

Harvard Law School: – Sales Negotiations – How to get to Win-Win, Negotiation Special Report, Cambridge (Mass.) 2013c, pp. 1–25.

Harvard Law School: Win-Win or Hardball? Learn Top Strategies from Sports Contract Negotiations, Free Report, Cambridge (Mass.) 2012c, pp. 1–9.

Medvec, Victori H./Leonardelli, Geoffrey J./Galinsky, Adam, D./Claussen-Schulz, Aletha: Choice and Achievement at the Bargaining Table: The Distributive, Integrative and Interpersonal Advantage of Making Multiple Equivalent Simultaneous Offers, IACM 18th Annual Conference, June 1, 2005, pp. 1–30.

Online Sources

Changing minds: http://changingminds.org/disciplines/negotiation/tactics/tactics.htm (last downloaded on 02.5.2018).

Harvard Law School – Program on Negotiation – Daily Blog: http://www.pon.harvard.edu/blog/ (last downloaded on 16.02.2018).

Karrass: http://www.karrass.com/blog/ (last downloaded on 02.5.2018).

Peter Barron Stark Companies – Blog: http://www.peterstark.com/category/negotiating-tactics/ (last downloaded on 02.5.2018).

Soll, Jack B./Milkman, Katherine L./Payne, John W.: A User's Guide to Debiasing, http://www.opim.wharton.upenn.edu/~kmilkman/Soll_et_al_2013.pdf, 2014, pp. 1–29 (last downloaded on 02.5.2018).

The Negotiator's Magazine: http://negotiatormagazine.com/index.php (last downloaded on 02.5.2018).

The New Palgrave Dictionary of Economics: http://www.dictionaryofeconomics.com/articles_az (last downloaded on 02.5.2018).

Voeth, Markus/Herbst, Uta/Sandstede, Christoph: Battle of the Sexes, Universität Hohenheim, 2006, available under: https://verhandlungsforschung.uni-hohenheim.de/fileadmin/einrichtungen/verhandlungsforschung/files/1battleofthesexes.pdf (last downloaded on 02.5.2018).

Index

S. Jung, P. Krebs, *The Essentials of Contract Negotiation*,
https://doi.org/10.1007/978-3-030-12866-1

MIX
Papier aus verantwortungsvollen Quellen
Paper from responsible sources
FSC® C105338

If you have any concerns about our products,
you can contact us on
ProductSafety@springernature.com

In case Publisher is established outside the EU,
the EU authorized representative is:
Springer Nature Customer Service Center GmbH
Europaplatz 3, 69115 Heidelberg, Germany

Printed by Libri Plureos GmbH
in Hamburg, Germany